Lecture Notes in Computer Science 4787

Commenced Publication in 1973
Founding and Former Series Editors:
Gerhard Goos, Juris Hartmanis, and Jan van Leeuwen

Dilip Krishnaswamy   Tom Pfeifer
Danny Raz (Eds.)

Real-Time Mobile Multimedia Services

10th IFIP/IEEE International Conference on Management
of Multimedia and Mobile Networks and Services, MMNS 2007
San José, USA, October 31 - November 2, 2007
Proceedings

 Springer

Volume Editors

Dilip Krishnaswamy
Qualcomm Inc.
Advanced Technology R&D
5665 Morehouse Drive, L-603U, San Diego, CA 92121, USA
E-mail: dilip@ieee.org

Tom Pfeifer
Waterford Institute of Technology (WIT)
Telecommunications Software & Systems Group (TSSG)
Carriganore Campus, Waterford, Ireland
E-mail: t.pfeifer@computer.org

Danny Raz
The Technion
Department of Computer Science
Haifa 32000, Israel
E-mail: danny@cs.technion.ac.il

Library of Congress Control Number: 2007937182

CR Subject Classification (1998): C.2, H.5.1, H.3, H.5, H.4

LNCS Sublibrary: SL 5 – Computer Communication Networks
and Telecommunications

ISSN   0302-9743
ISBN-10   3-540-75868-2 Springer Berlin Heidelberg New York
ISBN-13   978-3-540-75868-6 Springer Berlin Heidelberg New York

Springer is a part of Springer Science+Business Media

springer.com

© IFIP International Federation for Information Processing 2007
Printed in Germany

Typesetting: Camera-ready by author, data conversion by Scientific Publishing Services, Chennai, India
Printed on acid-free paper   SPIN: 12177622   06/3180   5 4 3 2 1 0

Preface

It is a great pleasure to present the proceedings of the 10th IFIP/IEEE International Conference on Management of Multimedia and Mobile Networks and Services (MMNS 2007).

The MMNS 2007 Conference was held in San Jose, California, USA during October 31 – November 2 as part of the 3rd International Week on Management of Networks and Services (Manweek 2007). As in the previous three years, the Manweek umbrella allowed an international audience of researchers and scientists from industry and academia – who are researching and developing management systems – to share views and ideas and present their state-of-the-art results.

The other events co-located with Manweek 2007 were the 18th IFIP/IEEE International Workshop on Distributed Systems: Operations and Management (DSOM 2007), the 7th IEEE Workshop on IP Operations and Management (IPOM2007), the 2nd IEEE International Workshop on Modeling Autonomic Communications Environments (MACE 2007), and the 1st IEEE/IFIP International Workshop on End-to-End Virtualization and Grid Management (EVGM 2007).

Under this umbrella, MMNS proved itself again as a top public venue for results dissemination and intellectual collaboration with specific emphasis on multimedia and mobility aspects of end-to-end services. These aspects of management are becoming a major challenge in the ability to deliver cost effective end-to-end multimedia-based services in the upcoming 4G wireless systems.

Contributions from the research community have met this challenge with 46 paper submissions from four continents, out of which 14 full high-quality papers and 4 short papers, presenting innovative work in progress, were subsequently selected to form the MMNS 2007 technical program. The diverse topics in this year's program include services and user experience, management aspects of wireless and cellular networks, monitoring and control, resource management, and multicast and IPTV management – all contributing to the management of real-time mobile multimedia services, as expressed in this year's motto.

The high-quality MMNS 2007 program is a delicate concoction based on the accepted papers of the original and novel contributions of all the authors who submitted their work to the conference, purified by the hard work of the MMNS 2007 Technical Program Committee members and the rigorous review process accomplished by this set of worldwide experts, cooked with the great help of the 2007 Manweek Organizing Committee, and spiced with the generous contribution of IFIP, IEEE and the sponsor companies, all of whom are gratefully thanked by the conference Technical Program Committee Chairs. In addition, we thank the Springer LNCS team for their support of these proceedings.

We have no doubt that the MMNS 2007 conference in the heart of Silicon Valley was another significant step towards the ability to develop, manage and control truly scalable end-to-end multimedia-based services over next-generation wireless networks.

October 2007

Dilip Krishnaswamy
Danny Raz
Tom Pfeifer

MMNS 2007 Organization

Technical Program Committee Co-chairs

Dilip Krishnaswamy QUALCOMM Inc., USA
Danny Raz Technion, Israel

Publication Chair

Tom Pfeifer Waterford Institute of Technology, Ireland

Publicity Chair

Sumit Naiksatam Cisco Systems, USA

Treasurers

Raouf Boutaba University of Waterloo, Canada
Brendan Jennings Waterford Institute of Technology, Ireland

Website and Registration Co-chairs

Edgar Magana UPC / Cisco Systems, USA
Sven van der Meer Waterford Institute of Technology, Ireland

Submission Chair

Lisandro Zambenedetti Granville Federal University of Rio Grande do Sul, Brazil

Manweek 2007 General Co-chairs

Alexander Clemm Cisco Systems, USA
Silvia Figueira Santa Clara University, USA
Masum Z. Hasan Cisco Systems, USA

Manweek 2007 Advisors

Raouf Boutaba University of Waterloo, Canada
Brendan Jennings Waterford Institute of Technology, Ireland
Sven van der Meer Waterford Institute of Technology, Ireland

MMNS 2007 Technical Program Committee

Ahmed Helmy	University of Southern California, USA
Aiko Pras	University of Twente, The Netherlands
Alan Marshall	The Queen's University of Belfast, UK
Alexander Clemm	Cisco Systems, USA
Bert-Jan van Beijnum	University of Twente, The Netherlands
Brendan Jennings	TSSG, Waterford Institute of Technology, Ireland
Burkhard Stiller	University of Zurich and ETH Zurich, Switzerland
Chadi Assi	CIISE, Concordia University, Canada
David Hutchison	Lancaster University, UK
Dirk Pesch	Cork Institute of Technology, Ireland
Ehab Al-Shaer	DePaul University Chicago, USA
Fan Bai	General Motors Research, USA
Gabriel-Miro Muntean	Dublin City University, Ireland
Gang Ding	Olympus Communication Technology of America, USA
George Pavlou	University of Surrey, UK
Gerard Parr	University of Ulster, UK
Go Hasegawa	Osaka University, Japan
Guy Pujolle	Université de Paris 6, France
Hanan Lutfiyya	University of Western Ontario, Canada
James Irvine	University of Strathclyde, UK
John Strassner	Motorola Labs, USA
John Vicente	Intel, USA
Jun Li	University of Oregon, USA
Kai Miao	Intel, USA
Karim Seada	Nokia Research Center Palo Alto, USA
Liam Murphy	University College Dublin, Ireland
Lukas Kencl	Charles University Prague, Czech Republic
Mallik Tatipamula	Juniper Networks, USA
Masum Hasan	Cisco Systems, USA
Mihaela van der Schaar	University of California Los Angeles, USA
Nazim Agoulmine	University of Evry, France
Nicola Cranley	Dublin Institute of Technology, Ireland
Pablo Arozarena	Telefónica Investigación y Desarrollo, Spain
Petre Dini	Cisco Systems, USA
Roger Zimmermann	National University of Singapore, Singapore
Sasitharan Balasubramaniam	TSSG, Waterford Institute of Technology, Ireland
Shlomo Greenberg	Ben Gurion University, Israel
Spyros Denazis	Hitachi Europe & University of Patras, Greece
Sven van der Meer	TSSG, Waterford Institute of Technology, Ireland
Theodore Willke	Intel, USA

Theodore Zahariadis   Ellemedia Technologies, Greece
Thomas Magedanz   Fraunhofer FOKUS, Germany
Tom Pfeifer   TSSG, Waterford Institute of Technology, Ireland
Viji Raveendran   QUALCOMM Inc., USA
Xin Liu   UC Davis, USA

MMNS 2007 Additional Reviewers

Alaa Seddik   University of Evry, France
Alain Maloberti   France Téléom / Orange, France
Alan Davy   TSSG, Waterford Institute of Technology, Ireland
Andreas Mauthe   Lancaster University, UK
Anna Sperotto   University of Twente, The Netherlands
Christina Thorpe   University College Dublin, Ireland
Dan Marconett   Intel, USA
Dragos Vingarzan   Technical University of Berlin, Germany
Fabricio Gouveia   Fraunhofer FOKUS, Germany
Jennifer McManis   Dublin City University, Ireland
John Fitzpatrick   University College Dublin, Ireland
Lopa Roychoudhuri   DePaul University Chicago, USA
Mark Grayson   Cisco Systems, USA
Mehdi Nafa   University of Evry, France
Min Xie   University of Notre Dame Indiana, USA
Paul Knickerbocker   University of Oregon, USA
Quoc Thinh Nguyen Vuong   University of Evry, France
Ramin Sadre   University of Twente, The Netherlands
Ritesh Maheshwari   State University of New York - Stony Brook, USA
Steven Davy   TSSG, Waterford Institute of Technology, Ireland
Sumit Naiksatam   Cisco Systems, USA
Sven Ehlert   Fraunhofer FOKUS, Germany
Tiago Fioreze   University of Twente, The Netherlands
Toby Ehrenkranz   University of Oregon, USA
Tohru Asami   University of Tokyo, Japan
Vamsi Gondi   Université d'Evry Val d'Essonne, France
Xiaohui Ye   University of California Davis, USA
Yang Yu   Motorola Research Lab., USA
Yibo Wang   University of Oregon, USA
Yongning Tang   DePaul University Chicago, USA
Zein Wali   DePaul University Chicago, USA

Table of Contents

Resource Management

Short Papers

Hybrid Overlay Networks Management for Real-Time Multimedia Streaming over P2P Networks

Mubashar Mushtaq and Toufik Ahmed

CNRS LaBRI Lab. – University of Bordeaux 1
351 Cours de la Libération, Talence Cedex 33405 – France
{mushtaq, tad}@labri.fr

Abstract. Recent growth of the multimedia content delivery over the Internet and the popularity of the peer-to-peer (P2P) architecture have opened new horizons for emerging novel services over the Internet. Currently, most of multimedia services are being offered to the end users by using set-top boxes installation on the client's premises, with integrated media storage capabilities and their adaptation. The organization of the end-clients in P2P fashion has great potential to change business models to offer new value-added multimedia services and therefore to generate substantial revenue for service providers. In this paper, we present a mechanism to organize the sender peers in hierarchical hybrid overlay networks. The objective of such organization is to facilitate the receiver peer (content consumer) to select best sender peers for the provision of better QoS (Quality of Service). To construct the hybrid overlay networks, peers offering the same video quality are placed together at the same level of overlay networks. The organization of sender peers within these overlays is subject to (1) the semantic of the video provided by the peer (base layer, or enhancement layers) and (2) the QoS offered by each peer along the end-to-end path. The proposed streaming mechanism is receiver-centric where receiver peer selects a number of sender peers from the overlay networks to receive media contents. The performance evaluation performed using ns-2 simulator shows that hybrid overlays organization mechanism is helpful to enhance the overall QoS by significant improvement in received video packets throughput, the packets drop ratio and transmission delay.

1 Introduction

P2P networking frameworks have recently received a lot of attention by the research community, as they provide an efficient infrastructure to use available networking resources in a more transparent, scalable and cost-effective way. P2P networks were initially designed and were considered suitable for huge contents distribution across networks. These networks possess distributed, scalable, cost-effective, cooperative resource sharing, self-organizing, and many more characteristics that have encouraged service providers (SPs) to deploy many real-time applications over large scale heterogeneous networks. This is considered as a giant shift of technology that has changed the way people interact with the technologies. The most important real-time

D. Krishnaswamy, T. Pfeifer, and D. Raz (Eds.): MMNS 2007, LNCS 4787, pp. 1–13, 2007.
© IFIP International Federation for Information Processing 2007

applications based on P2P framework include: video streaming, video on demand, P2P based IP-TV, P2P gaming, signaling for IP telephony, etc. Overlay networks are considered as the most promising infrastructure for the deployment of distributed applications. Many existing multimedia applications over P2P networks are based on the organization of the participating peers in overlay networks. Many research developments have been observed overlay networks organization that address the scalability, efficient management, and self organization of overlay networks. The well known overlay networks like Content Addressable Network (CAN) [1], Chord [2], and Pastry [3] have been proposed for the Internet routing to guarantee better quality of service.

On the other hand, recent advances in audiovisual content coding have favored a widespread growing of multimedia streaming and Video on Demand (VoD) services. A number of home holders are subscribing to these services by the service provider through a set-top box. These boxes are generally equipped with specific functions such as storage space, on which the client can store programs, movies, and other desired contents. The service provider has full access for indexing, tracking and to use the contents available in these set-top boxes. These characteristics enable service providers to use such boxes as independent content servers. In the rest of paper, we refer these boxes as peers when used in P2P networks. The terms set-top-box and peer are used interchangeably. In fact, most of these boxes are capable of performing media content adaptation in accordance with the end client's requirements. These features extend the usability of these boxes to that of media servers for the end clients possessing different characteristics, i.e. heterogeneous clients. Another point of heterogeneity is related to the end-user connection. Most of the end-clients (service subscribers) connect to the network using ADSL (Asymmetric Digital Subscriber Line) or CMTS (Cable Modem Termination System), where uplink capacity is 3-8 time lesser than that of the downlink. If media content is requested from a single box, it cannot be achieved. In fact, a single peer might not be able to meet the requirements of any one request. In this regard, we propose to select multiple sender peers to cooperate in the streaming mechanism using multi-source streaming. The use of multiple peers for the service delivery reduces the load on the central server, reduces the start-up delay, latency, and improves the overall Quality of Service (QoS) of the system.

In this paper, we present a quality adaptive mechanism for the multimedia streaming and video on demand services over P2P networks. This mechanism is based on the organization of sender peers in hybrid overlay networks. These overlay networks are formed on the basis of offered video quality and end-to-end probing among the sender and receiver peers.

The network topology for multimedia streaming and video on demand services is illustrated in the Fig. 1 where different service clients with variant characteristics are connected to the network. In this topology, we consider only those peers which have the requested media contents and are willing to participate in the streaming mechanism. The receiver peer selects multiple sender peers to receive the media contents from the overlay networks. The received media contents are combined to decode the received video with a higher quality. The sender peers are selected from the different overlays on the basis of receiver characteristics and its preferences.

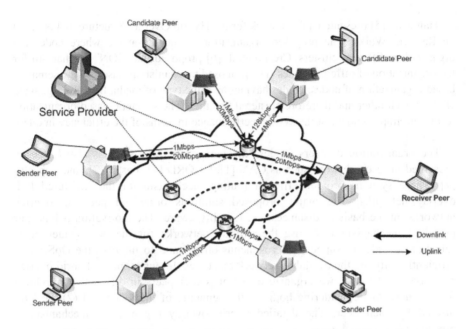

Fig. 1. Network Topology for Multimedia Streaming / Video on Demand

The rest of the paper is organized as follows. A brief motivation and some of the related work is presented in the section 2. Section 3 describes an overview of the scalable video coding (SVC) scheme. The proposed streaming mechanism based on the organization of sender peers in hierarchical overlay networks is given in section 4. The evaluation results of proposed mechanism using simulations are presented in section 5. Finally, concluding remarks are presented in section 6.

2 Motivation and Related Works

There have been significant studies carried out in the context of multimedia streaming applications and for the construction of overlay networks to enhance the QoS. Most of these studies have investigated and proposed solutions for the efficient routing algorithms, organization techniques, and self organization.

Zhang et al. [4] developed a framework for live media streaming that is based on data-driven overlay networks where each node periodically exchanges data availability information with other nodes. The management of nodes which join the networks is controlled by an origin node that is persistent during the life time of the streaming session. In the proposed mechanism, a scheduling algorithm is devised for heterogeneous clients. The nodes in the data-driven overlay network are organized in a Breath-First-Search (BFS) tree, where origin node is located at level '0' while any node at level 'k' can be reached in 'k' hops from the origin.

Tian et al. [5] presented a framework for the Hybrid Overlay Structure that is based on Random Walks. The proposed organization is locality-aware where nodes are organized in different clusters. Crespo et al. [6] proposed the "SON" mechanism for the organization of different nodes. The proposed mechanism is based on the semantic based organization of nodes. Nodes having the same type of media files are organized close to each other and therefore clustered together. The semantic based organization result into improvement of the system performance in terms of the efficiency in query search.

The organization of peers (nodes) in overlay networks systems also has been presented in research work such as CAN [1], CHORD [1], Pastry [2], and Tapestry [7]. These systems provide efficient routing mechanism for the structured P2P overlay networks. The major proposed solutions organized peers in overlay networks on the basis of distances, i.e. Locality-aware. The motivation behind our proposed mechanism is to use the overlay networks for the best sender peers selection in order to support heterogeneous clients and to improve the QoS while efficiently utilizing the available network resources. In our proposed hybrid overlay networks mechanism, we organize different sender peers in different hierarchical overlay networks considering both (1) the semantic of the video and (2) the QoS offered by each peer. The detailed hybrid overlay organization mechanism is presented in section 4.

3 Scalable Video Coding (SVC)

Multimedia content adaptation is considered as an important technique to provide QoS management for multimedia delivery over heterogeneous networks to meet the requirements of clients with distinct characteristics. Many video encoding schemes have been proposed for real-time applications operating for heterogeneous networks and terminals. Layered encoding and multiple description coding [8] are considered suitable for many applications including P2P services. At present, Scalable Video Coding (SVC) is considered most promising video encoding format for streaming application in heterogeneous networks and terminals [9]. A scalable video coding is used to produce highly compressed bit-streams, to generate a wide variety of bit-rates. An original SVC stream can be truncated to produce videos of different qualities, resolutions, and frame rates using respectively SNR (signal-to-noise ratio), spatial, and temporal scalabilities.

In this paper, we focus on the use of SVC video formats as an important component of the proposed P2P system while organizing the sender peers in hybrid overlay networks. The SVC characteristics make it more suitable for heterogeneous environments especially P2P networks. A layered stream representation of SVC in terms of spatial, temporal, and SNR resolution is shown in Fig. 2. In SVC encoding scheme, each quality tier is decodable with different characteristics. The first tier providing the basic quality of the video is called "Base Tier" while other tiers which are used to enhance the overall video quality of the base tier are called "Enhancement Tiers" [10].

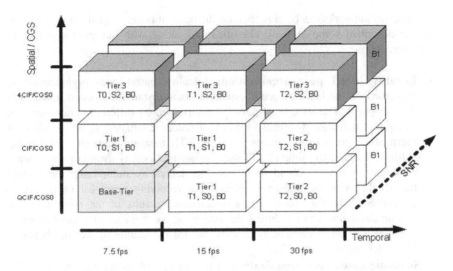

Fig. 2. Scalable Video Encoding – A Layered Stream Representation

4 Hybrid Overlay Networks Organization: Semantic and QoS-Awareness

In this section, we describe our proposed multimedia streaming mechanism over P2P networks. Our targeted P2P streaming solution is based on the collective communication among multiple senders towards a single receiver where the receiver peer orchestrates the overall streaming mechanism. Receiver peer maintains the list of the entire candidate peers which have the requested media contents and are ready to participate in the streaming process. A peer is considered as a candidate peer if it has the requested contents and it is willing to participate in the streaming mechanism. The sender peers are organized in different hybrid overlay networks based on the offered content (i.e. which SVC tier is provided per peer) and based on the QoS offered by the peer. The organization of peers in hybrid overlay networks and their management is described in the following sub-sections.

4.1 Overlay Networks Organization

Many overlay organization schemes have been proposed to address different issues including efficiency, scalability, self-organization, efficient routing. For this study, we have slightly different objective for the organization of the sender peers in overlay networks. We aim to facilitate the receiver peer to select the best sender peer to enhance the overall QoS for the offered services. In this paper, we organize the sender peers in hierarchical hybrid overlay networks. This hybrid peer organization is based on two important characteristics, (1) semantic aware peer organization, (2) quality aware or locality-aware peer organization. The main goal for this hybrid based organization is to bring sender peers closer to the receiver peer and to provide an efficient mechanism for the selection of best peers with the required video quality.

The overlay networks can be classified on the basis of peers' organization criterion. Here, we described some of these classifications along with our proposed Hybrid peers organization.

- **Locality based peer organization:** Locality based peer organization is performed on the basis of geographical/physical distances between sender and receiver peers. The locality of peers is determined by different parameters, for example, Euclidean distances, logical distances estimated using number of intermediate peers (e.g. number of Hops, TTL measurement, etc.), and using end-to-end round trip time (RTT) measurements. Locality-aware or QoS-aware techniques primarily intend to reduce the delays by minimizing the logical distance between the source peers and the receiving peers for each service request. Such locality based peers organization results in the minimizing of start-up delay and latency during the streaming mechanism. Our mechanism is based on RTT measurement as an indicator for the quality of the link between the sender and the destination.

- **Semantic based peer organization:** The structure of media contents is useful for the selection and organization of the appropriate peers in overlay networks. In semantic based organization, peers with the same media contents or offering the same video quality are placed together in overlay networks. Semantic based peers organization influences the delivery of important parts of the audiovisual content to the important peer. Such organization makes it convenient to search media contents rapidly. Semantic based peer organization can be a good choice for scalable video coding and in other coding schemes where media contents are distinguished according to priority. Our mechanism is best adapted to SVC coding or any schemes that can provide priority between sub-streams.

- **Hybrid peer organization:** We propose hybrid peers organization that is influenced by combining locality based (or quality-based) organization and semantic based organization schemes. In this hierarchical hybrid overlay organization, sender peers are arranged in hierarchical overlay networks. The streaming mechanism is receiver-centric. The sender peers offering the same video quality tiers of the same media types are placed at the same level in overlay networks. Sender peers within each level of overlay networks are organized according to locality-aware peer organization. We use round-trip-time "RTT" as an indicator of the offered QoS by each peer. In fact, the best peer is the one offering the best QoS (i.e. the lower RTT). This peer should be selected by the receiver to contribute the base tier of the video. In [11], we have noticed that "RTT" can be used to improve the overall QoS for the streaming applications in heterogeneous networks like P2P. The motivation behind using RTT is its relationship with the offered bandwidth on the end-to-end path. A simplified version of the equation given the bandwidth (data rate) of a particular TCP-like session is given in Eq. 1. The MTU represents the maximum transfer unit and the "Loss" represents the packet loss rate [12].

$$Bandwidth = 1.3 * MTU / \left(RTT * \sqrt{Loss} \right) \tag{1}$$

It is commonly agreed that the lower the "RTT" the more the offered data rate (bandwidth) is higher (c.f. Eq. 1). Thus, peers offering lower RTTs are considered as having a higher available bandwidth and that may be shared fairly among the services. This leads us to propose an efficient peer organization mechanism based on active measurement of peers. Any peer is considered as an important peer if it provides the lowest "RTT" and is assigned to contribute the SVC base video tier.

A hybrid organization of the sender peers in different hierarchies is illustrated in Fig. 3. Here, sender peers are divided into three different levels of overlay networks. The organization of these peers is carried out on the basis of the "RTT" probing and on the basis of offered video quality tiers. Overlay 1 consists of the peers offering the base SVC tier quality of video, overlay 2 and overlay 3 depicts the peers offering enhancement SVC tier 1 and enhancement SVC tier 2 respectively. Within each overlay network, peers are organized according to the end-to-end RTT probing carried out between the receiver and each sender peer. We exploit the "MinHeap" Tree structure for the organization of peers. A "MinHeap" is a minimum complete binary tree where the value in each node is less or equal to those in its children. In such tree structures 'n' peers can be organized in $\Theta(n \log n)$ time. The organization of peers inside the "MinHeap" tree structure is shown in Fig. 3. The peer offering minimum "RTT" is always present at the root of the overlay tree and provides an efficient mechanism to select the best peer offering the best.

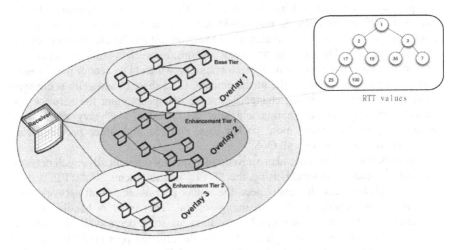

Fig. 3. Layered Organization

4.2 Management of the Sender Peers

The main components of the P2P based media streaming and video on demand services include: indexing of the media contents available to each sender peer, signaling among the peers for their activation, organization of sender peers in virtual overlay networks, media contents retrieval, selection of best sender peer to serve for subsequent request, sender peers switching, selection of quality adaptation path, etc..

In this paper, we did not discussed the issues of indexing, signaling, and data retrieval mechanisms and we are more concerned with the organization of peers in overlay networks for the efficient sender peers selection to enhance the overall QoS.

The management of senders peers in the P2P streaming mechanism is essential as (1) a single peer is not able to serve alone a service request due to its uplink capacity limitations, (2) some selected peers might leave the P2P network at any moment – for example, when the end-user may switch off its system, and (3) additional contributions from new source peers improves the overall Quality of Service (QoS).

- **Selection and Switching of Sender Peers:** We propose to select multiple sender peers from different overlay networks to address the aforementioned issues. We described earlier that scalable video coding is used for video encoding schemes, thus the selection of the best peers is performed by assigning the best quality tier (Base tier) to the best sender peer. A peer is consider as the best peer if it offers the lowest end-to-end "RTT" to the destination. The peers are organized using the "MinHeap" tree structure in different overlay networks thus the best peer in each overlay is located at the root of the "MinHeap" tree that is accessible to the receiver peer in $\Theta 1$ time.

P2P networks possess highly dynamic nature and show unpredictable behavior; any peer node can enter or leave the network without any prior notification. In this situation, P2P architecture is not considered reliable for multimedia streaming applications which require permanent connection establishment throughout the streaming process. During long streaming sessions, network conditions can change drastically. This may involve many factors among which (1) a sender peer crashes and /or stops contributing to the media content, (2) a shared bandwidth is changed since the network conditions change, (3) some new peers enter the network and provide better bandwidth sharing and low "RTT" value, (4) heavy traffic on a particular peer can cause more packet loss, and (5) high inter packets delay ultimately degrades the overall QoS.

Network fluctuations degrade received video quality dramatically. Such network fluctuations can be detected using the "RTT" measurements. If "RTT" values become high for a certain sender peer, the sender peer assumes that network links are no longer suitable for the streaming session. This issue is handled by the switching mechanism in two ways. First, if there are some peers available with low "RTT" values in the subset of tracked peers, the effected peer could be replaced with this peer to maintain a smooth video packet delivery. In other case, if no other best peer is available, stream switching is enforced instead of peers switching. In stream switching, receiver peer re-adjusts the received video streams dynamically. This can be done easily using SVC stream organization as it offers three-dimensional scalability (i.e. special, temporal and SNR). Thus, the received video quality is adapted to the actual available resources in the network by dropping the streaming of some SVC tiers. We implemented the exponential weighted moving average "EWMA" to prevent from oscillation effects while updating peers after each "RTT" calculation. EWMA is an Exponential Smoothing technique [13] that employs one exponential smoothing parameter to give more weight to recent observations and less weight to older observations and vice-versa.

Can the best peer always remain the best? Our targeted architecture for the proposed solution is based on many to one streaming, i.e. a single receiver selects multiple sender peers to receive different parts of the requested media contents. In this scenario, what happens when a number of receivers request for the same media contents? Every receiver peer should prefer to select the best sender peer to receive the contents with the highest quality, in this case due to a certain overload on the best peer; can it still remain the best peer? Nash presented in his classical "Nash Equilibrium" theory [14] that no player can end with higher scores if every player of the certain game choose the best policy. We can state that if every receiver peer intends to select the same best peer, no receiver can get the entire video with good quality and there might be a system crash due to the heavy load (in the case of large number of receiver peers). The best peer for a particular session will not then remain the best for the following session.

The proposed peer organization and their selection provide an efficient way of handling this issue. Firstly, our proposed solution is receiver-centric, and secondly it is based on the probing of sender peers using "RTT" as an indicator of the QoS. We noticed that the probed end-to-end "RTT" is not the same for all the receiver peers, and being the receiver-centric solution every receiver maintains the overlays of sender peers and candidate peers in its own prospective. In our mechanism, the best peer for a receiver might be the worst sender peer for other receiver peer.

- **Quality adaptation:** Quality adaptation determines the way to assign the video quality tiers to respective sender peers by selecting from different overlay networks. The hybrid overlay organization facilitates to determine the quality adaptation in an efficient manner as all the peers are classified on the basis of offered video quality and QoS. Fig. 4 describes scenarios how a receiver peer can determine quality adaptation based on its preferences. We have presented different quality adaptations patterns (i.e. horizontal adaptation, vertical adaptation, diagonal adaptation, ZigZag adaptation) which represent the patterns to select the sender peers to receive the video quality tiers.

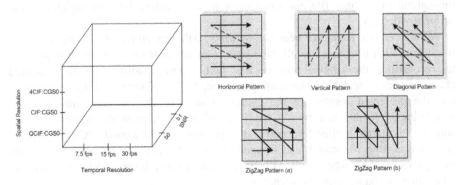

Fig. 4. Quality Adaptation Patterns

Horizontal and Vertical ordering is more suitable for cases where the receiver intends to receive video quality based on a single parameter, i.e. temporal, spatial, or SNR. ZigZag and Diagonal patterns provide the mechanism to select different sender peers to receive video quality based on multiple parameters. We suggest selecting multiple sender peers from the overlay networks based on ZigZag adaptation for our proposed streaming mechanism. In this way, a better QoS for the received video can be ensured on the basis of available resources.

5 Performance Evaluation

This section describes the simulation results for the proposed streaming mechanism performed using the ns-2 simulator.

5.1 Network Model

We consider Gnutella like P2P topology for the simulations and we organize different groups of peers on the basis of proposed hybrid overlay scheme. We distribute the SVC tiers equally among different overlays to examine the performance of the proposed mechanism. A receiver peer intends to receive the real-time video packets from multiple sender peers using P2P network. The receiver peers use "RTT" for the probing of sender peers and best peer selection is performed on the basis of lower "RTT". "RTT" values are only indicative that reflect the current network conditions and give sufficient information to choose the best peer.

We perform simulations to receive the video quality of CIF/CGS0 with 15 fps. The receiver peer activates a particular sender peer from each overlay group depending on the "RTT" value and the offered video quality based on ZigZag pattern (a) shown in Fig. 4. Each sending peer contributes different quality tiers of the original video file, so that it can be used to reconstruct a video file with the best quality at the receiver node. For the test cases, we generated 4 different quality tiers using MPEG-4 trace files where Base Tier offers 40 % throughput of original video, enhanced tier 1 offers 30 % throughput of original file, enhanced tier 2 offers 20 % throughput of original file and enhancement tier 3 offers 10% throughput of the original video file.

We noticed that no source peer is providing 100% throughput of the original video but if a receiver peer receives all the 4 tiers from different sender peers, it is possible to reconstruct the original media file with 100% quality with the selected characteristics of scalable video coding scheme. The simulation time was 60 seconds and the presented results are the average results of the multiple runs of these simulations. We attached two "CBR sources" to overcharge the network. "CBR source 1" is started at time 5 second and stopped at time 55 second. "CBR source 2" is started at time 10 second, and stopped at time 50. Both sources injected constant throughput of 512 Kbps with 512 Bytes UDP packet lengths. We simulate the adaptation mechanism for two scenarios.

- Scenario without Quality Adaptation: Simulation without applying any quality adaptation mechanism. In this case, P2P system works as in downloading modes. The sender peers are selected on a random basis.

- Scenario with the proposed Quality Adaptation: Simulation with quality adaptation mechanism is performed by best peer selection and their switching based on the proposed hybrid overlay networks as described in section 4.

5.2 Simulation Results

Fig. 5 shows the received video throughput at receiver peer for both scenarios. We observed that the quality adaptation mechanism improved the received throughput compared to the scenario without quality adaptation. We have noticed few packets drop even with quality adaptation mechanism. These packets drops are caused due to the heavy stress on the network created by CBR/UDP traffic which is presented in Fig. 6. Packet drop ratio is much lesser in the scenario with quality adaptation compared to scenario without adaptation so, our quality adaptation mechanism works fine for this case too. This enhanced throughput and lower packets drops results into the overall improvement in QoS.

We monitored all the active network links constantly and select only one sender peer from each overlay group, i.e. peer having lowest "RTT" and present at the root of "MinHeap" tree. The stream switching is done by selecting the best sender peer offering the better QoS (high bandwidth share). We performed peer switching and implemented EWMA mechanisms to avoid fluctuations caused by peers arrival or removal. Fig. 7(a), Fig. 7(b), Fig. 7(c), and Fig. 7(d) describe the comparison between received and original base tiers, enhancement tier 1, enhanced tier 2, and enhanced tier 3 respectively. We can see clearly that our proposed mechanism performs a smooth video delivery with higher quality, lower loss and delay. A summary of these results is given in Table 1.

The overall received 1-way packets delay (from sender peer to receiver peer) for both cases is presented in Fig. 8. The packets transmission delay has been significantly improved when quality adaptation mechanism is applied. We reconstructed the expected video file using the "AKIYO" video sequence for the received video quality at the receiver end to evaluate the PSNR (Peak signal-to-noise ratio) objective measurements. The comparison results for PSNR for the videos generated in both scenarios to the original video are shown in Fig. 9.

Table 1. A Summary of Simulation Analysis

	Received Video Quality (%)	Average Received Base Tier (%)	Average Received Enh. Tier 1 (%)	Average Received Enh. Tier 3 (%)	Average Received Enh. Tier 2 (%)	Average Packet Delay (ms)
With quality Adaptation	98	99	99	93	99	45
Without Quality Adaptation	76	60	96	57	100	60

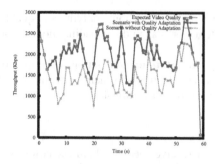

Fig. 5. Received Video Throughput

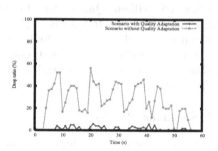

Fig. 6. Packets Drop Ratio

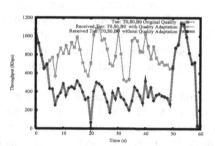

Fig. 7. (a) Base Tier

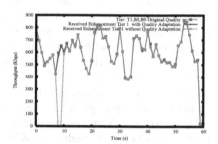

Fig. 7. (b) Enhancement Tier 1

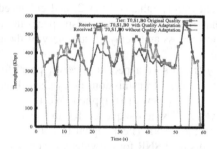

Fig. 7. (c) Enhancement Tier 2

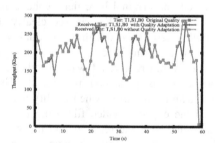

Fig. 7. (d) Enhancement Tier 3

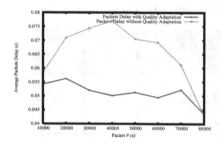

Fig. 8. 1-way Packets Delay

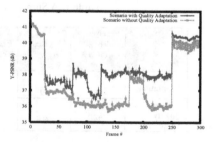

Fig. 9. PSNR

6 Conclusion

In this paper, we presented a hybrid overlay network mechanism for the multimedia streaming and video on demand services in P2P environment. The hybrid overlay networks are constructed on the basis of video quality offered by sender peers and active end-to-end probing of sender peers using "RTT". The overlay organization provides a mechanism to select the best sender peers in $\Theta 1$ time. The proposed mechanism is evaluated using simulations and a significant improvement in the received throughput especially for the important video quality tiers, lower packets drop ratio for the important quality tiers, and a considerable improvement in the received packets delay are observed.

References

1. Ratnasamy, S., Francis, P., Handley, M., Karp, R., Shenker, S.: A Scalable Content-Addressable Network. In: Proc. ACM SIGCOMM, pp. 161–172. ACM Press, New York (2001)
2. Stoica, I., Morris, R., Karger, D., Kaashoek, M.F., Balakrishnan, H.: Chord: A scalable peer-to-peer lookup service for internet applications. In: Proc. ACM SIGCOMM, ACM Press, New York (2001)
3. Rowstron, A., Druschel, P.: Pastry: Scalable, distributed object location and routing for large-scale peer-to-peer systems. In: proc. of the 18th IFIP/ACM International Conference on Distributed Systems Platforms (Middleware 2001), pp. 329–350 (November 2001)
4. Zhang, X., Liu, J., Li, B., Yum, T.-S.P.: CoolStreaming/DONet: A Data-Driven Overlay Network for Efficient Live Media Streaming. In: proc. of IEEE Infocom 2005, Miami, FL, USA (March 2005)
5. Tian, R., Xiong, Y., Zhang, Q., Li, B., Zhao, B.Y., Li, X.: Hybrid Overlay Structure Based on Random Walks. In: Castro, M., van Renesse, R. (eds.) IPTPS 2005. LNCS, vol. 3640, pp. 152–162. Springer, Heidelberg (2005)
6. Crespo, A., Garcia-Molina, H.: Semantic Overlay Networks for P2P Systems, technical report (last viewed May 15, 2007), available from http://infolab.stanford.edu/ crespo/publications/op2p.pdf
7. Zhao, B., Kubiatowicz, J., Joseph, A.: Tapestry: An infrastructure for fault-tolerant widearea location and routing. Technical report UCB/CSD-01-1141, U. C. Berkeley (April 2001)
8. Vitali, A., Fumagalli, M., Cefriel: Standard-compatible Multiple-Description Coding (MDC) and Layered Coding (LC) of Audio/Video Streams, Internet Draft, Network Working Group (July 2005)
9. Schwarz, H., Marpe, D., Wiegand, T.: SNR-Scalable Extension of H.264/AVC. In: proceedings of ICIP 2004, Singapore (2004)
10. Wu, D., Hou, T., Zhang, Y.-Q.: Scalable Video Coding and Transport over Broadband Wireless Networks. In: Proceedings of the IEEE (September 2000)
11. Mushtaq, M., Ahmed, T.: Adaptive Packet Video Streaming over P2P Networks Using Active Measurements. In: ISCC 2006. proceedings of the 11th IEEE Symposium on Computers and Communications, pp. 423–428. IEEE Computer Society, Los Alamitos (2006)
12. Mahdavi, J., Floyd, S.: TCP-Friendly Unicast Rate-Based Flow Control. Technical note sent to the end2end-interest mailing list (January 8, 1997)
13. Stuart Hunter, J.: The Exponentially Weighted Moving Average. J. Quality Technology 18(4), 203–207 (1986)
14. Nash, J.: Non-Cooperative Games. The Annals of Mathematics 54(2), 286–295 (1951)

Measuring Interaction QoE in Internet Videoconferencing*

Prasad Calyam[1], Mark Haffner[1], Eylem Ekici[1], and Chang-Gun Lee[2]

[1] The Ohio State University, Columbus, OH 43210
pcalyam@oar.net, mhaffner@oar.net, ekici@ece.osu.edu
[2] Seoul National University, Korea, 151-742
cglee@snu.ac.kr

Abstract. Internet videoconferencing has emerged as a viable medium for communication and entertainment. However, its widespread use is being challenged. This is because videoconference end-users frequently experience perceptual quality impairments such as video frame freezing and voice dropouts due to changes in network conditions on the Internet. These impairments cause extra *end-user interaction effort* and correspondingly lead to unwanted *network bandwidth consumption* that affects user Quality of Experience (QoE) and Internet congestion. Hence, it is important to measure and subsequently minimize the extra end-user interaction effort in a videoconferencing system. In this paper, we describe a novel active measurement scheme that considers end-user interaction effort and the corresponding network bandwidth consumption to provide videoconferencing interaction QoE measurements. The scheme involves a "Multi-Activity Packet-Trains" (MAPTs) methodology to dynamically emulate a videoconference session's participant interaction patterns and corresponding video activity levels that are affected by transient changes in network conditions. Also, we describe the implementation and validation of the *Vperf* tool we have developed to measure the videoconferencing interaction QoE on a network path using our proposed scheme.

1 Introduction

Internet videoconferencing is being used increasingly for remote meetings, distance learning, tele-medicine, etc. over the Internet. However, videoconferencing service providers are facing challenges in successfully deploying and managing large-scale videoconferencing systems on the Internet. This is because videoconference end-users frequently experience *perceptual quality impairments* such as video frame freezing and voice dropouts due to changes in network conditions i.e., "network fault events" caused by: (a) cross-traffic congestion at intermediate hops, (b) physical link fractures, and (c) last-mile bandwidth limitations.

To assist videoconferencing service providers in proactive identification and mitigation of network fault events, several metrics and active measurement tools

---

* This work has been supported in part by The Ohio Board of Regents.

D. Krishnaswamy, T. Pfeifer, and D. Raz (Eds.): MMNS 2007, LNCS 4787, pp. 14–25, 2007.
© IFIP International Federation for Information Processing 2007

have been developed. The metrics include network factors such as end-to-end available bandwidth, packet delay, jitter and loss. Active measurement tools such as Ping and Iperf [1] observe the performance levels of these network factors on the Internet paths. Studies such as [2] - [6] map the different performance levels of the measured network factors to metrics that indicate severity of the perceptual quality impairments in a videoconference session. The most widely-used metric to quantify end-user Quality of Experience (QoE) in terms of perceptual quality impairment severity is the "Mean Opinion Score" (MOS).

In addition to causing perceptual quality impairments, network fault events also cause *interaction difficulties* to the videoconference participants, which the existing metrics and tools do not measure. This observation along with an explanation on the need for schemes to measure human interaction difficulties in voice and video conferences is presented in [7]. The interaction difficulties correspond to instances during a session where a 'listening' participant is led to interrupt a 'talking' participant by saying "Can you please 'repeat' the previous sentence?" due to a voice drop-out caused by a network fault event occurrence. In extreme cases, prolonged network fault events impair the perceptual quality and aggravate the interaction difficulties to an extent that the participants decide to 'disconnect' and 'reconnect' the videoconference session. Upon reconnection, assuming the effects of the network fault events have subsided, the participants 'reorient' their discussion to progress further with the remaining "agenda-items" in the videoconference session.

These 'repeat', 'disconnect', 'reconnect', and 'reorient' actions during a videoconference session are unwanted interaction patterns because they increase the end-user effort required to complete a set of agenda-items in a videoconference session. In addition, video traffic in a videoconference session has high data rates (256 Kbps - 768 Kbps) and hence the video traffic of the unwanted interaction patterns increases the Internet traffic congestion levels. The end-user interaction effort and the corresponding network bandwidth consumption together can be measured using the "agenda-bandwidth" metric, which we define as the aggregate network bandwidth consumed on both sides while completing a set of agenda-items in a videoconference session. Unwanted interaction patterns result in *unwanted agenda-bandwidth*. The ability to measure the unwanted agenda-bandwidth and subsequently minimize it using suitable traffic engineering techniques [8] can foster efficient design of large-scale videoconferencing systems.

To measure the unwanted agenda-bandwidth i.e., interaction QoE in an automated manner by mimicking the interaction behavior of participants, it is not practical to use actual videoconferencing end-points and video sequences. Hence, in this paper, we describe a *novel active measurement scheme to measure the interaction QoE of a videoconference session*. This scheme described in Section 3 (after describing a videoconferencing system in Section 2) involves a "Multi-Activity Packet-Trains" (MAPTs) methodology. Here, an interaction behavior controller illustrated in Figure 1, generates probing packet trains to dynamically emulate a videoconference session's participant interaction patterns and corresponding video activity levels for a given session agenda input. During the session emulation, the network fault events, for example on Side-A, are detected by analyzing online performance of the received video streams from Side-B. Such detected events affect the smooth progress of the agenda-items and cause inter-action patterns with 'repeat', 'disconnect', 'reconnect', and 'reorient' actions. The interaction QoE is reported based on the session agenda progress, which is reflected in the agenda-bandwidth measurement. In Section 4, we describe the implementation of the *Vperf* tool that we have developed to measure the video-conferencing interaction QoE on a network path using our proposed scheme. In Section 5, we show Vperf's measurements in a network testbed that features a wide variety of network fault events. Finally, Section 6 concludes the paper.

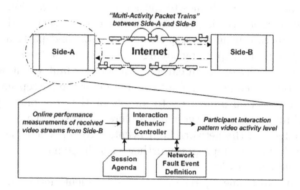

Fig. 1. MAPTs methodology

2   System Description

2.1   Video Traffic Characteristics

The combined voice and video traffic streams in a videoconference session are expressed in terms of sender-side encoding rate (b_{snd}) as shown in Equation (1).

$$b_{snd} = b_{voice} + b_{video} = tps_{voice}\left(\frac{b_{codec}}{ps}\right)_{voice} + tps_{video}\left(\frac{b_{codec}}{ps}\right)_{video} \quad (1)$$

where *tps* corresponds to the total packet size of either voice or video packets, whose value equals a sum of the payload size (ps), the IP/UDP/RTP header size (40 bytes) and the Ethernet header size (14 bytes); b_{codec} corresponds to the voice or video codec data rate values chosen. Commonly, G.711/G.722 voice codec and H.263 video codec are used in videoconferences. The peak encoding rate of $\lceil b_{voice} \rceil$ is generally 64 Kbps, whereas, end-points allow end-users to choose different $\lceil b_{video} \rceil$ settings depending on the desired video quality and the access link bandwidth at the end-user site. The end-users specify the $\lceil b_{video} \rceil$ setting as a "dialing speed" in a videoconference. Dialing speeds of 768 Kbps and higher are chosen by end-users with access links of T-1 or better, whereas, dialing speeds of 256 Kbps and 384 Kbps are chosen by end-users with cable-modem/DSL access links.

Owing to the sampling nature of voice codecs, voice streams contain a series of packets that are relatively small ($tps_{voice} \leq 534$ bytes) with fixed ps characteristics. As for the video ps, they are mainly influenced by the activity-level (a_{lev}) in the sent video sequence. This is because most video codecs use inter-frame differencing encoding, where only frames containing differences between consecutive frames are sent rather than sending every video frame. The a_{lev} refers to the temporal and spatial nature of the video sequences in a videoconference session. Broadly, video sequences can be categorized as having either low or high a_{lev}. Low a_{lev} video sequences feature slow body movements and a constant background (e.g. *Claire* video sequence). High a_{lev} video sequences feature rapid body movements and/or quick scene changes (e.g. *Foreman* video sequence). In our study, we consider the 'listening' end-user action to produce a low a_{lev} video sequence and the 'talking' end-user action to produce a high a_{lev} video sequence.

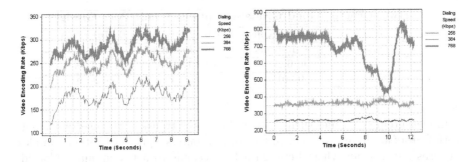

Fig. 2. b_{video} for *Claire* (low a_{lev})   **Fig. 3.** b_{video} for *Foreman* (high a_{lev})

To distinguish the low and high video a_{lev} characteristics in terms of the bandwidth consumption b_{video}, let us look at Figures 2 and 3. They show the instantaneous b_{video} values for the *Claire* and *Foreman* video sequences, respectively for the common dialing speeds. We can see that the bandwidth consumption for low a_{lev} video i.e., 'listening' end-user action is less than that for high a_{lev} video i.e., 'talking' end-user action, irrespective of the session's dialing speed. We will use this video encoding behavior observation in our MAPTs methodology explained in Section 3.

2.2   Network Fault Events

The network fault events correspond to the network condition changes that affect the b_{snd} traffic and cause unwanted interaction patterns between participants in a videoconference session. The network condition changes are measured in terms of the network factors: end-to-end network bandwidth (b_{net}), delay (d_{net}), jitter (j_{net}), and loss (l_{net}). If there is adequate b_{net} provisioned in a network path to accommodate the b_{snd} traffic, receiver-side traffic (b_{rcv}) will be equal to b_{snd}. Otherwise, b_{rcv} is limited to b_{net} - available bandwidth at the bottleneck hop as shown in Equation (2).

$$b_{rcv} = min(b_{snd}, min_{i=1..hops} b_{i^{th} hop})$$ (2)

Earlier studies have shown that the performance levels of network factors can be mapped to the MOS expressed in three grade ranges: [4, 5] for "Good", [3, 4) for "Acceptable" and [1, 3) for "Poor" as shown in Table 1. Specifically, [2] and [3] suggest that for Good grade, b_{net} should be at least 20% more than the dialing speed value to accommodate the voice payload and protocol overhead; b_{net} values less than 25% of the dialing speed result in Poor Grade. The ITU-T G.114 [4] recommendation provides the levels for d_{net}. The studies in [5] and [6] provide the performance levels for j_{net} and l_{net} on the basis of empirical experiments on the Internet.

Table 1. Performance levels of network factors and MOS for $\lceil b_{video} \rceil = 768$ Kbps

Network Factor	Good Grade	Acceptable Grade	Poor Grade
b_{net}	(>922] Kbps	(576-922) Kbps	[0-576) Kbps
d_{net}	[0-150] ms	(150-300) ms	(>300] ms
l_{net}	[0-0.5) %	(0.5-1.5) %	(>1.5] %
j_{net}	[0-20) ms	(20-50) ms	(>50] ms

In measurement studies such as [9] and [10], the transient changes of the network factors are found to occur in the form of bursts, spikes and other complex patterns and last anywhere between a few seconds to a few minutes. Considering the broad severity levels of the network fault events and the timescale within which end-point error-concealment schemes cannot ameliorate the voice and video degradation, we classify network fault events into two types: (i) Type-I, and (ii) Type-II. If the performance level of any network factor in the Good grade changes to the Acceptable grade over a 5 second period, we treat such an occurrence as a "Type-I" network fault event. Also, if the performance level of any network factor in the Good grade changes to the Poor grade over a 10 second period, we treat such an occurrence as a "Type-II" network fault event. Further, we consider the impact of a Type-I network fault event on end-user QoE to result in a 'repeat' action of a listening participant in a videoconference session. Along the same lines, we consider the impact of a Type-II network fault event on end-user QoE to result in the 'disconnect', 'reconnect' and 'reorient' actions between the participants in a videoconference session.

3   Multi-Activity Packet-Trains (MAPTs) Methodology

In this section, we explain our "Multi-Activity Packet-Trains" (MAPTs) methodology, which uses the active measurements principle where probing packet trains dynamically emulate participants' interaction patterns and corresponding video activity levels in a videoconference session.

3.1   Emulation of Participant Interaction Patterns

For simplicity, we assume that a videoconference session agenda involves a participant on side-A asking a series of questions to another participant on side-B. Each question or answer corresponds to a separate agenda-item. Further, if the participant on side-A is 'talking', we assume the participant on side-B to be 'listening' and vice versa. Hence, the total network bandwidth consumed by the participant on side-A asking questions, can be considered as the *request* of the videoconference session. Likewise, the total network bandwidth consumed by the participant on side-B while responding to the questions (or while satisfying the request) can be considered as the *response* of the videoconference session.

For such a videoconference session, we consider three different participant interaction patterns (PIP): PIP_1, PIP_2, and PIP_3. The PIP_1 corresponds to the participant interaction pattern when no network fault events occur during the videoconference session. Figure 4 shows the instantaneous request and response for the PIP_1 interaction pattern. The videoconference session starts with the participant on side-A doing the 'talking' for the introduction agenda-item. Following this, the agenda-items progress with each side participant 'talking' alternately without any network fault event interruptions. Finally, the session ends with the both-side participants 'talking' during the conclusion agenda-item.

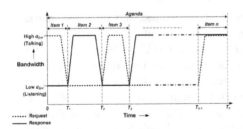

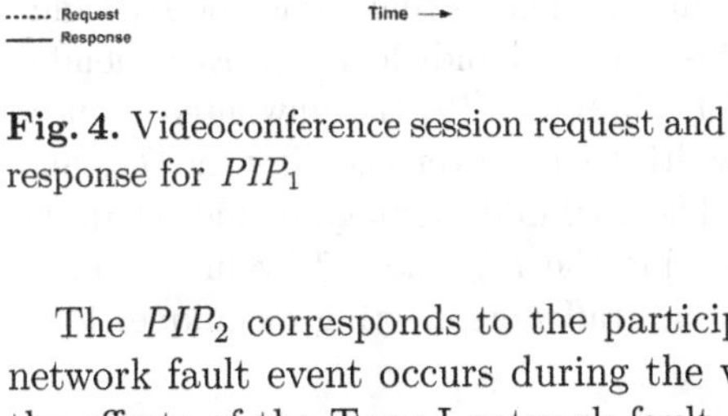

Fig. 4. Videoconference session request and response for PIP_1

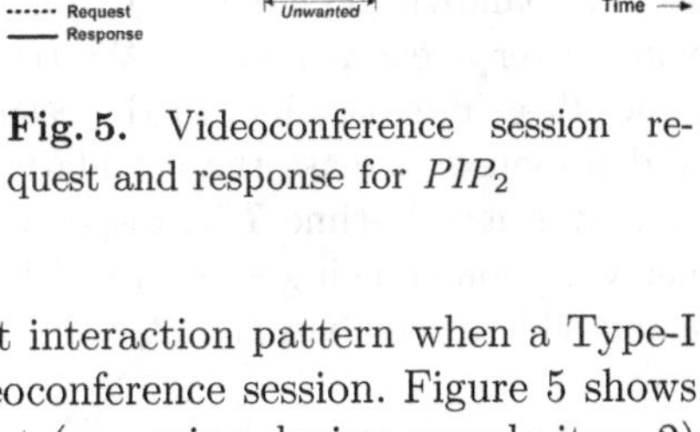

Fig. 5. Videoconference session request and response for PIP_2

The PIP_2 corresponds to the participant interaction pattern when a Type-I network fault event occurs during the videoconference session. Figure 5 shows the effects of the Type-I network fault event (occurring during agenda-item 2) on the instantaneous request and response in the videoconference session. We can see that once the Type-I network fault event affects the 'listening' side-A participant at time T'_{event}, the participant begins 'talking' to interrupt the 'talking' side-B participant and requests for a repeat of the previous statements. The time between T'_{event} and T_{repeat} corresponds to the time taken for the participant on side-B to complete responding to the repeat request made by the side-A participant. The revised time to finish the item 2 in this case is T'_2.

The PIP_3 corresponds to the participant interaction pattern when a Type-II network fault event occurs during the videoconference session. Figure 6 shows the effects of the Type-II network fault event (occurring during agenda-item 2) on the instantaneous request and response in the videoconference session. We can see that once the Type-II network fault event affects the 'listening' side-A participant at time T''_{event}, the participant begins 'talking' to interrupt the 'talking' side-B participant and requests for a session reconnection. The times $T_{disconnect}$, $T_{reconnect}$ and $T_{reorient}$, correspond to the 'disconnect', 'reconnect' and 'reorient' actions, respectively. The revised time to finish the item 2 in this case is T''_2.

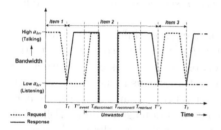

Fig. 6. Videoconference session request and response for PIP_3

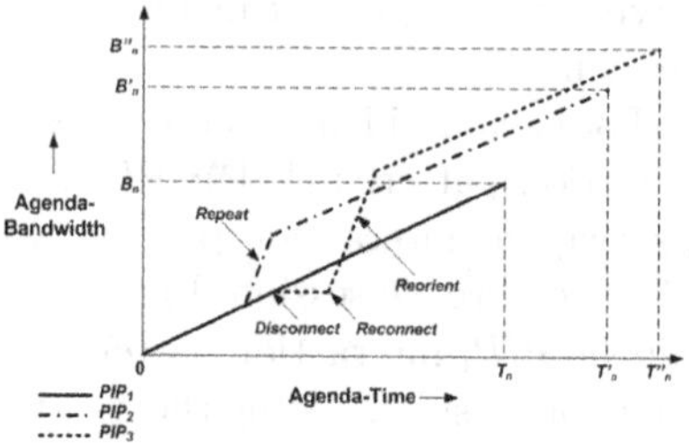

Fig. 7. Agenda-bandwidth for the three participant interaction patterns

Our next step is to determine the "unwanted" request and response (marked in Figures 5 and 6) and thus obtain the unwanted agenda-bandwidth in the session. Based on the agenda-bandwidth definition stated in Section 1, the agenda-bandwidth is calculated as a sum of all the instantaneous request and response bandwidth values over the session duration. The agenda-bandwidth measurements for PIP_1, PIP_2, and PIP_3 are shown in Figure 7. In the case of PIP_1, the agenda-bandwidth increases steadily and all the agenda-items consume B_n bandwidth over agenda-time T_n. We treat this agenda-bandwidth B_n over agenda-time T_n as our baseline. In the cases of PIP_2 and PIP_3, the unwanted request and response increase the agenda-bandwidth to B'_n over agenda-time T'_n and B''_n over agenda-time T''_n, respectively. The goal in designing an efficient Internet videoconferencing system will be to bring the B'_n and B''_n values as close as possible to the baseline B_n using suitable traffic engineering techniques [8].

3.2 Emulation of Video Activity Levels

We now describe the videoconferencing traffic model to be used by the probing packet trains that emulate the low and high a_{lev} video at the different dialing speeds: 256, 384 and 768 Kbps. Since there do not exist earlier proposed videoconferencing traffic models that can be used to emulate the low and high a_{lev}

video at different dialing speeds, we derive the videoconferencing traffic model parameters below using a trace-analysis based approach.

There are several video sequences available at [11] whose statistical characteristics (e.g. mean and covariance of frame quality) are widely known. Hence, researchers use them as a reference to compare the performance of their proposed techniques with other existing techniques. From these, we choose a set of 10 video sequences with 5 video sequences (*Grandma, Kelly, Claire, Mother/Daughter, Salesman*) belonging to the low a_{lev} category and 5 video sequences (*Foreman, Car Phone, Tempete, Mobile, Park Run*) belonging to the high a_{lev} category. The video sequences within a category are combined and used in a videoconference session initiated on an isolated LAN testbed with two Polycom View Station end-points that use the H.263 video codec. The b_{video} values for low and high a_{lev} traces for the common dialing speeds are shown in Figures 8 and 9, respectively. To emulate the time-series characteristics of the b_{video} values, we divide the instantaneous *tps* values with the corresponding instantaneous b_{video} values to obtain the instantaneous inter-packet time *ipt* values in the packet trains.

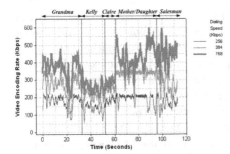
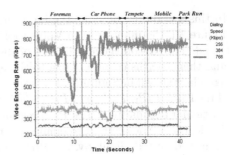

Fig. 8. b_{video} for combined low a_{lev} video sequences

Fig. 9. b_{video} for combined high a_{lev} video sequences

To derive the *tps* characteristics, we perform a statistical distribution "goodness of fit" testing. Our distribution-fit analysis suggests that the video *tps* distribution corresponds to the Gamma distribution given by Equation (3).

$$F(x) = \frac{1}{\Gamma(\alpha)\beta_{\alpha}} x^{\alpha-1} e^{\frac{-x}{\beta}} \tag{3}$$

Table 2 shows the Gamma distribution shape (α) and scale (β) parameters of the $x = tps$ data in the low and high a_{lev} video traffic traces at the different dialing speeds.

To derive the trend parameters for the b_{video}, we perform time-series modeling using the classical decomposition method [12]. Our model-fit analysis suggests b_{video} as a second-order moving average (MA(2)) process given by Equation (4).

$$X_t = Z_t + \theta_1 Z_{t-1} + \theta_2 Z_{t-2} \tag{4}$$

where Z_t is an i.i.d. noise process with mean 0 and variance σ^2. Table 2 also shows the MA(2) time-series model parameters for the low and high a_{lev} video traffic at the different dialing speeds. The θ_1, θ_2, μ and σ^2 parameters correspond to the MA1 and MA2 co-efficients, mean and variance, respectively.

Table 2. Gamma distribution and MA(2) parameters for low and high a_{lev}

Activity Level	Dialing Speed (Kbps)	α	β	θ_1	θ_2	μ	σ^2
Low	256	4.115	102.0	-1.2395	0.2395	192	200
Low	384	2.388	250.3	-1.1614	0.1614	253	400
Low	768	1.625	240.1	-1.2684	0.2684	301	500
High	256	4.321	110.0	-1.5213	0.5213	249	5
High	384	1.517	281.6	-1.4741	0.4741	349	140
High	768	1.142	446.1	-1.3024	0.3024	720	100

4   Vperf Implementation

In this section, we describe the implementation of the *Vperf* tool. As shown in Figure 10, the inputs to the Vperf tool include the session agenda and dialing speed. The session agenda consists of the L and H video a_{lev} packet train order and their lengths corresponding to the agenda-items. A simple example session agenda is shown in Figure 11. It consists of three sections that correspond to the three PIPs: PIP_1, PIP_2, and PIP_3. Each row in the PIP_1 section corresponds to a particular agenda-item. The PIP_2 section row is used to specify the length of the H video a_{lev} packet train to emulate a 'repeat' action if a Type-I network fault event is detected. Similarly, the PIP_3 section rows are used to specify the length and video a_{lev} of the packet trains to emulate the 'disconnect', 'reconnect' and 'reorient' actions if a Type-II network fault event is detected. Note that the N during the reconnect action corresponds to no video a_{lev} portion of the session. Vperf generates b_{video} from Side-A to Side-B and vice versa according to the specified session agenda and dialing speed parameters. For a particular L or H video a_{lev} specified in the session agenda, the Vperf tool uses the tps and ipt traffic model parameters (obtained from Section 3.2) specified in the "Traffic Model" file.

For these inputs, the outputs from Vperf tool are as follows: Based on the emulated traffic performance, Vperf continuously collects online measurements of b_{net}, d_{net}, j_{net}, and l_{net} network factors on a per-second basis and appends them to an "Interim Test Report". It also produces a total average of these measurements, agenda-bandwidth and agenda-time measurements at the end of the session in the form of a "Final Test Report". To generate these measurements for an emulated session, it uses the "Interaction Behavior Controller" component. This component processes the interim test report and detects the occurrence of Type-I and Type-II network fault events by looking up the detection rules (refer to Table 1) specified in the "Network Factor Limits" file. When a Type-I or Type-II network fault event occurrence is detected, the interaction behavior controller

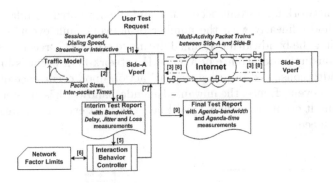

Fig. 10. Vperf tool components and their workflow

PIP-Type	Side-A Train (a_{iev})	Side-B Train (a_{iev})	Train Duration (Seconds)	
	L	H	30	
	H	L	10	
	L	H	30	
PIP$_1$	H	L	20	
	L	H	30	
	H	L	20	
	L	H	20	
	H	L	20	
PIP$_2$	H	H	5	◄── Repeat
	H	H	5	◄── Disconnect
PIP$_3$	N	N	15	◄── Reconnect
	H	H	5	◄── Reorient

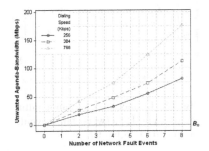

Fig. 11. An example Vperf tool session agenda specification

Fig. 12. Impact of increasing number of Type-I network fault events on Agenda-bandwidth

alters the emulation of the session agenda based on the participant interaction patterns explained in Section 3.1.

5   Performance Evaluation

In this section, we describe the videoconference session performance measurements collected on an isolated network testbed consisting of two measurement servers separated by the NISTnet network emulator [13]. The NISTnet was dynamically configured with different WAN profiles that featured the occurrence of varying number of Type-I and Type-II network fault events during videoconference session emulation by the Vperf tool. The session agenda input to the Vperf tool contained the packet trains video a_{iev} and train durations for the PIP_1, PIP_2 and PIP_3 cases as shown in Figure 11.

Figures 12 and 13 show the unwanted agenda-bandwidth measurements from the Vperf tool for increasing number of NISTnet-generated Type-I and Type-II network fault events, respectively. Each measurement is an average of 10 emulation runs. As expected, the amount of unwanted agenda-bandwidth is zero when there is no network fault event occurrence and the unwanted agenda-bandwidth increases almost linearly with the number of network fault events occurrence. We know that the bandwidth consumed during 'disconnect', 'reconnect' and 're-orient' actions upon occurrence of a Type-II network fault event is higher than the bandwidth consumed in just a 'repeat' action upon occurrence of a Type-I network fault event. Hence, the unwanted agenda-bandwidth is greater for Type-II network fault event cases than Type-I network fault event cases, regardless of the dialing speed.

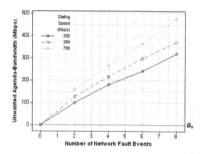

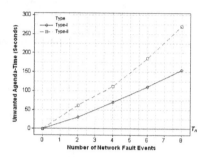

Fig. 13. Impact of increasing number of Type-II network fault events on Agenda-bandwidth

Fig. 14. Impact of increasing number of Type-I and Type-II network fault events on Agenda-time at 768 Kbps dialing speed

Similar to the unwanted agenda-bandwidth, the unwanted agenda-time also increases linearly as the number of network faults events increase. Figure 14 shows such an increase for Type-I and Type-II network fault events at the 768Kbps dialing speed. We know that the time involved in the 'disconnect', 'reconnect' and 'reorient' actions upon occurrence of a Type-II network fault event is higher than the time involved in just a 'repeat' action upon occurrence of a Type-I network fault event. Hence, we can see that the unwanted agenda-time is greater for Type-II network fault event cases than Type-I network fault event cases, regardless of the dialing speed. Similar unwanted agenda-time characteristics were observed at the 256 Kbps and 384 Kbps dialing speeds also.

6   Conclusion

In this paper, we presented a novel active measurement scheme used to measure the videoconferencing interaction QoE on a network path. The scheme involved a "Multi-Activity Packet-Trains" (MAPTs) methodology where probing packet trains dynamically emulated participants' interaction patterns and corresponding video activity levels in a videoconference session that are affected by network fault events on the Internet. We detailed the characteristics of the probing packet trains with a videoconferencing traffic-model derived using a trace-analysis approach. Lastly, we described the implementation and validation of the *Vperf* tool we have developed that uses our MAPTs methodology.

Besides the basic participant interaction patterns and network fault event types considered in this paper, there are obviously several others that commonly occur in Internet videoconferencing. To formally define and classify them, detailed studies with actual end-users need to be conducted. Hence, there is a wide scope of investigation yet to be explored that can help us better understand the causes and effects of videoconference session performance failures affecting end-user interaction QoE over the Internet.

References

1. Tirumala, A., Cottrell, L., Dunigan, T.: Measuring End-to-end Bandwidth with Iperf using Web100. In: Proc. of PAM (2003)
2. Tang, H., Duan, L., Li, J.: A Performance Monitoring Architecture for IP Videoconferencing. In: Proc. of IPOM (2004)
3. Implementing QoS Solutions for H.323 Videoconferencing over IP, Cisco Systems Technical Whitepaper Document Id: 21662 (2007)
4. ITU-T Recommendation G.114, One-Way Transmission Time (1996)
5. Calyam, P., Sridharan, M., Mandrawa, W., Schopis, P.: Performance Measurement and Analysis of H.323 Traffic. In: Barakat, C., Pratt, I. (eds.) PAM 2004. LNCS, vol. 3015, Springer, Heidelberg (2004)
6. Claypool, M., Tanner, J.: The Effects of Jitter on the Perceptual Quality of Video. In: Proc. of ACM Multimedia (1999)
7. Rix, A., Bourret, A., Hollier, M.: Models of Human Perception, BT Technology Journal 17 (1999)
8. Jha, S., Hassan, M.: Engineering Internet QoS, Artech House Publication (2002) ISBN: 1580533418
9. Markopoulou, A., Tobagi, F., Karam, M.: Loss and Delay Measurements of Internet Backbones, Elsevier Computer Communications (2006)
10. Ciavattone, L., Morton, A., Ramachandran, G.: Standardized Active Measurements on a Tier 1 IP Backbone, IEEE Communications Magazine (2003)
11. Arizona State University Video Trace Library (2007), http://trace.eas.asu.edu
12. Brockwell, P., Davis, R.: Introduction to Time Series and Forecasting. Springer, New York (2002)
13. NISTnet Network Emulator, http://snad.ncsl.nist.gov/itg/nistnet

Predicting Calls – New Service for an Intelligent Phone

Santi Phithakkitnukoon and Ram Dantu

Network Security Laboratory, Department of Computer Science and Engineering,
University of North Texas, Denton, TX 76203, USA
{santi, rdantu}@unt.edu

Abstract. Predicting future calls can be the next advanced feature of the intelligent phone as the phone service providers are looking to offer new services to their customers. Call prediction can be useful to many applications such as planning daily schedule and attending unwanted communications (e.g. voice spam). Predicting calls is a very challenging task. We believe that this is a new area of research. In this paper, we propose a Call Predictor (CP) that computes the probability of receiving calls and makes call prediction based on caller's behavior and reciprocity. The proposed call predictor is tested with the actual call logs. The experimental results show that the call predictor performs reasonably well with false positive rate of 2.4416%, false negative rate of 2.9191%, and error rate of 5.3606%.

Keywords: Caller, Callee, Communications, Incoming calls, Outgoing calls, Arrival time, Inter-arrival time, Inter-arrival/departure time, Reciprocity, Behavior, Kernel density estimation, Probability density function (pdf), Call matrix, Receiving call probability.

1 Introduction

Prediction plays an important role in various applications. The prediction is widely applied in the areas such as weather, environmental, economic, stock, disaster (earthquake, flooding), network traffic, and call center forecasting [1, 2, 3, 4]. Companies use predictions of demands for making investment and efficient resource allocation. The call centers predict workload so that they can get the right number of staff in place to handle it. Network traffic prediction is used to assess future network capacity requirement and to plan network development so as to better use of network resources and to provide better quality of services. Prediction is also applied in the human behavior study by combining the computer technology and social networks [5, 6, 7, 8]. There is also some work reported on telephone telepathy based on psychology [9].

Predicting the expected calls for a busy business executive can be very useful for scheduling a day. Match making services can use calling patterns for the compatibility studies [10]. Moreover, the prediction of incoming calls can be used to avoid unwanted calls and schedule a time for wanted calls. For example, the problem of spam in VoIP networks has to be solved in real time compared to email systems. Compare receiving an email spam at 2:00 AM that sits in the inbox until you open it the next morning to receiving a junk phone call that must be answered immediately.

D. Krishnaswamy, T. Pfeifer, and D. Raz (Eds.): MMNS 2007, LNCS 4787, pp. 26–37, 2007.

Over the past few years, there has been a rapid development and deployment of new advanced phone features, including internet access, e-mail access, scheduling software, built-in camera, contact management, accelerometers, and navigation software as well as the ability to read documents in variety of format such as PDF and Microsoft Office. In 2005, Google filed a patent including detail about the Google Phone (GPhone) that could predict what a user is searching for or the words they are typing in a text messages by taking into account the user's location, previous searching/messaging history, and time of the day. However, none of these features offers ability to predict future calls.

Let us consider a simple caller-callee scenario shown in Fig. 1. In order to have an efficient scheduling of transactions, the caller wants to know the willingness of taking calls of the callee, which could be determined by the callee's presence. At the same time, the callee wants to know (predict) the incoming calling pattern (calling schedule) of the caller. *This raises two interesting problems; (1) predicting the incoming calling pattern of the caller, and (2) determining the presence of the callee. In this paper, we attempt to solve the first problem. The second problem and its solution will be addressed in our future work.*

Caller

Wants to know the callee's
presence before initiating a call

Callee

Wants to predict the caller's
incoming calling schedule

Fig. 1. A simple caller-callee scenario

To the best of our knowledge, no scientific research has been reported in predicting the incoming calls for phone services. Predicting of incoming calls using just the call history is a challenging task. We believe that this is a new area of research. One way of predicting incoming calls from specified callers is to compute the probability of receiving calls associated with them. In this paper, we present a model for predicting the next-day calls based on caller and user's past history. Section 2 presents the architecture of a Call Predictor (CP) that computes the probability of receiving calls from a specified caller and makes the next-day call prediction. Section 3 presents the CP framework which describes our real-life data sets and carries out the receiving call probability computation. The performance of the proposed CP is then measured and discussed in Section 4.

2 Call Predictor

The Call Predictor (CP) for computing the probability of receiving calls from a specified caller and making next-day call prediction can be deployed either in conjunction with perimeter controllers such as voice spam filters or firewalls, or in end systems such as multimedia phones. The basic architecture of the CP is shown Fig. 2.

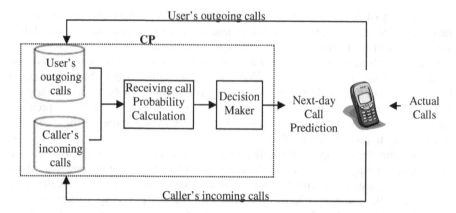

Fig. 2. Architecture of Call Predictor (CP). The CP calculates the probability of receiving next-day calls from specified callers based on the past call history (incoming and outgoing calls) and makes next-day call prediction. The call database is updated with the actual call activities.

For any time that phone user requests for a call prediction of a particular caller, the CP computes the probability of receiving calls of the next 24 hours based on the caller's past history (*Caller's incoming calls*) and the previous outgoing calls from the phone user to the caller (*User's outgoing calls*). Both of these histories are maintained by the CP by logging the call specific information for every call received and mode by the user. The computed receiving call probability is checked with a preconfigured threshold value to make a decision as to predict "call" or "no call" for each of the next 24 hours.

3   Call Prediction Framework

To predict the future incoming calls, the behavior learning models must be used. These models should incorporate mechanisms for capturing the caller's behavior (based on call arrival time and inter-arrival time), the user's behavior (based on call departure time), reciprocity (based on call inter-arrival/departure time), the probability model of receiving calls from caller, and finally, the next-day call prediction.

3.1 Real-Life Data Sets

Every day calls on the cellular network include calls from different sections of our social life. We receive calls from family members, friends, supervisors, neighbors, and strangers. Every person exhibits a unique calling pattern. These calling patterns can be analyzed for predicting the future calls to the callee.

To study calling pattern, we collected the actual call logs of 20 individuals at our university. These 20 individuals are faculties, staffs, and students. We are in process of collecting many more call logs. The details of the data collecting process are given in [11]. We found it difficult to collect the data set because many people are unwilling to give their call logs due to privacy issues. Nevertheless, the collected datasets include people with different types of calling patterns and call distributions.

As part of the data collecting process, each individual downloaded three months of detail telephone call records from his/her online accounts on the cellular service provider's website. Each call record in the dataset had the 5-tuple information as shown below:

Call record: (date, start time, type, caller id, talk time) where
    date - date of communication
    start time - the start time of the communication
    type - type of call i.e., "Incoming" or "Outgoing"
    caller id - the caller identifier
    talk time - amount of time spend by caller and the individual during the call

We then used the collected data for deriving the traffic profiles for each caller who called the individuals. To derive the profile, we inferred the arrival time (time of receiving a call), inter-arrival time (elapsed time between adjacent incoming calls), and inter-arrival/departure time (elapsed time between adjacent incoming and going calls).

3.2 Probability Computation

In our daily life, when we receive a phone call, at the moment of the first phone ring before we look at the caller ID, we often guess who the caller might be. We base this estimation on:

- *Caller's behavior:* Each caller tends to have a unique calling pattern. These patterns can be observed through history of calling time (we normally expect a call from a caller who has history of making several calls at some particular time, for example, your spouse likes to call you while you drive to work in the morning and after work in the evening therefore when your phone rings while you are on the way to work or back home, you likely to guess that it is a phone call from your spouse), periodicity of call history (we can expect that a caller who calls periodically will repeat the same pattern, for example, your friend calls you at about 2:00 PM every Tuesday therefore you expect a call from him/her at about 2:00 PM for next Tuesday).
- *Reciprocity:* The communication activity patterns between the caller and the user in the past. These patterns can be observed in terms of number of user's outgoing calls per caller's incoming call and call inter-arrival/departure time.

Therefore, we believe that receiving a call is influenced by caller's past incoming calls and call interaction history between caller and phone user. The patterns of caller's incoming calls can be observed from call arrival time and inter-arrival time. The patterns of call interaction between caller and phone user can be observed from the number of outgoing calls per incoming call and the inter-arrival/departure time.

The calling pattern based on caller's call arrival time can be captured by using nonparametric density estimation. The most popular method for density estimation is the kernel density estimation (also known as the Parzen window estimator [12]) which is given by Eq. (1).

$$a(x) = \frac{1}{Nh} \sum_{i=1}^{N} K\left(\frac{x - x_i}{h}\right).$$ (1)

$K(u)$ is kernel function and h is the bandwidth or smoothing parameter. The most widely used kernel is the Gaussian of zero mean and unit variance which is defined by Eq. (2).

$$K(u) = \frac{1}{\sqrt{2\pi}} e^{-u^2/2}.$$ (2)

The choice of the function and h is crucial. Several optimal bandwidth selection techniques have been proposed [13, 14]. In this paper, we use AMISE optimal bandwidth selection using the Sheather Jones Solve-the-equation plug-in method [15]. Fig. 3(a) shows an example histogram of call arrival time. It should be noted that the widow of observation is shifted to start at 5:00 AM and end at 4:59 AM in order to capture the entire calling pattern in the middle. The corresponding estimated probability density function (pdf) using kernel density estimation is shown in Fig. 3(b).

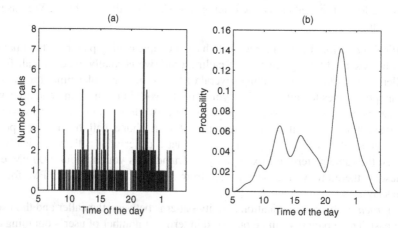

Fig. 3. (a) An example histogram of call arrival time. (b) The estimated probability density function using kernel density estimation of the example histogram of call arrival time shown in Fig. 3(a). Note that observation window is 5:00 AM to 4:59 AM.

We define a *Call Matrix* as a matrix whose entries are call indicators where rows are hours of the day and columns are days of observation. The call indicator (*CI*) indicates if there is at least one incoming call or going call or both incoming and outgoing call or no call. *CI*'s values and its indications are given in Eq. (3) and an example Call Matrix of 15 days of observation is shown in Fig. 4.

$$CI = \begin{cases} 0, \text{ no call} \\ 1, \text{ at least one incoming call} \\ 2, \text{ at least one outgoing call} \\ 3, \text{ at least one incoming call and one outgoing call .} \end{cases} \tag{3}$$

Hour of the day

Hour	1	2	3	4	5	6	7	8	9	10	11	12	13	14	15	Predicting
24	0	0	1	0	2	1	0	3	0	0	1	1	0	3	0	
23	1	2	2	0	0	2	2	0	1	3	0	0	2	1	2	
22	2	0	1	2	0	0	1	2	0	0	1	2	0	0	1	
21	0	0	1	0	0	0	2	1	0	0	0	0	0	1	0	
20	0	0	0	2	0	0	2	1	0	0	2	1	0	0	2	
19	1	0	3	2	1	0	3	1	2	0	2	1	3	2	1	
18	0	2	0	2	1	3	2	0	1	1	1	0	0	2	2	
17	2	3	0	0	0	2	3	1	0	0	2	1	2	0	0	
16	0	1	1	2	0	0	0	3	2	2	0	0	1	1	2	
15	2	3	2	0	1	0	0	0	0	2	2	3	1	1	1	
14	0	0	0	2	0	0	0	2	0	0	2	2	0	1	1	
13	0	0	2	3	0	0	1	1	0	0	1	1	0	0	2	
12	1	1	0	1	1	0	3	3	0	0	2	1	1	1	1	
11	2	3	0	0	0	2	2	0	1	0	0	1	2	0	1	
10	0	1	0	2	0	0	0	0	2	0	0	0	2	0	0	
9	0	1	2	2	1	0	0	2	3	0	0	2	0	1	1	
8	0	0	0	1	2	0	2	0	0	0	1	1	0	0	2	
7	0	0	2	0	0	2	0	0	0	0	0	2	1	0	0	
6	0	0	0	0	0	0	0	2	0	0	0	0	2	0	0	
5	0	0	0	0	0	0	0	0	0	0	0	0	0	0	0	
4	0	0	0	0	0	0	0	0	0	0	0	0	0	0	0	
3	0	0	2	0	0	0	0	0	3	0	0	1	0	0	2	
2	1	0	0	1	0	0	2	0	2	1	0	0	0	2	1	
1	0	1	0	0	1	2	1	0	0	1	2	2	1	1	1	

Day of observation

Fig. 4. An example Call Matrix of 15 days of observation

The caller's behavior can also be observed through the call inter-arrival time. However, the inter-arrival time in our normal sense is the elapsed time between temporally adjacent calls, which we believe that it does not accurately represent the caller's behavior based on inter-arrival time. Due to the human nature that requires state of natural rest, sleeping time causes the inaccuracy in the average inter-arrival time. In fact, it increases the average inter-arrival time from the true value. Therefore, we believe that the more accurate angle to observe calling pattern based on inter-arrival time is to scan over each hour of the day through days of observation, i.e. capturing inter-arrival time patterns by observing each row of the Call Matrix.

Let a random variable X_k be inter-arrival time of kth hour where $k = 1, 2, 3,..., 24$. A Normal distribution $N(\mu_k, \sigma_k^2)$ is assumed for the call inter-arrival time since no information is available that $Pr(X_k \leq \mu_k - c) < Pr(X_k \leq \mu_k + c)$ or vice versa therefore it can be safely assumed that $Pr(X_k \leq \mu_k - c) = Pr(X_k \leq \mu_k + c)$ where μ_k is the mean and σ_k^2 is the variance of inter-arrival time of kth hour which can be calculated by Eq. (4) and Eq. (5).

$$\mu_k = \frac{1}{N-1} \sum_{n=1}^{N-1} x_k(n). \tag{4}$$

$$\sigma_k^2 = \frac{1}{N-1} \sum_{n=1}^{N-1} (x_k(n) - \mu_k)^2. \tag{5}$$

N is the total number of calls and $x_k(n)$ is the nth inter-arrival time. The inter-arrival time is now treated as a random variable X_k that consists of number of small random variables $\{x_k(1), x_k(2), x_k(3), ..., x_k(N-1)\}$, is normal random variable which has probability density function (pdf) given by Eq. (6).

$$i_k(x_k) = \frac{1}{\sqrt{2\pi\sigma_k^2}} e^{-(x_k - \mu_k)^2/2\sigma_k^2}. \tag{6}$$

For example, if a caller calls on average every 3 days, the chances of receiving a call one day earlier (day 2) or day one later (day 4) are the same.

As previously mentioned that receiving a call is influenced by not just caller's behavior but also reciprocity, one way to observe the calling patterns based on reciprocity is to monitor the number of outgoing calls per incoming call. This can give us a good approximation of when the next incoming call can be expected. A normal distribution $N(\mu_k, \sigma_k^2)$ is also assumed for the same reason as in the inter-arrival time case, where Y_k is a random variable representing the number of outgoing calls per incoming call of the kth hour where μ_k is the mean and σ_k^2 is the variance of which can be calculated by Eq. (7) and Eq. (8).

$$\mu_k = \frac{1}{M} \sum_{n=1}^{M-1} y_k(n). \tag{7}$$

$$\sigma_k^2 = \frac{1}{M} \sum_{n=1}^{M-1} (y_k(n) - \mu_k)^2. \tag{8}$$

M is the total number of incoming calls of kth hour and $y_k(n)$ is the number of outgoing calls beween the nth and $(n+1)^{th}$ incoming call. Therefore, the pdf is given by Eq. (9).

$$n_k(y_k) = \frac{1}{\sqrt{2\pi\sigma_k^2}} e^{-(y_k-\mu_k)^2/2\sigma_k^2}. \tag{9}$$

An example of calculating $n_k(y_k)$ is shown in Fig. 5.

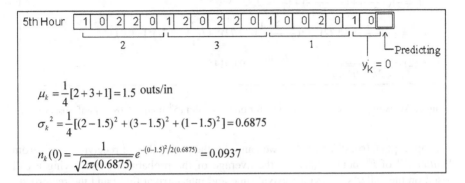

Fig. 5. An example of calculating $n_k(y_k)$ for one hour slot (5th hour) of 18 days of observation

Another angle to observe the calling patterns based on reciprocity is to monitor the inter-arrival/departure time. This gives us the chance (probability) of receiving a call from the caller given the time of the last outgoing call to the caller.

Let Z_k be a random variable mapping to the inter-arrival/departure time of the kth hour. A normal distribution $N(\mu_k, \sigma_k^2)$ is also assumed for the the same reason previously mentioned. The mean (μ_k) and variance (σ_k^2) are given by Eq. (10) and Eq. (11).

$$\mu_k = \frac{1}{L-1}\sum_{n=1}^{L-1} z_k(n). \tag{10}$$

$$\sigma_k^2 = \frac{1}{L-1}\sum_{n=1}^{L-1}(z_k(n)-\mu_k)^2. \tag{11}$$

L is total number of incoming calls of kth hour and $z_k(n)$ is the average inter-arrival/departure time of the nth incoming call to all right-hand-side outgoing calls (in the Call Matrix's row) before reaching the $(n+1)^{th}$ incoming call (an example is illustrated in Fig. 6). The pdf of inter-arrival/departure time is given in Eq. (12).

$$t_k(z_k) = \frac{1}{\sqrt{2\pi\sigma_k^2}} e^{-(z_k-\mu_k)^2/2\sigma_k^2}. \tag{12}$$

An example of calculating $t_k(z_k)$ is shown in Fig. 6.

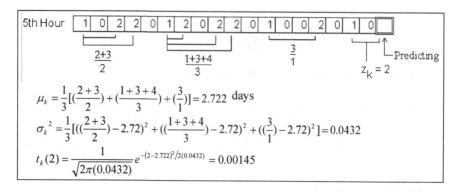

Fig. 6. An example of calculating $t_k(z_k)$ for one hour slot (5th hour) of 18 days of observation

From Eq.(1), (6), (9), and (12), we can infer the probability of receiving a call from "Caller A" of kth hour ($P_A(k)$) as the average of the probability of receiving a call based on the caller's behavior (arrival time and inter-arrival time) and the reciprocity (number of outgoing calls per incoming call and inter-arrival/departure time), which is given by Eq. (13) where $k = 1, 2, 3, ..., 24$.

$$P_A(k) = \frac{1}{4}\left[\sum_{j=60(k-1)+1}^{60k} a_k(j) + i_k(x_k) + n_k(y_k) + t_k(z_k)\right]. \tag{13}$$

There is another group of callers who never receive any calls back from the user, i.e. no reciprocity. More likely these callers are telemarketers or voice spammers. Since there is no history of call interaction between the callers and the user, the Eq. (13) reduces to the averaging over the probability based on only the caller's behavior, which is given by Eq. (14). Likewise, for the regular callers where some hour slots (rows of Call Matrix) have no reciprocity, Eq. (13) also reduces to Eq. (14).

$$P_A(k) = \frac{1}{2}\left[\sum_{j=60(k-1)+1}^{60k} a_k(j) + i_k(x_k)\right]. \tag{14}$$

To present the accuracy of the receiving call probability model, a phone user is randomly selected to represent all the individuals. Fig. 7 shows 30 consecutive days of receiving call probability calculation for an arbitrary caller where the receiving call probability is represented with a green surface and the actual calls during these 30 days of observation are represented with vertical black pulses.

It can be observed from Fig. 7 that most of the calls are received when the computed receiving-call probability is high. At the same time, no call is received during 0:00 AM to 9:00 AM period where the probability of receiving call is low.

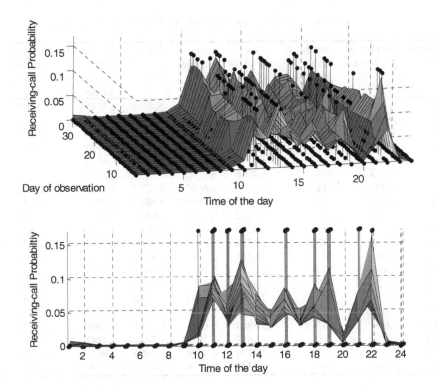

Fig. 7. A randomly selected phone user with 30 consecutive days of computed receiving-call probability of an arbitrary caller plotted with the actual received calls represented with vertical pulses. Top figure is the 3-dimensional view. Bottom figure is the front view (looking from the first day of observation).

4 Performance Analysis

The CP is tested with the actual call logs. Its performance is then measured by false positives, false negative, and error rate. A false positive is considered when a call is predicted but no call is received during that hour. A false negative is considered when no call is predicted but a call is received during that hour. Error rate is defined as a ratio of the number of fault predictions to the total number of predictions.

An experiment is conducted with 20 phone users (as mentioned in Section 3.1). The call logs of the first 2 months are used to train the CP, which is then tested with the call logs of the following month (next 30 days). Each of the 30 days of testing, the new prediction is consequently made by the CP at midnight (0 AM) with all available call history (up to that day) taken into account. The computed receiving call probability is checked with a threshold value to make a decision as to predict "call" or "no call" for each of the next 24 hours. The average number of calls per day is computed and rounded to the next largest integer M. The threshold is dynamically set as M hour slots are selected to make "Call" prediction and the rest of the $(24-M)$ time slots are predicted "No Call." The experimental results are shown in Table 1.

Table 1. The experimental results of 20 phone users

Phone user	Number of predictions	Number of fault predictions	False positive (%)	False negative (%)	Error rate (%)	Number of fault predictions per day	Average tolerance (hours)
1	6,432	332	2.5683	2.9214	5.4896	1.3175	1.9070
2	14,472	503	1.4486	2.2042	3.6528	0.8767	1.4618
3	1,968	133	4.0278	2.7183	6.746	1.6190	2.5676
4	13,512	609	1.9651	2.5916	4.5568	1.0936	1.8395
5	8,136	547	3.9371	4.2595	8.1966	1.9672	2.8694
6	5,616	579	6.4966	5.6342	12.1308	2.9114	2.7092
7	6,000	211	2.4096	1.6697	4.0793	0.9790	1.9995
8	10,178	178	1.1033	0.8860	1.9893	0.4774	1.3011
9	1,776	224	6.4342	8.1774	14.6117	3.5068	2.1220
10	8,352	659	3.4785	4.7221	8.2005	1.9681	2.8823
11	17,400	870	2.6798	2.5612	5.2409	1.2578	1.8337
12	2,088	67	2.6235	0.6944	3.3179	0.7963	1.5622
13	7,416	374	2.6365	2.9602	5.5968	1.3432	2.0133
14	3,720	167	2.6730	3.1831	5.8561	1.4054	2.3980
15	7,632	357	2.2900	3.0674	5.3574	1.2857	2.4452
16	19,416	1,090	2.7982	3.3569	6.1551	1.4772	2.7210
17	6,840	652	3.8854	5.6129	9.4984	2.2796	1.6221
18	2,808	216	3.5417	4.2014	7.7431	1.8583	1.8703
19	2,208	181	3.5779	4.6196	8.1975	1.9674	2.7001
20	5,040	146	1.0417	1.8750	2.9167	0.7000	1.6675

There are total of 151,008 predictions made with 8,095 total fault predictions. The average false positive is 2.4416%, the average false negative is 2.9191%, and the average error rate is 5.3606%. Therefore the overall average number of fault predictions per day (24 predictions) is 1.2866 and the average tolerance is 2.1246 hours. The average tolerance is a measure of how far off (in hours) the predicted call from the actual call when fault prediction occurs.

5 Conclusion

In this paper, we propose a Call Predictor that computes receiving call probability and makes the next-24-hour call prediction. The receiving call probability is based the caller's behavior and reciprocity. The caller's behavior is measured by the caller's call arrival time and inter-arrival time. The reciprocity is measured by the number of outgoing calls per incoming call and the inter-arrival/departure time.

The kernel density estimation is used to estimate the probability model for the calling pattern based on caller's arrival time. The normal distributions are assumed for the inter-arrival time, number of outgoing calls per incoming call, and the inter-arrival/departure time. The final receiving call probability model is the average of the receiving call probabilities based on these four parameters.

To validate the model, the cell phone call records of real-life individuals at our university are used to test the call predictor. The results show that the call predictor exhibits a reasonably good performance with low false positives, false negatives, and error rate.

Clearly, there are still many parameters that need to be identified to capture the calling patterns. This work is intended to be the first piece of many more to come in this new area of predicting future calls which can be useful to many applications such as planning a daily schedule and preventing unwanted communications (e.g. voice spam). Also, the prediction technique proposed here is preliminary and other approaches need to be considered in order to minimize the number of false positives and negatives. We will continue to investigate other parameters to characterize the behaviors of the phone users and explore other prediction techniques to improve the performance of the call predictor as our future direction.

Acknowledgements. This work is supported by the National Science Foundation under grants CNS-0627754, CNS-0619871, and CNS-0551694.

References

1. Magalhacs, M.H., Ballini, R., Molck, P., Gomide, F.: Combining forecasts for natural stream flow prediction. IEEE annual meeting of the fuzzy information, 390–394 (2004)
2. Guang, C., Jian, G., Wei, D.: Nonlinear-periodical network traffic behavioral forecast based on seasonal neural network model. IEEE international conference on communications, circuits, and systems 1(1), 683–687 (2004)
3. Tych, W., Pedregal, D.J., Young, P.C., Davies, J.: An unobserved component model for multi-rate forecasting of telephone call demand: the design of a forecasting support system. International jouornal of forecasting 18(4), 673–695 (2002)
4. Hansen, J.W., Nelson, R.D.: Neural networks and traditional time series methods: a synergistic combination in state economic forecasts. IEEE Transaction on neural network 8(4), 863–873 (1997)
5. Eagle, N., Pentland, A., Lazer, D.: Infering social network structure using mobile phone data. In: PNAS (in submission, 2007)
6. Eagle, N., Pentland, A.: Reality mining: Sensing complex social systems. Personal and Ubiquitous Computing 10(4) (2006)
7. Eagle, N., Pentland, A.: Eigenbehaviors: Identifying structure in routine. In: Proc. Roy. Soc. A. (in submssion, 2006)
8. Eagle, N., Pentland, A.: Social serendipity: Mobilizing social software. IEEE Pervasive Computing 4(2) (2005)
9. Sheldrake, R., Smart, P.: Testing for telepathy in connection with e-mails. Perceptual and Motor Skills 10, 771–786 (2005)
10. Eagle, N.: Machine Perception and Learning of Complex Social Systems, PhD Thesis, Massachusetts Institute of Technology (2005)
11. Dantu, R., Kolan, P.: Survey of Calling Patterns. University of North Texas Internal Survey (2006), http://secnet.csci.unt.edu/nuisance/index.htm
12. Parzen, E.: On estimation of a probability density function and mode. Ann. Math. Statist. 3(33), 1065–1076 (1962)
13. Jones, M., Marron, J.S., Sheather, S.J.: A brief survey of bandwidth selection for density estimation. J. Amer. Stat. Assoc. 433(91), 401–407 (1996)
14. Wand, M.P., Jones, M.C.: Multivariate plug-in bandwidth selection. Computational Statistics 9, 97–117 (1994)
15. Sheather, S.J., Jones, C.: A reliable data-based bandwidth selection method for kernel density estimation. Journal of the Royal Statistical Society, Series B 53, 683–690 (1991)

Q3M – QoS Architecture for Multi-user Mobile Multimedia Sessions in 4G systems

Eduardo Cerqueira[1], Luis Veloso[1], Augusto Neto[1], Marília Curado[1], Paulo Mendes[2], and Edmundo Monteiro[1]

[1] University of Coimbra, Pinhal de Marrocos, 3030-290 Coimbra, Portugal
{ecoelho, lmveloso, augusto, marilia, edmundo}@dei.uc.pt
[2] DoCoMo Euro-Labs, Landsbergerstr, 312, 80687 Munich, Germany
mendes@docomolab-euro.com

Abstract. Fourth generation systems (4G) will provide multimedia group communication sessions to multiple mobile users with distinct requirements. This way, it is expected the control of the quality level, connectivity and ubiquitous access for multi-user multimedia sessions across heterogeneous and mobile networks with seamless capability. This paper analyses the requirements of a control architecture to provide *Quality of Service* (QoS), connectivity and seamless handover management for multi-user sessions in 4G systems, and introduces the *QoS Architecture for Multi-user Mobile Multimedia* (Q3M) proposal. In addition, simulation results present the efficiency of this approach concerning the session setup time and packet losses during handover.

Keywords: Multi-user Multimedia Sessions, Seamless Mobility, Quality of Service, Heterogeneous Mobile Networks.

1 Introduction

Fourth generation systems are expected to allow mobile users to access group communication sessions over heterogeneous wired and wireless networks with QoS support. Examples of these sessions are IPTV, video streaming, push media and other multicasting multimedia-alike sessions. Since the content is simultaneously destined to multiple users, this type of sessions are called multi-user sessions. Based on well-know codecs, such as MPEG4, multi-user sessions can also be scalable. Each scalable session can be composed by a set of flows, with well-defined priorities, rates and QoS requirements. Hence, the importance of each flow must be used to adapt the overall quality of the session to the capability of different networks service classes.

The delivery of multi-user session may be done through different wired and wireless access technologies [1]. This heterogeneity may go from cellular and wide area access technologies (e.g., *Worldwide Interoperability for Microwave Access* (WiMAX)), to local area access technologies (e.g., *Wireless Local Area Networks* (WLAN)), and broadcast media such as *Digital Video Broadcasting-Terrestrial* (DVB-T) and *DVB-Handheld* (DVB-H). This diversity requires an infrastructure to

D. Krishnaswamy, T. Pfeifer, and D. Raz (Eds.): MMNS 2007, LNCS 4787, pp. 38–49, 2007.

reduce operational costs and enhance efficiency in the usage of network resources, where these requirements are satisfied by an all-IP 4G mobile system.

In addition to the access technologies heterogeneity, the 4G systems are expected to be heterogeneous also at the network layer, due to the diversity of connectivity control mechanisms and different address realms. For instance, in terms of unicast mobility management, the use of *Hierarchical Mobile IP* (HMIP) allows users to use a sequence of two global IP addresses, inside and outside each access-network. In the field of IP multicast, which is the most suitable technology to distribute multi-user sessions, there are already several address realms associated with multicast models such as, the *Any-Source Multicast* (ASM), *Source-Specific Multicast* (SSM) and *Small-Group Multicast* (SGM).

However, to allow the distribution of multi-user sessions throughout heterogeneous access and transport technologies, it seems to be mandatory to cluster homogeneous network devices into domains (named clusters in this paper) and to create of open interfaces between such clusters and existing standards. Therefore, a control architecture should be built as modular and decentralized as possible. The modularization facilitates the inclusion of emerging technologies, while the decentralization permits a higher scalability. Both of these characteristics might be sustained by an edge-networking approach in which the functionality of each cluster is controlled by a group of organized edge devices.

Since each cluster may implement a different connectivity scheme (e.g., IP unicast, IP multicast, *Multimedia Broadcast Multicast Service* (MBMS) or any type of Layer 2 connectivity), the architecture must control the multi-user session connectivity cluster by cluster. This functionality allows the session continuity independent from the connectivity scheme offered inside or between clusters. Hence, each multi-user session must have a global identifier, independent from hosts location or IP address. Furthermore, in order to support emerging mobile-aware sessions, to increase the satisfaction of the users and to avoid the interruption of sessions, an architecture must provide ubiquitous access, QoS and mobility control across heterogeneous clusters with no perceived service degradation for the user.

From the QoS point of view, different QoS models (e.g., such as *Differentiated Service* (DiffServ), IEEE 802.11e and IEEE 802.16) can be implemented by clusters to provide QoS assurances for multi-user sessions along end-to-end heterogeneous paths. Hence, inside or between clusters, QoS mapping procedures must be done to map the requirements of the session into the appropriated service class. Since QoS mapping alone is not sufficient to assure the quality level of sessions, due to the use of different QoS models, class of services with distinctive configurations and available bandwidth capacities, QoS adaptation schemes must be used to avoid the session blocking and to keep those sessions with acceptable quality level, independently of the movement of users or even re-routing events (caused by a link or network agent failure). From the mobility point of view, an architecture must support inter and intra-cluster handovers with seamless capability. For instance, by using caching and buffering mechanisms to reduce packet losses during handover and by reserving network resources in advance to allow a faster session re-establishment.

Summing up, an IP-based control architecture for multi-user multimedia sessions must allow senders to offer their content and receivers to access them ubiquitously. It must also provide open interfaces, QoS, connectivity and seamless mobility control.

This paper first analyzed the requirements for a control architecture for multi-user sessions over an IP-based 4G mobile system. Following, the *QoS Architecture for Multi-user Mobile Multimedia* (Q3M) proposal is presented, together with an illustration of its functionalities and an insight to its performance.

The next section presents relevant related work. The Q3M architecture is described in Section 3. Section 4 illustrates an example of the Q3M overall functionality. An evaluation is shown in Section 5. Conclusions are summarized in Section 6.

2 Related Work

There are IETF standards that address some of above mentioned needs, such as the DiffServ model to provide QoS assurance, the *Next Step in Signaling* (NSIS) QoS *Signaling Layer Protocol* (NSLP) for signaling resource reservations for unicast sessions, the *Session Initiation Protocol* (SIP) to control the access to announced sessions, the *Protocol Independent Multicast for the SSM* (PIM-SSM) for packet distribution to groups of users. The MIP, HMIP and the *Fast Handovers for MIPv6* (FMIPv6) to control handovers in unicast networks. FMIPv6 adds seamless experience to the users, by transferring and buffering packets from old to new access-routers. The *Context Transfer Protocol* (CXTP) can reduce latency and packet losses, by transferring the session-context among access-routers. However, each of these standards does not cover by itself all aspects for the development of an architecture to provide connectivity, QoS, and seamless handover for multi-user sessions.

In addition to the IETF solutions, architectures for QoS, mobility and heterogeneous systems have been proposed. The FAMOUS architecture [2] aims to support broadband services to fast moving users. This proposal only supports single-user sessions and uses a tunnel-based approach to control connectivity, restricting network operations. The MUSE project [3] proposes QoS architecture for stationary users to access broadband services in unicast environments. However, mobility is not supported and the QoS control is based on a static guideline mapping approach to map the session requirements into four proprietary classes, which reduces the system flexibility. The DAIDALOS project [4] provides an architecture that supports the distribution of unicast and multicast sessions across heterogeneous mobile systems. However, the DAIDALOS architecture uses a centralized approach to control per-flow QoS resources and multicast tree creation, reducing thus the system scalability. The EuQoS project [5] supports a QoS architecture based on brokers to control network resources and an *Application Layer Multicast* (ALM) to distribute packets using unicast connections. However, it does not take heterogeneous connectivity scheme or IP multicast into account. Instead, it uses an ALM that requires extra modules on the end-hosts and does not avoid sending redundant data over the same physical link. A 4G architecture to provide QoS, resource reservation and mobility is introduced in [6]. This architecture uses QoS brokers to control network resources for the sessions and hierarchical FMIPv6 schemes to provide the continuity of unicast sessions, but it does not avoid packet losses nor assure seamless experience for ongoing sessions. This architecture does not also take the use of heterogeneous QoS models into account and the packet differentiation in wireless links is not supported.

From the related work analysis it is evident that the IETF solutions are not sufficient to provide QoS, connectivity and seamless mobility for multi-user session. Additionally, several architectures do not support multicast sessions and only control network resources and handover in unicast networks. Moreover, the use of centralized approaches to control QoS and mobility reduces the flexibility and scalability of the system. To overcome the identified limitation, the University of Coimbra is working together with NTT DoCoMo Euro-labs in an all-IP 4G control architecture called *QoS Architecture for Multi-user Mobile Multimedia* (Q3M).

3 The Q3M Architecture

The Q3M architecture controls multi-user sessions across heterogeneous clusters through a modular integration of three components: the *Multi-User Session Control* (MUSC) [7], the *Multi-service Resource Allocation* (MIRA) [8] and the *Cache-based Seamless Mobility* (CASM) [9]. The coordination of these components provides ubiquitous access, resource reservation, QoS mapping, QoS adaptation, connectivity and seamless mobility control for multi-user session in 4G systems.

MUSC, MIRA and CASM use interfaces to allow a tighter communication between themselves and external solutions, such as SIP, *Session Description Protocol* (SDP), PIM-SSM, *Internet Group Management Protocol* (IGMPv3), *Multicast Listener Discovery* (MLDv2), DiffServ elements and Wireless Controllers. For instance, the interaction between MIRA and Wireless Controllers, such as used by WiMAX or IEEE 802.11e [10], allows QoS support in wireless links. The interface among CASM and Wireless Controllers gives seamless support for mobility control functions accomplished by the former. These interfaces are represented in Fig. 1.

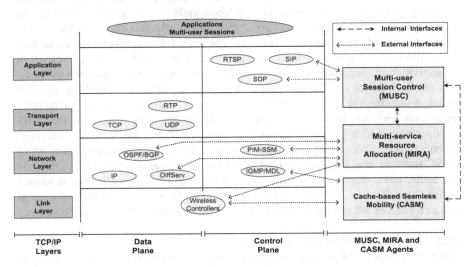

Fig. 1. Q3M components in a TCP/IP stack view

The referred components are implemented in an element named Q3M-Agent (Q3MA). A Q3MA is called *access-Q3MA* when located at wired or wireless access-routers. Furthermore, Q3MAs can have distinct roles in different edges for different sessions: in an edge-router, a Q3MA is called an *ingress-Q3MA* for sessions whose traffic is entering the cluster in that edge element, or *egress-Q3MA* if the traffic is leaving the cluster.

3.1 Q3M Components

This sub-section details the Q3M components.

3.1.1 Multi-user Session Control

MUSC manages the mobility of multi-user session, as well as the ubiquitous access of users to those sessions. The cooperation between MUSC agents allows QoS mapping, QoS adaptation and connectivity of multi-user sessions along heterogeneous end-to-end path. The ubiquitous access control is done in the access-agent through an interface with SIP and CASM to allow fixed and mobile users to access multi-user sessions respectively. The interface with CASM provides the control of mobility with a seamless capability, by allowing sessions to be configured in advance on new paths and by reducing the number of packet losses during handover. In ingress and egress-agents, the QoS mapping is based on the association between the session quality requirements and the available network services provided by MIRA. If such mapping is not optimal, for instance due to a congestion period, the session is not blocked but a QoS adaptation to the current network conditions is done. The adaptation mechanism can request the allocation of extra resources to the selected service class, the mapping of flows into another class, or the dropping/joining of low priority flows of sessions.

If the ingress or egress-agent is in the frontier between unicast and/or multicast address realms, MUSC configures its connectivity translator mechanisms, allowing multi-user sessions to be distributed independently of underlying connectivity technology. In unicast-aware networks, the packet distribution is handled in a multicasting way to save network resources. The packet duplication is performed near to the receivers (application layer multicasting). The coordination of a chain of connectivity translators supports any layout of heterogeneous networks and end-hosts.

A receiver-driven and source-initiated protocol, called MUSC-P, is used to exchange information between MUSC agent using a soft-state approach to maintain per-session and per-flow state. MUSC-P is being specified based on the NSIS framework, in which it can be included as an extra NSLP. MUSC-P is a receiver-driven protocol because it is triggered at access-agents. It is source-initiated since MUSC starts the configuration of its agents at the agent nearest to the source, or at the first agent, in the path towards the source, discovered which contains the requested session. This functionality gives support for building QoS-aware distribution trees as well as it reduces the session setup time and signaling overhead to establish sessions.

3.1.2 Multi-service Resource Allocation

MIRA aims to build QoS-aware distribution trees associated with multi-user sessions in environments with asymmetric routing. MIRA controls network resources for unicast and multicast sessions in a per-class basis, where it is done inside and between networks based on DiffServ model *and Service Level Specifications* (SLS) respectively. MIRA also provides QoS guarantees on the wireless link through the interaction with a wireless resource allocation controller. Therefore, MIRA gives support for QoS mapping and QoS adaptation operations and assures the QoS level for each flow of a multi-user session controlled by MUSC.

In multicast-aware networks, MIRA follows the SSM model for controlling multi-user distribution and it also allocates a SSM channel (e.g., source and multicast group) to be used for each flow of a session. In unicast-aware networks, a pair of IP unicast addresses and transport ports is allocated to identify each flow of a session. Based on the information about the distribution channel identifiers provided by MIRA, MUSC controls the session connectivity independently of the address realm implemented along the end-to-end session path. In SSM-aware environments, MIRA provides support so that the multicast routing protocol (e.g., PIM-SSM) creates QoS-aware multicast trees taking into account the path from the sender to the receiver. This is done through updating the *Multicast Routing Information Base* (MRIB) with the QoS path during the resource allocation work, enabling thus PIM-SSM to create the trees without suffering with asymmetric routes.

The control information is supplied to MIRA agents through the *MIRA Protocol* (MIRA-P), which is being specified as a new NSIS QoS-NSLP with multicast support. MIRA-P operates edge-to-edge and controls the state maintenance by soft-state: periodically signaling the paths with the amount of state to be kept and to collect network resource capability information for admission control. MIRA does not compromise inter-network links performance since it configures the network resources based on SLS, without requiring signaling exchanges on those links.

3.1.3   Cache-Based Seamless Mobility

CASM supplies users with a seamless moving experience among access-Q3MAs belonging to the same neighbor-clusters. This is done based on the use of caches in access-Q3MAs and buffers in mobile devices to reduce packet loss. In the presence of a handover, the data in the buffer of the mobile receiver will continue to be read by the application. When the handover is resumed, the mobile receiver updates its buffer by fetching the missing packets from the cache in its new access-Q3MA. The latency experimented by the user depends on the size of the buffer and handover duration.

In its enhanced configuration, CASM uses of an interface to receive information concerning the new probable access-Q3MAs to which the user can move, being the number of access-agents dependent on the prediction granularity [11]. Upon receiving information about the candidate access-Q3MAs, the session context is transferred among access-Q3MAs. The use of an interface with mobility prediction controllers together with CASM context transfer mechanism allows the session setup in advance by interacting with MUSC, increasing the assurance of low latency.

CASM-P is the CTXP-based signaling protocol used to transfer the context of multi-user sessions between old and the predicted access-Q3MAs. It also collects information about the capability provided by the latter. At the old access-Q3MA, the probed information, combined with knowledge regarding the access technologies, such as signal-to-noise ratio, gives support to the handover decision. After handover, the interaction between CASM and MUSC allows the release of the session resources on the old path and on the predicted paths that the mobile device is not going to use (if no other users are subscribed to the same flow of the session).

3.2 Q3M Interfaces

Interfaces are used to exchange control information between Q3M components and existing solutions as follows.

The MUSC-CASM interface is used in access-Q3MAs to support seamless mobility. When a new session is accepted by MUSC, CASM is triggered to create a cache for the new session (if the session does not exist). During handover, CASM triggers MUSC in predicted access-agent(s) to setup the session and to collect information concerning the capability and connectivity of the new paths. At the previous access-agent, the interaction between CASM and MUSC allows the release of resources associated with the session on the old path.

The MUSC-MIRA interface is implemented in all Q3MAs providing end-to-end connectivity and QoS support over heterogeneous clusters. MUSC triggers MIRA by querying it about the QoS characteristic of the cluster network services. After selecting a network service for the flows of the session, MUSC requests to MIRA the allocation of the resources required by each flow. As a response, MUSC gets from MIRA information about the unicast flow or multicast tree to which the flow was associated inside or between clusters. When there are no more users in a flow of a session, MUSC triggers MIRA to release the resources associated with each flow.

MUSC interacts with SIP to allow users to join or leave a multi-user session. Applications compose a SIP/SDP message to join announced sessions. This message is received by a SIP-proxy in the access-cluster, which can accomplish some authentication, authorization and accounting procedures. After performing its operations, the SIP-proxy forwards the session information to the receiver's access-Q3MA based on SIP Location Servers. The reception of this information activates the MUSC access-control. After the conclusion of the MUSC operations, the application is informed, by means of a SIP/SDP message, that its request was accepted or not. For multicast-aware devices placed in multicast-aware access-clusters, MUSC also informs the receiver about the multicast channel to be joined by each session-flow (as a consequence, IGMPv3 or MLDv2 messages are sent to the access-router).

MIRA interacts with DiffServ elements to collect information about the network services (loss, delay, jitter, and available bandwidth) by checking the *Per-Hop-Behaviour* (PHB) table on each network node from the ingress to egress. Based on the session-flow information provided by MUSC (flow rate and network service to be used), MIRA adjusts the bandwidth share of the PHB of the selected network service in each router of the cluster ingress-egress path. The interface between MIRA and wireless technologies is being considered, such as 802.11e and 802.16. Therefore, MIRA is configured with information about the wireless service class capabilities, allowing QoS support on the wireless interface.

The MIRA-PIM-SSM interface allows the former to update the MRIB on each router, or to directly configure the SSM channel on outgoing interfaces.

The interface CASM-IGMPv3/MLDv2 allows users in multicast-aware clusters to join the multicast channels allocated for each flow of a session in new access-agents.

4   Example of Q3M Overall Functionality

Fig. 2 shows the interaction of the Q3M components to setup a session (*S1*) in fixed and mobile scenarios. Therefore, the application on *R1* uses a SIP/SDP message to subscribe the announced session (*step i*). The SIP-proxy forwards the message to the receiver's access-Q3MA based on previous registration. Afterwards, the MUSC access-control is notified and triggers MUSC-P in Q3MA-12 to send a message towards the source with *IP Router Alert Option* enabled. This message is received by the Q3MA closest to the source of the signaled path, or by the first Q3MA, in the path towards the source, found with the requested session, as happens in Q3MA-33.

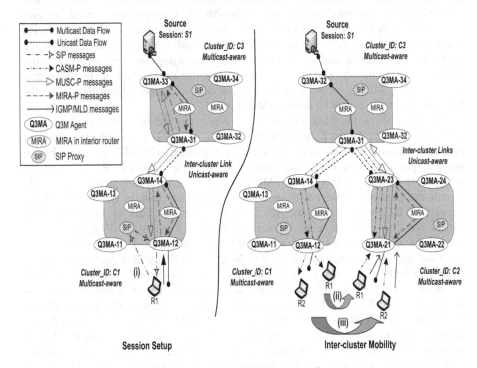

Fig. 2. Example of Q3M Functionality

In Q3MA-33, MUSC triggers MIRA to query about network services in the cluster path towards Q3MA-12. Based on the response, MUSC selects the preferred service class and requests MIRA to configure the required bandwidth. After admission control, MIRA updates the resources of the requested QoS class and configures the multicast (configuring the MRIB) on the path towards the egress Q3MA-31. When all intra-cluster operations succeed, MIRA informs MUSC about the multicast SSM channel allocated for each flow of the session. This information allows MUSC to start translating all incoming packets of *S1* to the indicated intra-cluster multicast trees.

After the operations in Q3MA-33, MUSC in Q3MA-31 is triggered by MUSC-P, updating its translation state about the SSM channel used for the flows of *S1* in *C3*.

The interaction with MIRA occurs as described before. Since Q3MA-31 is an egress-agent, PIM-SSM is triggered to create multicast trees for each flow of the session in the QoS-aware reserved-path. MIRA also collects QoS information by checking the inter-cluster SLSs, instead of querying the network. Since unicast is used between clusters, MIRA gets from the SLS the unicast IP address of the next Q3MA (Q3MA-14) as well as a pool of available ports. Based on this connectivity information, a pair of source and destination ports is allocated for each flow of *S1*. It allows MUSC to translate all packets coming from the intra-cluster to the pair of source and destination IP addresses and ports allocated for each flow between *C3* and *C1*.

When the MUSC-P response message reaches the access-Q3MA-12, MIRA is required to control the multicast tree creation inside *C1* and to inform the available service class on the wireless interface. After MUSC QoS and connectivity control operations, MIRA is triggered to configure the required bandwidth in the selected wireless service class. Afterwards, MUSC interacts with CASM to activate/update the cache for the session and gives information concerning session-context. Finally, MUSC sends a correspondent successful SIP message to the receiver. In a multicast access-cluster, MUSC includes, in the SIP response message, information about the SSM channel to be joined by using IGMPv3 or MLDv2.

The situation on the right side of Fig. 2 represents the inter-cluster mobility, in which *R1* (*step ii*) moves away from the access-Q3MA-12. Upon detection the next probable access-Q3MA to which the receiver is moving, CASM is triggered by the mobility prediction controller and receives information about the IP address of the new access-Q3MA (in this case Q3MA-21). After the handover prediction, CASM signals the predicted Q3MA with session-context information. In Q3MA-21, CASM triggers MUSC, which configures the session on the new path by interacting with MIRA for the reservation of network resources. The MUSC-P messages and procedures are performed only between Q3MA-21 and Q3MA-31 and not end-to-end, since the session is already active in the Q3MA-31. In Q3MA-21, CASM configures a session cache to avoid packet losses. After this, a reply is sent to CASM in Q3MA-12.

Based on the QoS configuration of the session on the new path and the signal-to-noise ratio, CASM in Q3MA-12 takes a handover decision to Q3MA-21. Hence, CASM informs MUSC about the handover, allowing MUSC to adjust the number of receivers and to possibly remove the state of the session. In this case, no state is removed, since *R2* is still subscribed. During handover, the application consumes packets from the *R1* buffer while packets continue to arrive to the cache in Q3MA-21. After attaching to the new access-Q3MA, CASM sends a fetch message to request the missing packets and to sync the packet reception with the cache in Q3MA-21. Furthermore, CASM triggers the IGMPv3/MLDv2 to join the new multicast channel allocated to the flow of the session.

After the mobility of *R1*, *R2* (*step iii*) also moves away from the Q3MA-12. In Q3MA-12, the mobility prediction controller notifies CASM that the Q3MA-21 is the candidate access-agent, allowing the session transfer and the configuration of the session on the new path by MUSC. Since flows of the requested session are already active on the new path, MUSC only adjusts its state about the number of receivers, allows the configuration of QoS resources on the wireless link and replies to CASM. After the local reply, CASM sends a message to its peer in Q3MA-12. After handover, the fetching of packets from the network cache to the *R2* buffer is done as explained for *R1*. In the old access-agent, CASM is triggered to release the cache. On the old path, the state of the session is released by soft-state operations (interaction between MUSC and MIRA). This occurs because the state associated with each flow of *S1* is not refreshed by MUSC-P messages before the clean-up time-out expires.

5   Q3M Evaluation

Simulations were done using the *Network Simulator* 2.28 (NS2) to analyze the impact of the Q3M architecture on the expectation of mobile receivers and on the performance of the network. This paper focus on the analysis of the convergence time and signaling overhead of the Q3M components, as well as the impact of the Q3M cache and buffer mechanisms on the user-perceived quality level.

A random topology was generated by *Boston University Representative Internet Topology Generator* (BRITE) following the same inter-cluster mobility scenario illustrated in Fig. 2. In the topology, each of the three clusters has sixteen routers (four Q3MAs and twelve MIRA interior routers). The intra and inter-cluster links have a bandwidth of 10 Mb/s and their propagation delay is attributed according to the distance between the edges. Moreover, two receivers are connected to the same access-Q3MA. These receivers get one *Variable Bit Rate* video with an average rate of 86 Kb/s. The packet distribution is accomplished by PIM-SSM. Since the usage of mobility prediction is still under investigation, it is assumed that CASM transfers the session context and notifies MUSC in the predicted access-Q3MA before the handover. This allows the pre-configuration of the session in new paths (e.g., pre-reserve of QoS-aware distribution tree and the cache configuration).

Table I presents the results of the convergence time of the Q3M components before and after the attachment of the moving receivers to the new access-agent. The convergence time before the attachment includes CASM, MUSC and MIRA signaling and their procedures to configure the cache, QoS mapping, adaptation and connectivity, and network service class, respectively. The convergence time after the attachment encompasses CASM operations to fetch the missing packets.

Table 1. CASM, MUSC and MIRA convergence time

Mobile Receiver	Before Handover			After	Total (ms)
	CASM	MUSC	MIRA	CASM	
R1	24.12	13.48	10.97	1.78	50.35
R2	24.12	-	-	1.78	25.9

The results demonstrate that CASM requires more time to transfer the session-context and to configure its mechanism than MUSC or MIRA. The MUSC session setup time would be higher if the requested session for *R1* would be activated in an agent near the source. The MIRA convergence time is small, because only intra-cluster operations are performed to reserve network resources in the selected class. Since the resources associated with the session requested by *R2* are already configured on the path ending in the new access-agent, the MIRA and MUSC convergence time are negligible. Only local operations are done to configure the number of receivers, quality level and connectivity functions associated with the session and to reply to CASM. This functionality allows a reduction of 60% in the overall signaling overhead and 50% in the time required to setup the same session for a second receiver in the same access-agent. After handover, each receiver needs to wait less than 2 ms to receive packets, because the session is already installed. This period includes the CASM procedures to fetch the missing packets during handover.

The benefit of the Q3M architecture to recover missing packets when the handover duration varies from 50 to 1000 ms and considering a buffer size with 100 KB is presented in Fig. 3. The results show the influence of the Q3M solution on the session quality level achieved by recovering missing packets after handover. For instance, the proposal recovers 47 packets when the handover duration is 500 ms (including the convergence time of Q3M components) and the cache size is of 50 KB.

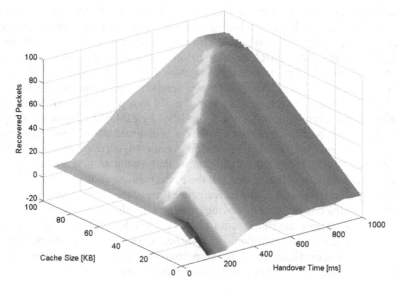

Fig. 3. Recovered packets

6 Conclusions

This paper presents the Q3M solution for a unifying IP-based architecture to support seamless multimedia multi-user sessions in 4G systems. With Q3M architecture, users are unaware of the network technology diversity, and experience seamless mobility. The seamless characteristic of the Q3M solution is achieved by a modular integration of the control of group communication sessions, network resources, and device mobility. By implementing most of the network computation at the edges, a cost reduction is expected. Operators will also be able to provide services with high availability times due to the high robustness of the decentralized architecture.

The evaluation shows that the Q3M architecture has a convergence time and a signaling overhead reduced for a second receiver for the same session in the same access-agent. Moreover, Q3M provides seamless experience to the user by reducing the packet losses and latency during handover. Finally, further evaluations to verify the impact of the Q3M architecture in an experimental environment and the standardization of its protocols as well as the study of mobility prediction schemes to achieve higher seamless handover will be done in future work.

References

1. Hartung, F., et al.: Advances in Network-Supported Media Delivery in the Next-Generation Mobile Systems, IEEE Communications Magazine 44(8) (August 2006)
2. Greve, F., et al.: FAMOUS: A Network Architecture for Delivering Multimedia Services to FAst MOving USers. In: Wireless Personal Communications, vol. 33(3-4), Kluwer Academic Publishers, Dordrecht (2005)
3. Rojan, G., et al.: Policy Based QoS Architecture in MUSE. In: Proc. of Annual IEEE Conference on Computer Communications, Barcelona, Madrid (April 2006)
4. Miloucheva, I., et al.: QoS Based Multicast Architecture for Heterogeneous Mobile IPv6 Environment. In: Proc. International Conference on Telecommunication, Madeira, Portugal (May 2006)
5. Dugeon, O., et al.: End-to-End Quality of Service over Heterogeneous Networks (EuQoS). In: Proc. of Fourth IFIP International Conference on Network Control and Engineering for QoS, Security and Mobility, Lannion, France (November 2005)
6. Jamalipour, A., Mirchandani, V., Kibria, M.: QoS-aware Mobility Support Architecture for Next generation Network, Wireless Communications & Mobile Computing 5(8) (December 2005)
7. Cerqueira, E., et al.: Multi-user Session Control in the Next Generation Wireless System. In: Proc. of ACM Workshop on Mobile Management and Wireless Access, Malaga, Spain (October 2006)
8. Neto, A., et al.: Resource Reservation Protocol Supporting QoS-aware Multicast Trees for Next Generation Networks. In: Proc. of IEEE Symposium Computer and Communications, Aveiro Portugal (July 2007)
9. Veloso, L., et al.: Seamless Mobility of Users for Media Distribution Services. In: Proc. of IEEE Performance Computing and Communications Conference, New Orleans, USA (April 2007)
10. Cicconetti, C., et al.: Quality of Service Support in IEEE 802.16 Networks, IEEE Network 20(5) (March-April 2006)
11. Sricharan, M., et al.: An Activity Based Mobility Prediction Strategy for Next Generation Wireless Networks. In: Proc. of IFIP Conference on Wireless and Optical Communications Networks, Bangalore, India (April 2006)

A Novel WiMAX Structure with Mesh Network

Jie Zeng and XiaoFeng Zhong

Department of Electronic Engineering, Tsinghua University, Beijing, P.R. China 100084
zengjie516@163.com

Abstract. IEEE802.16 (WiMAX) is a wireless metropolitan area network standard with high transmission speed and great coverage. Point to multi-point (PMP) is the traditional WiMAX transmission mode. Wireless mesh network (WMN) is an attractive and useful structure which is suggested to be adopted in WiMAX. A smart WiMAX structure with mesh is proposed in our paper, which supports direct data transmission between SSs (subscribe stations) with the control of the BS if possible. This mesh model is easy to achieve, and could improve the system performance such as throughput and propagation delay. With the help of the BS, several key problems in pure wireless mesh network are satisfactorily solved, such as coexistence, interference and billing. Simulation results are presented in this article to show the enhancement gain of the system performance by the smart model. The idea of virtual cell is put forward to benefit analysis, and the performance with AMC scheme is considered too. More concrete descriptions and explanations are given in the article.

Keywords: IEEE 802.16, WiMAX, wireless mesh network (WMN), adaptive modulation code (AMC), throughput.

1 Introduction

WiMAX (Worldwide Interoperability for Microwave Access) based on IEEE 802.16 standards is a wireless metropolitan area network (WMAN) which supports point to multi-point broadband wireless access(BWA). The IEEE wireless standard has a range of up to 30 miles, and offers wireless access at lower cost with higher bandwidth.It can afford transmission speed of up to 75 megabits per second. Therefore, WiMAX is considered one of the most attractive technologies for last-mile BWA problem in metropolitan areas and underserved rural areas. Mobile WiMAX based on the 802.16e-2005 enables WiMAX systems to address portable and mobile applications in addition to fixed and nomadic applications, and it seeks to support most client mobile requirements in the future market. The Mobile WiMAX Air Interface adopts Orthogonal Frequency Division Multiple Access (OFDMA) for improved multi-path performance in non-line-of-sight environments, Scalable OFDMA (SOFDMA)is introduced in the IEEE 802.16e Amendment to support scalable channel bandwidths from 1.25 to 20 MHz. Mobility broadens the market prospects of WiMAX, and creates a new research focus.

D. Krishnaswamy, T. Pfeifer, and D. Raz (Eds.): MMNS 2007, LNCS 4787, pp. 50–63, 2007.

Wireless mesh network, also known as ad hoc network, has become a significant technique for the next generation wireless networks. WMN is a self-organizing multi-hop system formed by user nodes,it can connect and communicate with other user nodes directly without pre-existing infrastructure. WMN provides a reliable and flexible system that can be quick-and-easy extended to thousands of devices. The signature of WMN is that each node acts as a relayed point for other nodes instead of being organized by a centralized control device. It has the reconstructive ability to fit the change of environments and the failure of some nodes. In addition, the distance of one-hop is much shorter; the power for transmission can be reduced obviously. Since the nodes in the multi-hop networking use much lower power to communicate with the neighboring nodes, the radio interference between them could be cut down. The channel quality and channel utilization efficiency will be greatly enhanced, resulting in higher capacity and better performance of the whole network.

WMN has so many advantages that it has done a good job in the improvement of IEEE802.11 network, known as the WiFi mesh. Similarly, it has been proposed to be adopted in WiMAX. To establish the multi-hop WMN connection and the single-hop PMP operation, IEEE 802.16a standard defined the basic signaling flows and message formats. The Mesh mode specifications are integrated into IEEE 802.16 revisions which are published later such as IEEE 802.16d and IEEE 802.16e.

The following is the key advantages of WiMAX mesh mode:

1) Greater coverage and better support of Non-Line of Sight (NLoS) transmission
2) Lower path loss and better performance
3) Higher throughput and lower delay
4) Rapid deployment and easy installation
5) Better robustness and flexibility

The name and the description of MAC Management messages for mesh network are given in IEEE802.16 standard, further work needs to be carried out to customize the specific application.

2 System Model

In order to achieve links characterized by high performances, the IEEE Standard 802.16a defines two different air-interfaces: PMP and Mesh. In PMP mode, connections are established among the BS and SS, hence, data transmissions between two SSs are routed through the BS. Within the Mesh network, traffic can occur directly among SSs since the protocol permits to set up data connections among neighbors. A station in the wireless network terms Mesh BS, acts like a BS in PMP mode and interfaces the network to the backhaul links. The MAC protocol for the Mesh mode has been designed to support both centralized (Mesh CS) and distributed (Mesh DS) schedulings.

A novel mesh structure is proposed as an extension to the traditional PMP WiMAX network, as is shown in fig. 1. When two subscribe stations (SS) are neighboring each other, they could exchange data packets directly with higher data rate and lower power after establishing the mesh link by the base station (BS) in the cell.

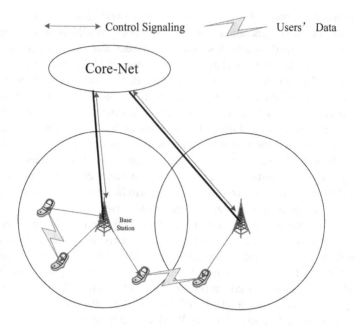

Fig. 1. Direct data transmission between SSs

Obviously, the scheduling idea we propose is simple to achieve and has a great system throughput enhancement. Through the control of a base station, cooperation shortcomings brought by DS mesh could be overcome, and the channel resources could be utilized more effectively. As a communication transfer and control center, the BS plays a very important role-key to the overall optimization. The main consideration in this issue is the system performance optimization within the coverage of one base station cell, and the cooperation between BSs to establish a mesh link needs pending further study.

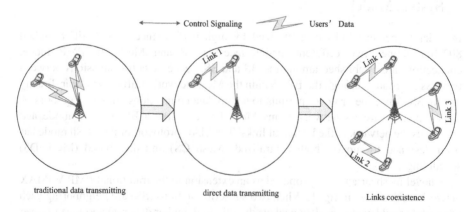

Fig. 2. Direct data transmission between SSs in one cell and different transmitting modes

The scheduling mode can be simplified as is shown in the following fig. 2 when only one cellular area is considered. Within the scope of a cell, we allow more than one direct data transmission between SSs at the same time on condition that there is no interference. The system throughput could be much more improved since more than one mesh links work at one time.

Basic conclusions need to be given here preparing for the in-depth discussions afterwards.

Due to the difference of transceiver parameters(such as Transmitting power, Receiver sensitivity, antenna height and gain) between BS and SS, the coverage of SS to SS link is much shorter than that of SS to BS at the same bit rate. We assume that the radius of the cell is R, the distance between a pair of SSs is d, and a threshold for mesh communicating is D. Without considering the adaptive modulation control, a pair of SSs will communicate directly if and only if d is not larger than D as proposed, otherwise they will transmit data with conventional mode through the BS.

If we put a pair of SSs in the cell randomly, fig. 3 gives the Cumulative Distribution curve of d/R.

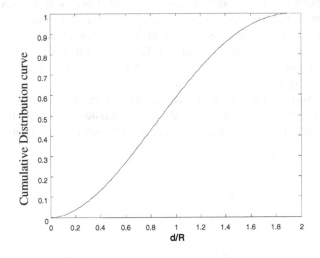

Fig. 3. The Cumulative Distribution curve of d/R for a random pair of SSs

The transmission range between SSs is smaller than that between BS and SS according to the difference of transmission power, receiver sensitivity and the channel conditions (LoS or NLoS). Giving an estimate on the value of D/R makes sense, and enables a better discussion on this network structure. WINNER Work Package 5 (WP5) [1] refers to the multi-dimensional radio channel modeling, when the scenarios suburban macro-cell and urban macro-cell defined in the document is suitable for WiMAX. The WINNER channel models show the key features(such as large-scale parameters, antenna gain, path-loss models and probability of LoS) in wireless communication. The typical urban macro-cell model is chosen for an estimate on the value of D/R. The path-loss models have the form as in formula (1), and "dis" is the distance between transmitter and receiver:

$$P_{loss}=35.0 \log_{10} (dis[m]) +38.4 \qquad 50 \text{ m} < dis < 5 \text{ km} \qquad (1)$$

Generally, the base station transmitter power (TPBS) is from 30dBw to more than 43dBw, and we choose 38dBw as the typical value. The transmitting power of the SS (TPSS) is from less than 10dBw to 33dBw (excessive estimate), and 28dBw is chosen as the typical value. Since we assume that the reception terminals and the channel path-loss models are the same, the transmission distance is just determined by the transmitting power at the same bit rates. According to the discussion, formula (1) comes up to formula (2) as following:

$$TP_{SS} - TP_{BS} =35.0 \log_{10} (D/R) \qquad (2)$$

Using the assumed transmitter power of BS and SS, the typical D/R can be calculated 0.52. The more reasonable range of D/R can be assumed from 0.3 to 0.7. Basing on the proposed scheduling idea, the average throughput will be increasing while the value of D/R increase.

A strongpoint in the model proposed is that there will be several direct non-interference transmission links in a cell when the threshold for mesh communicating D is suitable. A strongpoint in the model proposed is that there will be several non-interference direct transmission links in a cell when D is suitable. The coexisting restrictions of the direct transmission links should be discussed, since the scenario will bring more systematic throughput enhancements.

In the pure wireless mesh network, there are many solutions and schemes suggested to deal with the coexistence of several direct transmission links [2]~[3]. A two-link coexisting condition will be discussed here to seek the detailed restriction shown in fig. 4.

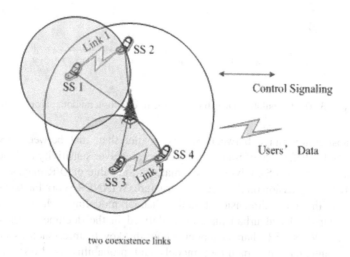

two coexistence links

Fig. 4. Two coexistence links scenario

Basing on the power control, the adaptive modulation and coding (AMC) scheme adopted in the direct data transmission, virtual cells can be used to describe the scope of different bit rates and interference as shown in fig. 5.

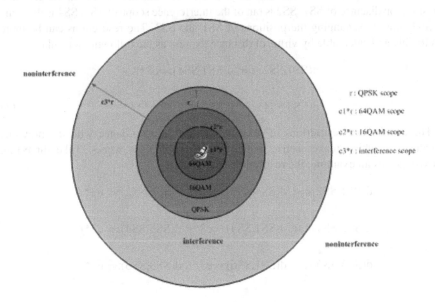

Fig. 5. Scope of different bit rates and interference

The virtual cell defined here is different from the traditional cell divided by the coverage of the BS, and is customized by the transmitter (BS or SS) launch capability. Since higher-order modulation means higher received power at the same BER (Bit Error Rate), there is smaller transmission scope according to the transmitting capability limit. As shown in fig. 5, different modulation modes have different transmission scopes. The typical modulation modes are QPSK, 16QAM and 16QAM. Several parameters are used to describe the application range. We assume that the QPSK transmission scope is r, the 64QAM scope is c_1*r, and the 16QAM scope is c_2*r. These adjustable parameters are set by the different wireless communication systems, and the typical value is given as follows: r=1000m, c_1=0.3, c_2=0.6. Interference between different transmission links is also considered, and virtual cell is also adopted to described the interference range c_3*r. According to the large-scale transmission path-loss model, the signal to interference ratio (SIR) is more than 9dB if the jamming 2 times the effective transmission distance away. In this condition the two links will coexist with the help of power control scheme as mentioned above, and the typical value of c_3 will be 2~3.

Essentially, the above-mentioned parameters are affected by the parameter r and three adjustable factors: c_1, c_2, c_3. For different transmission equipments as BS and SS, the factors will be different as a result of the different equipment performances, transmissions and channel models. The factors are inconstant due to the various wireless communication systems. However, the three factors are of universal significance, and they will be determined when the equipment's performance is confirmed.

Two link coexisting can be regarded as this concretion: SS1 sends message to SS2 and SS3 sends message to SS4 simultaniously. The restrictions are: SS2 is in the effective transmission distance of SS1, SS2 is out of the interference scope of SS3; SS4 is the same as SS2 simply exchanging the positions of SS1 and SS3. The restrictions can be more intelligible and calculable by virtue of distance express as the following formula:

$$d(SS1,SS2){<=}r, d(SS1,SS4){>=}c3 \bullet r,$$

$$d(SS3,SS4){<=}r, d(SS3,SS2){>=} c3 \bullet r \tag{3}$$

The coexistence restrictions of several links are in accordance with the previous conclusions, which makes sense in the coming simulation works. Take three-link coexistence as an example, the restrictions are:

$$d(SS1,SS2){<=}r, d(SS3,SS2){>=}c3 \bullet r, d(SS5,SS2){>=} c3 \bullet r$$

$$d(SS3,SS4){<=}r, d(SS1,SS4){>=}c3 \bullet r, d(SS5,SS4){>=} c3 \bullet r$$

$$d(SS5,SS6){<=}r, d(SS1,SS6){>=}c3 \bullet r, d(SS3,SS6){>=} c3 \bullet r \tag{4}$$

3   Performance Evaluation

In this section we analyze the performance of the proposed network.

3.1   Throughput Enhancement in Mesh Mode

In the following simulations: T is the total simulation time. Tmax is the maximum traffic holding time, the actual traffic holding time is uniformly distributed from 0 to tmax. Num is the number of total traffic links. The throughput of traditional WiMAX cell is normalized as 1, and all the links take the same QPSK modulation. The following figs. 6, 7 and 8 give the simulation results of the mesh modes of WiMAX throughput enhancements.

The direct mesh communicating will achieve double throughput enhancement for a single link. Considering the SSs distance probability and threshold D, the average system throughput will be increased by nearly 20% when the value of D/R is justifiably selected as 0.6 show in fig. 6 and 7. For different systems the threshold D can be changed, fig. 8 shows how the system throughput changes when the D/R changes. Obviously, more direct communications link when D/R is large,because this means more throughput enhancement, the simulation results verify the same conclusions. Fig. 9 gives a more clear relationship between throughput enhancement and the value of D/R. According to the curve and the analysis above, it is recommended to choose achievable largest threshold D in the system, such as 0.7.

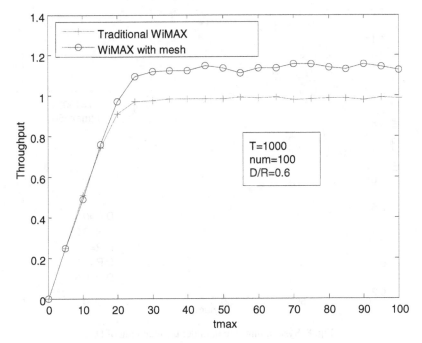

Fig. 6. System throughput under the changing of tmax

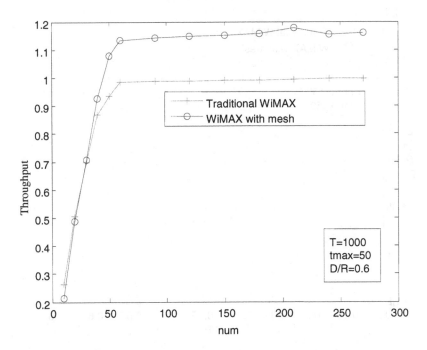

Fig. 7. System throughput under the changing of num

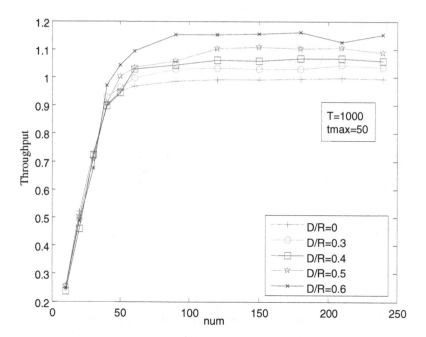

Fig. 8. System throughput under the changing of D/R

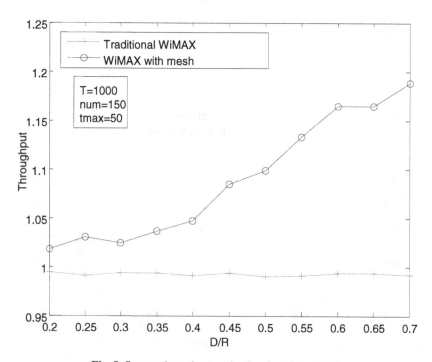

Fig. 9. System throughput under the changing of D/R

3.2 Throughput Enhancement with AMC

Throughput enhancement with AMC is discussed in the following simulation. With the adaptive modulation and coding scheme that are defined in IEEE802.16e specification, the neighboring SSs of shorter distance could achieve higher data rate, which will lead to more throughput enhancement. The parameters of the virtual cell need to be confirmed to support the simulation:

In the traditional WiMAX, the SS will work on different modulation ranks of 64QAM, 16QAM and QPSK when the distance between SS and BS is 0.3R, 0.6R and R. In the virtual cell of the BS, rate1=c1=0.3, rate2=c2=0.6.

In the WiMAX mesh mode, the SS will work on different modulation ranks of 64QAM, 16QAM and QPSK when the distance between a pair of SSs is 0.3D, 0.6D and D. In the virtual cell of the SS, rate3=c1=0.3, rate4=c2=0.6.

Rate1~4 are parameters in the simulation, they are set in a certain system. Fig. 10 gives the throughput comparison with AMC, which will be increased by nearly 40% in a cell while the AMC scheme gains 20% throughput enhancement.

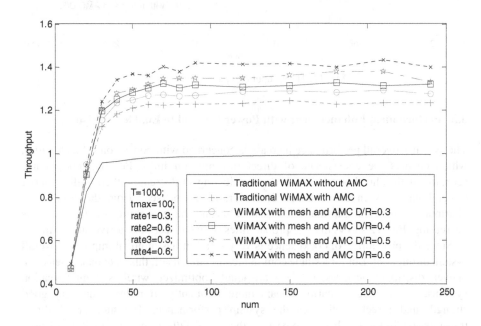

Fig. 10. Throughput comparison with AMC

The virtual cell parameters change in different systems, since the SSs are more likely to communicate in high modulation ranks, the virtual cell parameters of the SS may be set as rate3=c1=0.6, rate4=c2=0.9. This adjustment will bring changes in system performance as is shown in fig. 11, throughput enhancements therefore directly link and are more likely to work in high transmission speed.

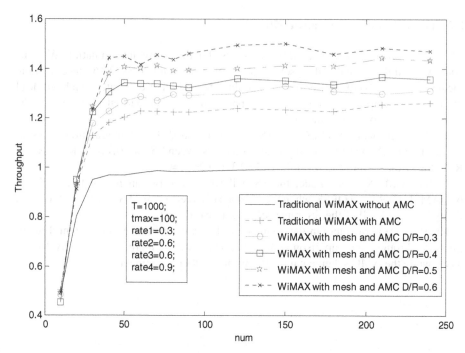

Fig. 11. Throughput comparison with AMC

3.3 Performance Enhancement with Power Control to Enable Coexistence

The system's overall performance increase is concerned with power control techniques, which enables the coexistence of direct transmission links. For link coexistence scenario, if the threshold for mesh communicating D decreases, there will be more direct links work in one channel. However, it can be seen from the cumulative distribution curve of d/R that decreased D means the probability of direct link is decreasing. Fig. 12 shows that the probabilities of two direct links arrive at one time.

Since the probability of coexistence is very small, it has minimal impact on overall system throughput. But for a single communication link itself, this state makes sense. In uneven distribute business, or even artificially optimized wireless communication systems, coexistence scenario appears more frequently. It reflects the very good strength and directly enhances the system performance. The number of direct transmission links which can coexist in the given D/R is present in Fig. 13 as a performance indicator.

It is very obvious that by support of the power control techniques, when D is decreased, more links can communicate simultaneously without interference in a cell. This coexistence scenario can be applied to some specific scenes which have frequent and close communication. For example, in one building, the main wireless business is the communication within the same office.

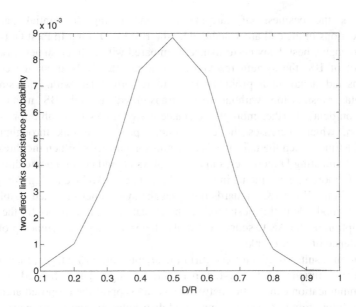

Fig. 12. Probabilities of two direct links arrive at one time

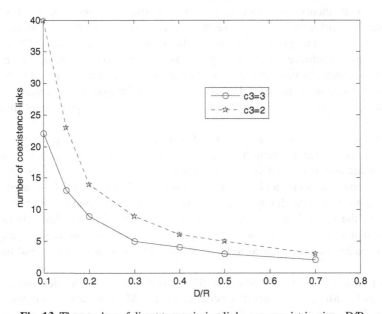

Fig. 13. The number of direct transmission links can coexist in given D/R

4 Conclusion and Further Work

The structure referred in the article is based on the mesh network under the control of the BS according to the characteristics of WiMAX. The greatest advantage of such a structure is the easiness of carrying out and taking substantial gains. The communications in the cell are scheduled by the BS; FIFO (First In First Out) mode is adopted to enable best delay performance. Compared with pure mesh network without the control of BS, the system resources are more effectively used, the coexisting restrictions and management problems are no more hard to deal with. For a single link, direct data transmission without being transmitted through BS means shorter transmission delay. Further more, the distance between SSs is suitable for high level modulation, which increases the transmission speed. The link throughput could enhance 2+ times when the pair of SSs transmits data directly. When the threshold for mesh communicating D increases, more pairs of SSs could communicate directly, and this leads to more enhancements in system throughput. AMC technology proposed to be adopted in the WiMAX standards improves the system performance visibly, and it also plays a good role in the mesh model. The virtual cell is a good tool for the analysis and description of the AMC scope, and it also helps solving interference problems in the coexistence of several links.

Simulation results are given to confirm the architecture advantages; they also give constructive comments on the system parameters design. The enhanced designs for direct communication capabilities between SSs can support the proposed architecture, and it's the future trend of the development of distributed communication systems.

From the emergence of the concept, wireless mesh network has achieved good results in both theory and practice. However, as evolved over from the traditional computer networks, WMN has several inevitable shortages in telecommunication business. The structure proposed combines the advantages of WiMAX and WMN, and is very simple to achieve. The service quality is well defined in WiMAX, which brings reliable telecommunication applications. The transmission delay of individual business could be reduced using mesh, and the average system throughput also enhances much. The combination of WiMAX and WMN achieves remarkable improvements in system performance, too.

In this article, we focus on the network structure, the working model and system performances. In-depth research needs to be carried out in specific business QoS requirements and BS scheduling optimization. Simulation results in this article are based on one cell scope and paired communication business. FIFO is used as the business processing scheduling program, which can be considered as the most optimal manner of the single link latency. But FIFO may not be the best choice in times of transmission congestion. To seek the optimum of the overall throughput, some communication businesses need to be rejected and the coexisting of several links are desirable.

Mesh network under the control of BS is discussed in this article, which is also known as CS Mesh. From another perspective, DS Mesh means the coexistence of different links and restrictions of data transmission. The structure proposed requires corresponding changes when used in pure mesh or DS mesh network.

In all, our smart structure combines the advantages of two advanced technologies, and is highly feasible. The scheduling optimizing could be highly targeted to adapt well to the future telecommunications development.

References

1. IST-2003-507581 WINNER D5.4 v. 1.4 Final Report on Link Level and System Level Channel Models
2. Whitehead, P.: Mesh Networks; a new Architecture for Broadband Wireless Access Systems. In: RAWCON (2000)
3. Redana, S., Lott, M., Capone, A.: Performance Evaluation of Point-to-Multi-Point (PMP) and Mesh Air-Interface in IEEE Standard 802.16a. In: Vehicular Technology Conference, 60th edn., pp. 3186–3190. IEEE, Los Alamitos (2004)

Monitoring Flow Aggregates with Controllable Accuracy

Alberto Gonzalez Prieto and Rolf Stadler

KTH Royal Institute of Technology
Stockholm, Sweden
{gonzalez, stadler}@ee.kth.se

Abstract. In this paper, we show the feasibility of real-time flow monitoring with controllable accuracy in today's IP networks. Our approach is based on Netflow and A-GAP. A-GAP is a protocol for continuous monitoring of network state variables, which are computed from device metrics using aggregation functions, such as SUM, AVERAGE and MAX. A-GAP is designed to achieve a given monitoring accuracy with minimal overhead. A-GAP is decentralized and asynchronous to achieve robustness and scalability. The protocol incrementally computes aggregation functions inside the network and, based on a stochastic model, it dynamically configures local filters that control the overhead and accuracy. We evaluate a prototype in a testbed of 16 commercial routers and provide measurements from a scenario where the protocol continuously estimates the total number of FTP flows in the network. Local flow metrics are read out from Netflow buffers and aggregated in real-time. We evaluate the prototype for the following criteria. First, the ability to effectively control the trade off between monitoring accuracy and processing overhead; second, the ability to accurately predict the distribution of the estimation error; third, the impact of a sudden change in topology on the performance of the protocol. The testbed measurements are consistent with simulation studies we performed for different topologies and network sizes, which proves the feasibility of the protocol design, and, more generally, the feasibility of effective and efficient real-time flow monitoring in large network environments.

1 Introduction

Several key management tasks, such as SLA verification, accounting and intrusion detection depend on monitoring state variables in the network. For many such tasks, the IP flow has emerged as the appropriate level of abstraction and granularity for monitoring. This has made flow monitoring an active research topic [14][17][18]. Its high relevance in practical scenarios has led the IETF to create the *IP Flow Information Export* (IPFIX) working group, focused on standardizing different aspects of flow monitoring, such as information models and information exchange protocols [15].

One of the key challenges in flow monitoring is controlling the trade off between the costs (e.g., processing resources, memory requirements, management traffic) and the accuracy of the monitored metrics. Examples of research efforts in this area are [16][17][18].

D. Krishnaswamy, T. Pfeifer, and D. Raz (Eds.): MMNS 2007, LNCS 4787, pp. 64–75, 2007.

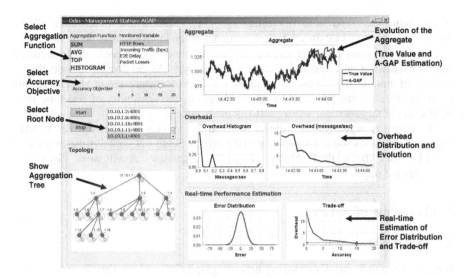

Fig. 1. Interface on the management station for evaluating A-GAP on the testbed. It shows the effect of changing the accuracy objective from 0 to 15 flows. at time 14:42:30 in a testbed scenario. As a consequence, A-GAP reduces the overhead at the cost of an increased error in estimating the aggregate. The interface provides also real-time estimation of the error distribution and of the trade-off curve accuracy vs overhead.

A relevant technique in this context is aggregation. It consists on computing network-wide metrics from device-level metrics across a network. Examples of aggregation functions are SUM, AVERAGE, MIN, MAX, and HISTOGRAM. Sample flow aggregates are the total number of VoIP flows, the most popular flow destination, or a histogram of flow sizes in a network domain. Monitoring flow aggregates enables administrators to learn the volume of traffic different applications generate and infer the performance requirements of end users. Monitoring flow aggregates also permits identifying elephant flows, a key task in traffic engineering [20].

While it is often crucial to know how accurate aggregate estimates are, network management solutions deployed today usually provide only qualitative control of the accuracy and do not support the setting of an accuracy objective [4].

The focus of this paper is on providing continuous estimates of flow aggregates with controllable accuracy in today's IP networks.

Our solution is based on Netflow [14] and A-GAP [11], a generic aggregation protocol with controllable accuracy. Router-level flow metrics are read from Netflow buffers. A-GAP continuously aggregates these router-level metrics into network-wide metrics by (i) creating and maintaining a self-stabilizing spanning tree and (ii) incrementally aggregating the metrics along the tree. A-GAP is push-based in the sense that changes in monitored metrics are sent towards the management station along the aggregation tree. The protocol controls the management overhead by filtering updates that are sent from monitoring nodes to the management station. The filters periodically adapt to the dynamics of the monitored variables and the network environment. All operations in A-GAP, including computing the aggregation function and filter configuration, are executed in a decentralized and asynchronous fashion to ensure robustness and achieve scalability. [11] contains the description of the stochastic model A-GAP uses for filter computation and performance prediction.

This paper reports on our prototype for flow monitoring with controllable accuracy and its evaluation on a testbed of commercial routers. At the cost of introducing an overlay of monitoring nodes, no changes to the routers are required. The results presented validate the protocol design and suggests the feasibility of real-time flow monitoring in large-scale dynamic network environments.

The paper is organized as follows. Section 2 provides an overview of A-GAP. Section 3 discusses the implementation of A-GAP. Section 4 contains the evaluation scenarios and the testbed results. Section 5 discusses related work. Section 6 concludes the paper.

2 Overview of A-GAP

2.1 Problem Statement

We consider a dynamically changing network graph $G(t) = (V(t), E(t))$ in which nodes $n \in V(t)$ and edges/links $e \in E(t) \subseteq V(t) \times V(t)$ may appear and disappear over time. Each node n has an associated local variable $w_n(t)$. The term *local variable* is used to represent a local state variable or device counter that is being subjected to monitoring. Local variables are updated asynchronously with a given sampling rate.

The objective is to engineer a protocol on this network graph that provides a management station with a continuous estimate of $\Sigma_n w_n(t)$ for a given accuracy. The protocol should execute with minimal overhead in the sense that it minimizes the (maximum) processing load over all nodes. The load is expressed as the number of updates per second a node has to process. The accuracy is expressed as the *average error* of the estimate over time.

Throughout the paper we use SUM as aggregation function. Other functions can be supported as well, as discussed in [11].

2.2 A-GAP

A-GAP is based on GAP (Generic Aggregation Protocol), an asynchronous distributed protocol that builds and maintains a BFS (Breadth First Search) spanning tree on an overlay network [1]. The tree is maintained in a similar way as the algorithm that underlies the 802.1d Spanning Tree Protocol (STP) [5]. In GAP, each node holds information about its children in the BFS tree, in order to compute the partial aggregate, i.e., the aggregate value of the local management variables from all nodes of the subtree where this node is the root. GAP is event-driven in the sense that messages are exchanged as results of events, such as the detection of a new neighbor on the overlay, the failure of a neighbor, an update to an aggregate or a change in the local management variable.

A drawback of such an approach is that it can cause a high load on the root node or on nodes close to the root, specifically in large networks. In order to reduce this overhead, A-GAP introduces filters in the nodes. When the partial aggregate (or the local variable in the case of a leaf node) of a node n changes, then n sends an update to its parent if the difference between the value reported in its last update and the current value exceeds the local filter width F^n.

Minimizing the Protocol Overhead. Estimating the network variable at the root node with minimal overhead for a given accuracy can be formalized as an optimization problem. Let n be a node in the network graph, ω^n the rate of updates received by node n from its children, E^{root} the distribution of the estimation error at the root node, and ε the accuracy objective. We formulate the problem as

$$\text{Minimize } Max_n \{\omega^n\} \quad \text{s.t.} \quad E\left(\left|E^{root}\right|\right) \leq \varepsilon \qquad (1)$$

whereby ω^n and E^{root} depend on the filter widths $(F^n)_n$, which are the decision variables.

We have developed a stochastic model for the monitoring process. The model is based on discrete-time Markov chains and describes individual nodes in their steady state. For each node n, it relates the error of the partial aggregate of n, the step sizes that indicate changes in the partial aggregate, the rate of updates n sends and the width of the local filter. The model is described in detail in [11]. The model permits us to compute the distribution of the estimation error at the root node and the rate of updates processed by each node.

A-GAP continuously estimates the evolution of the management variables that the protocol aggregates, one of the variables in our model. Based on these estimates, all others model variables, such as the error distributions and incurred overhead, are dynamically computed. Such an approach lets A-GAP adapt quickly, compared to an approach whereby all model variables are estimated.

A Local Heuristic. An optimal solution to (eq. 1) can be computed using a (centralized) grid search algorithm, a well-known optimization technique, where the model variables for all nodes in the aggregation tree are computed bottom-up. Such an approach, however, is not feasible for large networks, since the computational cost of this algorithm grows exponentially with the number of nodes. A-GAP realizes a distributed heuristic, which attempts to minimize the maximum processing load on all nodes by minimizing the load within each node's neighborhood. A-GAP maps (eq. 1) onto a local problem for each node n as follows:

$$\text{Minimize } Max_\pi \{\omega^\pi\} \quad \text{s.t.} \quad E\left(\left|E_{out}^n\right|\right) \leq \varepsilon^n, \qquad (2)$$

where π is the set composed by the node n and its children. This means that node n attempts to minimize the maximum load in a neighborhood for a given accuracy objective ε^n of its partial aggregate.

The node attempts to solve (eq. 2) by periodically re-computing the filters and accuracy objectives of its children, based on the stochastic model. Re-computing the filters $(F^c)_c$ allows node n to influence its own load ω^n, while re-computing the accuracy objective ε^c of a child c allows the node to influence the load ω^c on c.

A-GAP computes the local filters and accuracy objectives in a decentralized and asynchronous fashion, as described in detail in [11].

The two keys configuration parameters of A-GAP are (i) the maximum number of children whose filters and accuracy objectives are recomputed during a control cycle $|\Omega|$, and (ii) the period of the control cycle τ. As discussed in [11], both parameters influence the adaptability and computational cost of A-GAP.

3 Implementation

A-GAP executes on a distributed management architecture, whereby each network device participates in the monitoring task by running a *management process*, either internally on the network element or on an external associated device. In our testbed, the management processes execute on Linux PCs, or alternatively, on low-cost mini-computers. Each computer, which we also call a *monitoring node*, runs the management process associated with one of the routers. Monitoring nodes communicate with each other via overlay links.

Figure 2 shows the design of a monitoring node. The *node manager* is responsible for executing the commands from overlay peers and the management station. These include the invocation of services and protocols. Local services a node supports are overlay maintenance, node/link failure detector, reliable communication and local device access. The overlay maintenance service constructs and maintains the overlay that interconnects the monitoring nodes. The failure detector detects the failing of a neighboring node. The reliable communication service provides reliable and secure message passing across overlay links. The device access service provides access to local variables on the network device through SNMP, CLI, Netflow, etc.

A monitoring node is implemented in Java. A-GAP alone is in the order of 2500 lines of code. The heuristic used for solving the problem shown in (eq. 2) is implemented using JSci (v0.94) for solving systems of linear equations [2]. Message exchange between monitoring nodes is implemented using XML. All protocol invocations and services run as threads in a single JVM.

The interface on the management station shown in figure 1 facilitates the evaluation of A-GAP. It allows setting configuration parameters of the protocol, including the aggregation function, the accuracy objective, and the root node of the aggregation tree. Once the protocol has set up the aggregation tree on the overlay, the tree topology is displayed in the lower left corner. On the right side, the interface provides real-time information on A-GAP's performance. First and foremost, the estimate of the aggregate and its evolution over time (top right). Second, the distribution of the estimation error for the current networking conditions and objective (bottom center). Third, the estimated trade-off curve between the protocol overhead and the error objective for the current networking conditions (bottom right). The current operating point on the curve is displayed as well. Furthermore, the interface provides data from an application that monitors the execution of

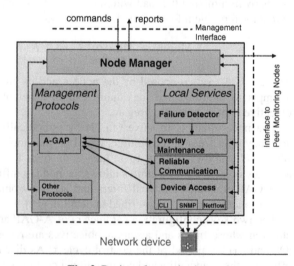

Fig. 2. Design of a monitoring node

A-GAP, namely, the true aggregate over time, as well as the distribution and evolution of the management overhead (blue curves in figure 1). These metrics are pushed by the management processes to a collecting node. The interface is built with JFreeChart (v.1.0.2) [3] that draws the graphs in real-time.

4 Evaluation

4.1 Testbed Setup

Figure 3 gives the setup of our testbed for the evaluation and shows an aggregation tree on the overlay created by A-GAP. The testbed includes 16 Cisco 2600 Series routers and 16 rack-mounted PCs running the monitoring nodes. Routers and PCs are connected through four 100Mbps Ethernet switches (a Netgear FSM750S and three Netgear FSM726S). An NTP server synchronizes the clocks on the PCs for the purpose of estimating the "true" aggregate. A Spirent Smartbits 6000 programmable traffic generator injects flows into the testbed.

4.2 Measured Metrics

During the experiments, we collect the following metrics. First, we trace A-GAP's *estimation of the aggregate* by logging all updates of the aggregate at the root node. Second, we trace the value of the *local variable* of each node (obtained by reading the router's Netflow cache) by logging all updates to this variable on the node. The first and the second metrics are used to compute the *estimation error*, which we define as the average difference between the sum of all the local variables (called the *true value* throughout the paper) and the *estimation of the aggregate* by A-GAP. Third, we trace the *management overhead* of each node by counting the number of updates each node receives during a control cycle. This data is used to compute the *maximum load* over all nodes in the testbed.

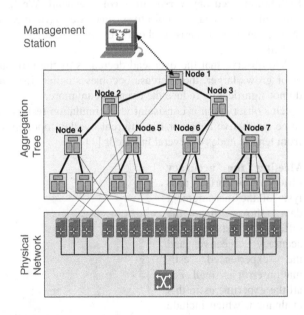

Fig. 3. Testbed configuration. The area at the bottom represents the physical network: 16 commercial routers. Each router is associated with a monitoring node. Monitoring nodes communicate via an overlay (middle area). The management station on top interacts with the root node of the aggregation tree.

4.3 Scenarios Description

The local management variable in the experiments is the number of FTP flows entering the network through that node. Therefore, the monitored aggregate is the number of FTP flows in the network. The traffic generator injects flows into the testbed following a random walk process with barriers. For the experiments in this paper, the aggregate takes values between 0 and 450 flows.

The local variables are sampled asynchronously, once every second, and are read from the Netflow caches of the Cisco routers through CLI.

During all experiments, the overlay topology does not change, and the aggregation tree set up by the protocol has the structure given in figure 3. The control cycle of A-GAP is set to 5 seconds, and the number of children whose filters are recomputed during a control cycle is set to 2.

All experiments start with an initialization phase of some 30 seconds, in which the aggregation tree is set up and the model variables are estimated or computed. This is followed by a transient period of up to 60 seconds. After that, the measurement period starts, which is 350 seconds for all experiments. The accuracy objective is set at the beginning of the experiment and it is not changed during a run.

4.4 Measurement Results

Estimation accuracy versus protocol overhead. We have run a set of experiments with different accuracy objectives, and we have measured the protocol overhead in function of the experi-enced error. Every point in figure 4 corresponds to a run on the testbed.

We observe that the overhead decreases as the estimation error increases. As the error grows larger, the decrease becomes smaller. Estimation errors above 10 flows do not significantly reduce the overhead anymore.

This observation is consistent with simulation results of A-GAP, where we see the same qualitative behavior for different overlay topologies and network sizes ranging from tens of nodes to several hundreds [11].

Meeting the accuracy objective. A further analysis of the measurement data shows that the difference between the accuracy objective and the experienced estimation error is small. For all the experiments in this evaluation, which include dozens of runs, it has been less than one flow (considering that typical aggregate values in our experiments are around 200 flows).

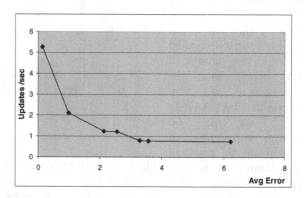

Fig. 4. Testbed measurements: management overhead incurred by A-GAP as a function of the accuracy of the estimation

The difference between accuracy objective and the experienced estimation error has two main causes. First, updates from different nodes in the network experience different delays in reaching the root, which distorts the evolution of the estimate at the root node. (This distortion is not captured by our stochastic model [11], since, for reasons of simplicity, it does not consider networking and processing delays). A second cause is the inaccuracy in the stochastic model variables used for filter computation, for instance, as a result of errors in the estimation of the evolution of the local variables.

These measurement results demonstrate that we can effectively control the accuracy of the estimation that A-GAP provides. Second, we can control the trade off between the accuracy of the estimation and the protocol overhead. Specifically, the larger the error A-GAP is allowed to make, the smaller the overhead it incurs.

Robustness: A router gets disconnected. In this experiment, we assess the adaptability of A-GAP to the disconnection of a router (and the computer running its associated management process). The disconnection happens instantly and the failure detectors in the neighbors of the disconnected node detect the failure in a sub-second.

When a failure is detected, A-GAP reconstructs the spanning tree. At the same time, the partial aggregates in some nodes are recomputed. The local mechanism for filter re-computation assures that the filters in the nodes adapt to the new tree structure.

In this particular experiment, node 6 (shown in figure 3) is disconnected from the network at time $\cong$ 101 seconds. The spanning tree is reconstructed on the overlay (not shown in the figure). Figure 5 shows traces of the experiment. In the upper graph, which shows the maximum load across all nodes, we see no apparent transient period. In the lower graph, which shows the estimation of the aggregate provided by A-GAP and the true value, we observe a spike during a transient period of a sub-second. For this experiment, the accuracy objective is 4 flows, and we see that the objective is achieved both before and after the failure.

This observation is consistent with the properties of protocols that use aggregation trees [9][1] and with our results from simulating A-GAP [11], where we observe brief spikes

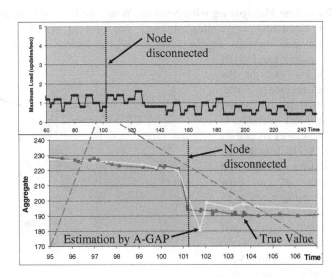

Fig. 5. Estimation error at the root node and management overhead caused by a node disconnection

in estimation errors. During tree reconstruction, some local variables may be considered more than once, or not at all, in the estimation of the global aggregate, which explains the spike in the estimation error at the root node. Specifically, in this experiment, the local variables of the children of node 4 are not considered at the root until updates from their new parents in the tree reach the root.

When simulating A-GAP for large networks, we have seen a significant peak in the overhead for cases where tree reconstruction involves a large number of nodes–a phenomena that we did not expect to see in our small testbed.

Distribution of the estimation error. In this experiment, we evaluate the capability of A-GAP for providing performance estimation. Based on our stochastic model, A-GAP can provide, for a given error objective, the distribution of the estimation error and the expected overhead at the nodes.

Figure 6 shows the error distribution for a run where A-GAP constructs a tree as shown in figure 3. The accuracy objective is 4 flows. One curve shows the error distribution estimated by A-GAP, the other gives the result from measuring the errors on the testbed.

We observe that both curves are close to each other, and the estimation by A-GAP is accurate in this sense. We see also that both distribu-tions have long tails. The maximum poss-ible error (i.e., the sum of all filter widths) in this run is 26. The estimated probability of having such a large error, though, is very small, in the order of 10-13. The actual maximum error during the experiment is 14. (The observation that the maximum error is a rare event is also made by other authors [9][12]. This confirms our choice of the average error as control parameter for the protocol, rather than the maximum error, which other authors advocate [10].)

Other measurements from our testbed also show that A-GAP accurately estimates the expected protocol overhead. Results can be found in [13].

Real-time Monitoring with Netflow. While we have developed A-GAP as a protocol for estimating aggregates of local variables in real-time, the accuracy of this estimation depends on the accuracy of the local variables, which capture device counters, local MIB objects, etc. In the measurements pre-sented in this paper, the local variable is the number of entries in a Netflow cache. Netflow keeps an entry of a flow traversing a router as long as its latest packet has traversed the router within the interval [now()-Δt, now()]. (In our setup Δt is 10 seconds.). As Netflow defines

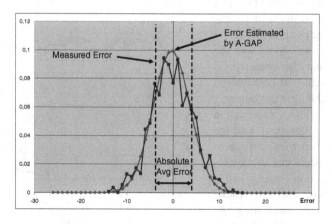

Fig. 6. Distribution of the error predicted by A-GAP and the actual error at the root node

flows in terms of packet inter-arrival times, counting the flows in a Netflow cache generally overestimates the number of flows currently traversing a router. In this sense, the figures in this paper overestimate the number of flows on the testbed. By taking into account flow statistics, such as flow duration, a more accurate estimation of the number of flows that currently traverse a router can be computed, and we are implementing such an algorithm on the monitoring nodes. Note though that local algorithms for obtaining the local variables are needed by but independent of A-GAP.

4.5 Comparative Evaluation on a Simulator

In order to compare the results from the testbed with those from the simulation-based evaluation of A-GAP [11], we have run testbed experiments where the local variables are based on the packet traces used in the simulations. The traces were captured on two 1 Gbit/s links that connect University of Twente to a research network. We have compared testbed results with simulation experiments for the same A-GAP configuration and traces. For the simulation runs, the link speeds in the overlay are set to 100 Mbps. The communication delay is set to 4 ms, and the time to process a message at a node is set to 1 ms. For a more detailed description of the simulation framework and set up, see [11].

This comparative evaluation is one way to strengthen our prediction on how A-GAP would perform in large networks that we have simulated [11]. This would be case, if the simulation results for the testbed configuration turn out to be very similar to the measurement results from the actual testbed. Alternatively, this comparative evaluation will give us some insight into potential limitations of our simulation-based studies.

Our results [13] (not included in this paper due to space restrictions) show that the trade-off curves for a simulation run and testbed measurements are very close. The difference in overhead is below 3,5%.

When considering the difference between the accuracy objective and the estimation error, we observe that the simulation gives results that are closer to the objective, but the differences between testbed and simulation results are very small. We explain this difference with the fact that the simulation model is simplified compared to the reality of the testbed.

5   Related Work

Recently, there has been significant research in real-time monitoring of network aggregates with the goal of achieving accuracy at low cost. For an overview, see [10]. Most of the proposed approaches have been evaluated using simulation. An example of a scheme that has been evaluated in a prototype implementation is described in [6]. The scheme in [6] differs from A-GAP in two ways. First, it is centralized in the sense that the management station computes the filter widths for all nodes, and all nodes communicate directly with the management station. Like A-GAP, [6] requires an execution environment on the nodes. Second, the accuracy objective in [6] is the maximum error, while A-GAP uses the average error as objective (which we argue is more significant for practical applications). [6] reports on an evaluation in a similar testbed setting. The authors show that they can effectively control the trade off between accuracy and overhead and provide a trade off curve that is qualitatively similar to figure 4.

[7] and [8] report on implementations of real-time monitoring of aggregates in the context of sensor networks. Similar to A-GAP, the above two works are based on in-network aggregation along spanning trees. They aim at providing periodically a snapshot of the aggregate, while A-GAP gives a continuous estimation of the aggregate. The focus of [7] and [8] is on studying the impact of lossy links on the accuracy of the estimated aggregate.

6 Conclusions

In this paper we have presented testbed results from our prototype for flow monitoring with controllable accuracy on a testbed with 16 commercial routers. Our prototype is based on Netflow and A-GAP. A-GAP is decentralized and asynchronous, two key properties for achieving robustness and scalability. At the cost of introducing an overlay of monitoring nodes, no changes to the routers have been required.

The experimental results show that we can effectively control the *trade off between estimation accuracy and protocol overhead* for A-GAP on a testbed. For the scenarios considered in this paper, A-GAP reduces the overhead by one order of magnitude, when allowed an error of 8 flows (figure 4), which is a relative error of less than 1%. The results also show that the protocol adapts quickly to a node failure on the testbed, in a manner that is consistent with what we expect from simulation results.

We also demonstrate the capability of A-GAP for *providing accurate performance estimation in real-time*. The management station can obtain, in real-time, an accurate view of (i) the distribution of the estimation error for the aggregate, and (ii) the expected overhead for each node in the system.

All the above results are consistent with simulation results that have been obtained for different topologies and much larger network sizes (up to some 700 nodes) [11]. Furthermore, the experimental results discussed in section 4.5 show that the behavior of our A-GAP implementation is very similar to that of the protocol running in a simulation environment. This validates our simulation model, proving that its assumptions and simplifications are reasonable. As a consequence, we are much more confident in the simulation results reported in [11], which have been obtained for different topologies and much larger network sizes, and the overall understanding of the behavior of A-GAP.

Together with [11], the results in this paper validate the protocol design and suggest the feasibility of real-time monitoring in large-scale dynamic network environments, in an efficient and effective manner.

Both simulation and testbed experiments [13] have shown that the choice of the *overlay topology can have a significant impact on A-GAPs performance*, and we plan to study this aspect in more detail A second issue that we plan to focus on is reducing the cost of computing the filters in A-GAP. We currently solve the local problem in (eq 2) through exhaustive search, and are searching for an efficient heuristic that yields close to optimal results. Future work also includes the design of algorithms for flow identification. In this paper, the identification of FTP flows is based on the transport port of the flow. This simple algorithm might not be valid for all applications. For instance, a popular VoIP application as Skype can use randomly chosen ports [19].

Acknowledgments. This paper describes work undertaken in the context of the Ambient Networks –an FP6 IST project that is partially funded by the Commission of the European Union.

References

1. Dam, M., Stadler, R.: A Generic Protocol for Network State Aggregation, Radiovetenskap och Kommunication (RVK), Linkoping, Sweden (June 2005)
2. JSci (December 2006), http://jsci.sourceforge.net/
3. JFreeChart (December 2006), http://www.jfree.org/jfreechart/
4. Olston, C., et al.: Adaptive Precision Setting for Cached Approximate Values. In: ACM SIGMOD 2001, Santa Barbara, USA (May 2001)
5. IEEE. ANSI/IEEE Std 802.1D, 1998 Edition. IEEE (1998)
6. Olston, C., Jiang, J., Widom, J.: Adaptive Filters for Continuous Queries over Distributed Data Streams. In: ACM SIGMOD 2003, San Diego, USA (June 2003)
7. Madden, S.R., et al.: TAG: a tiny aggregation service for ad-hoc sensor networks. In: 5th Symposium on Operating Systems Design and Implementation, Boston, USA (December 2002)
8. Zhao, J., et al.: Computing aggregates for monitoring wireless sensor networks. In: 1st IEEE International Workshop on Sensor Network Protocols and Applications, Anchorage, USA (May 2003)
9. Boulis, A., Ganeriwal, S., Srivastava, M.B.: Aggregation in sensor networks: an energy - accuracy tradeoff, Elsevier Ad-hoc Networks Journal (s.i. on sensor network protocols and applications) (2003)
10. Gonzalez Prieto, A.: Adaptive Management for Networked Systems, Licentiate thesis, KTH Royal Institute of Technology, Sweden (June 2006), Available at http://www.ee.kth.se/~gonzalez
11. Gonzalez Prieto, A., Stadler, R.: A-GAP: An Adaptive Protocol for Continuous Network Monitoring with Accuracy Objectives, IEEE Transactions on Network and Service Management 4(1) (June 2007)
12. Sharaf, M.A., et al.: Balancing energy efficiency and quality of aggregate data in sensor networks. ACM International Journal on Very Large Data Bases 13(4), 384–403 (2004)
13. Gonzalez Prieto, A., Stadler, R.: Implementation and Evaluation of A-GAP: Adaptive Monitoring with Controllable Accuracy, KTH Technical Report (January 2007), Available at http://www.ee.kth.se/~gonzalez
14. Cisco Netflow, http://www.cisco.com/warp/public/732/netflow/index.html
15. IETF IP Flow Information Export working group, http://www.ietf.org
16. Keys, K., Moore, D., Estan, C.: A robust system for accurate realtime summaries of internet traffic, SIGMETRICS Perform. Eval. Rev. 33(1), 85–96 (2005)
17. Molina, M., Chiosi, A., D'Antonio, S., Ventre, G.: Design principles and algorithms for effective high-speed IP flow monitoring. Computer Communications 29(10), 1653–1664 (2006)
18. Yang, L., Michailidis, G.: Sampled based estimation of network traffic flow characteristics. In: IEEE Infocom 2007, Anchorage, USA (May 2007)
19. Suh, K., Figueiredo, D.R., Kurose, J., Towsley, D.: Characterizing and detecting skype-relayed traffic. In: IEEE Infocom 2006, Barcelona, Spain (April 2006)
20. Mori, T., et al.: Identifying elephant flows through periodically sampled packets. In: 4th ACM SIGCOMM conference on Internet measurement, Taormina, Italy (October 2004)

OMA DM Based Remote RF Signal Monitoring of Mobile Devices for QoS Improvement*

Joon-Myung Kang[1], Hong-Taek Ju[2], Mi-Jung Choi[1], and James Won-Ki Hong[1]

[1] Dept. of Computer Science and Engineering, POSTECH, Korea
{eliot,mjchoi,jwkhong}@postech.ac.kr
[2] Dept. of Computer Engineering, Keimyung University, Korea
juht@kmu.ac.kr

Abstract. As mobile devices and functionalities have increased and become intelligent, many related problems have occurred. Especially, the degraded quality of service caused by the shadow area has given the end-users much inconvenience. In addition, the credibility of the service providers, the network operators, and the manufacturers of the mobile devices have also decreased. In order to solve these problems, we need to monitor the radio frequency (RF) signal related information such as the received signal strength (RSS) for finding the shadow areas. So far, no appropriate method has been given. In this paper, we propose a RF signal monitoring method for the quality of service (QoS) improvement based on the Open Mobile Alliance (OMA) Device Management (DM) standard. We have defined the management objects (MOs) for finding the shadow areas and design the management operations for collecting the MOs at the central server. We have developed based on MOs and the management operations. We also present the result of the performance evaluation of our proposed management operations.

Keywords: Mobile Device Management, RF Signal Monitoring, QoS, OMA DM, OMA DM DiagMon.

1 Introduction

Recently, the tremendous growth of the mobile computing and the wireless network communications has accelerated the introduction of various mobile devices in the wireless network environment. They have become more sophisticated and intelligent in order to satisfy the end user's various requirements in terms of technology convergence [1, 2]. As the service for the mobile devices has become various and the real time multimedia service has increased, the quality of service (QoS) in the mobile network has been an important factor for the end users and the service providers.

---

* This research was supported by the MIC (Ministry of Information and Communication), Korea, under the ITRC (Information Technology Research Center) support program supervised by the IITA (Institute of Information Technology Assessment)" (IITA-2006-C1090-0603-0045).

D. Krishnaswamy, T. Pfeifer, and D. Raz (Eds.): MMNS 2007, LNCS 4787, pp. 76–87, 2007.
© IFIP International Federation for Information Processing 2007

Many research topics and results have focused on monitoring and guaranteeing the QoS in the Internet [21].

Especially, the degraded QoS by the shadow area is critical in the mobile network. The shadow area is caused by the appearance of new buildings or the reduced capability of the base stations. The status of the received signal strength (RSS) is directly related to the QoS of the mobile device and determines the shadow area. Hence, if we can remove the shadow area through the quick and exact measurement of the RSS at the central server, then the QoS can be much improved. The usual method to find the shadow area is to measure the RSS with the direct visit to the region. However, it requires more time and labor. In order to solve this problem, if the mobile device collects and reports the relevant information about the radio frequency (RF) signal including RSS to the central server when the QoS is lower than the predefined threshold, it can be solved efficiently.

In this paper, we propose a RF signal monitoring method to discover the shadow areas for the QoS improvement. However, it is difficult to collect the relevant information on the RF signal of the mobile device due to the large size of data, and low bandwidth and high error rate of the mobile network environment. Furthermore, the data collection from the mobile device requires a complex process. That is, the central server must initialize the relevant function of the mobile device for monitoring. Next, it must start it. And then, the mobile device must collect and report the relevant information to the central server. When analyzing the RF signal data, the system information of the mobile device like network interface type, the type and the number of antenna, etc., is also necessary.

The Open Mobile Alliance (OMA) Device Management (DM) framework [3, 4], which is the international standard for the mobile device management, provides an appropriate solution to overcome these limitations. The DM protocol has been designed to collect large-scale data in mobile network environment. Additionally, it includes the management operations to collect the information. The standard managed objects (MOs) [5] include the system information as the basic requirement. In this paper, we present the design and the implementation of the system for RF signal monitoring based on OMA DM. We also present the results of the performance evaluation for validating the efficiency of our proposed method.

The remainder of this paper is organized as follows. Section 2 describes the OMA DM, OMA DM DiagMon standard and the mobile device management as the related work. Section 3 describes the management architecture, management information, and management operations of the proposed system. Section 4 presents the system development. The results of performance evaluation are given in Section 5. Finally, conclusions are drawn and future work is discussed in Section 6.

2 Related Work

In this section, we present the specification of the OMA DM and the OMA DM DiagMon standard. We describe the major components of OMA DM such as bootstrapping, device description framework (DDF), and OMA DM protocol. We introduce the functions and the current status of the OMA DM DiagMon Working Group (WG). We also describe the previous work and the systems related to the mobile device management.

2.1 OMA DM and OMA DM DiagMon

The OMA DM WG is one of the major WGs in OMA which has been established by mobile operators, information technology companies, wireless equipment vendors, and content providers in 2001. It has defined the management information and the management protocol for the mobile device called OMA DM protocol [6], which is a SyncML [7] based protocol aimed at providing a remote synchronization of mobile devices. The OMA DM standard includes three logical components such as DDF [8], bootstrapping [9], and OMA DM Protocol [6]. DDF provides the necessary information of MOs in devices for the server. Bootstrapping configures initial setting of devices. The OMA DM protocol defines the order of communicated packages by the server and client. Each device that supports OMA DM must contain a management tree [10], which organizes all available MOs in the device as a hierarchical tree structure where all nodes can be uniquely addressed with a uniform resource identifier (URI) [11]. The management tree is not completely standardized yet. OMA allows each device manufacturer to easily extend the management tree by adding new management functions in their devices by defining and adding the management nodes to the existing management tree. We show how this can be done in Section 3.

Table 1 shows the OMA DM commands, which are similar to SNMP operations [12, 13]. A management session is composed of several commands. The server retrieves the MO content or the MO list from the DM client by the '*GET*' command. The server can add a new MO by the '*ADD*' command. Moreover, the server can replace or delete MOs by '*REPLACE*' or '*DELETE*' command. The client can notify the management session by '*ALERT*' command, while the server can execute a new process to the client by '*EXEC*' command. We can design the monitoring process by a composition of these commands.

Table 1. OMA DM Commands

OMA DM Command	Feature	Description
GET	Reading a MO content or MO list	The server retrieves the content from the DM Client or the list of MOs residing in a management tree.
ADD	Adding a MO or MO content	A new dynamic MO is inserted
REPLACE	Updating MO content	Existing content of an MO is replaced with new content
DELETE	Removing MO(s)	One or more MOs are removed from a management tree
ALERT	Management session start	Convey notification of device management session
EXEC	Executing a process	New process is invoked and return a status code or result

The OMA DM WG has proposed device management diagnostics and device monitoring functionality. The overall goal of OMA DM DiagMon [14] is to enable management authorities to proactively detect and repair problems even before the users are impacted, or to determine actual or potential problems with a device when needed [15]. The OMA DM DiagMon includes the following management areas: diagnostics policies management, fault reporting, performance monitoring, device interrogation, remote diagnostics procedure invocation, and remote device repairing. The OMA DM WG publishes the standard documents as the following sequence:

WID (Work Item Document), RD (Requirement Document), AD (Architecture Document), TS (Technical Specification), and EP (Enablers Package). The OMA DM DiagMon WG is currently working on TS. DiagMon only defines MOs for common cases of diagnostics and monitoring. We have expanded MOs for RF signal monitoring based on the MOs defined by the OMA DiagMon.

2.2 Mobile Device Management

The mobile device management has recently become an important area of research. Rajiv and Hans presented the Smart Box Management (SBM) [1], which is an end-to-end remote management framework for Internet enabled devices. In SBM, client devices securely communicate over the public Internet for device management specific services such as remote registration, remote configuration, dynamic updates (downloads) and device diagnostic uploads with the SBM server. SBM uses HTTP to leverage a Web-based device management infrastructure that offers several benefits: ubiquity, security, reliability and a high degree of user friendliness. However, they do not consider the standard framework or protocol such as OMA DM. Instead, they have defined their own proprietary protocol. They also do not present how to manage and diagnose mobile devices clearly.

Sandeep *et al.* proposed a universal manager that manages both mobile and non-mobile devices in an enterprise [2]. They implemented the SyncML-based mobile devices integrated with SNMP based enterprise manager. Also, they developed a multi-protocol gateway which is a software entity that represents a terminal in the enterprise management system. The software makes the enterprise management system believe that the terminal is like a manageable entity in the enterprise. This study is a good trial for applying SyncML solution to the mobile device management.

Thanh *et al.* presented the Device Management Service (DMS) [16], which is considered as one big "Virtual Terminal" with multiple input and output capabilities for all the different communications devices. They presented some use-cases. State *et al.* presented an open-source agent toolkit built around the SyncML model [17]. It is also a trial to realize the SyncML device management framework. They considered only the framework of the agent part.

Nokia [18] has developed and deployed many mobile devices that support the OMA DM standard. They have developed a mobile device management solution in which an administrator is able to manage mobile devices remotely. They have been providing their solution for managing their mobile phones based on the OMA DM standard to the Nokia Forum [19].

All of the work mentioned above focus on the remote mobile device management based on their own management protocol or standard protocol. However, the current status is for configuring simple management information or retrieving it. In this paper, we propose a practical and useful application such as the RF signal monitoring for the QoS improvement.

3 Management Architecture

Our goal is to provide an efficient method in order to improve the QoS by the measurement of the RF signal from the mobile devices. Our proposed system is composed of the DM Server and DM Client. The DM Server sends the initialization and execution request of the RF signal monitoring function to the DM Client. The DM Client, which is equipped in various mobile devices such as PDA, cell phone, lap top, etc., replies the result of the request by the DM Server. In this section, we present the device management tree (DM tree) as MOs and the management operations.

3.1 Management Information

We have defined the DM trees for the RF signal monitoring (shown in Fig. 1) by expanding the *DiagMon* node and *DiagFunc* node defined by the OMA DM DiagMon WG. These are not the standard nodes yet but are under consideration of the standards. The DM tree for RF signal monitoring is to measure the RSS of the mobile device. We have created the *RF* node for the RF signal monitoring. Each node has its own *access control list (ACL)*, *format*, and *scope* attributes, which are denoted in the parenthesis in each node of Fig. 1. *ACL* represents which command is permitted to access the node. *Format* represents the type of the node. *Scope* represents whether the node is permanent or dynamic. If the node is permanent, we cannot change the node when we define DM tree. For example, the DM server can request *GET*, *DELETE*, and *EXEC* command on *RF* node because its *ACL* is (G, D, E). Its *format* is node. Its *scope* is dynamic because we can change *RF* node.

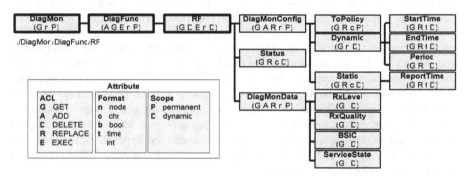

Fig. 1. DM tree for RF Signal Monitoring

We have defined three children nodes under the *RF*: *DiagMonConfig*, *Status*, and *DiagMonData*. The *DiagMonConfig* node is a placeholder for the configuration information. This interior node has the following three children nodes:

- *ToPolicy:* the type of reporting schedule (value: *Dynamic*, *Static*)
- *Dynamic:* collects data from *StartTime* to *EndTime* and reports it periodically. (e.g., if the *Period* is equal to 0, then reports it immediately.)
- *Static:* reports the data at the *ReportTime*.

The *Status* node specifies the operational state of the reset and RF function. Its value is one of the followings:

- *None:* the collection of reset data is stopped
- *Prepared:* the Exec command of data collection is received

- *Active:* the collection of data is started
- *Processed:* the data is collected
- *Reported:* the collected data is sent

The *DiagMonData* node is a placeholder for the RF signal data. The children nodes contain the relevant information for monitoring the RF signal. We can determine the shadow area using this data. It includes the following children nodes.

- *RxLevel:* the level of the received signal (value: 0 ~ 63, 63 is highest)
- *RxQuality:* the quality of the received signal (value: 0 ~ 7, 0 is best)
- *BSIC:* Base Station Identity Code, the information of the region
- *ServiceState:* the state of the service (value: *SERVICE, NOT_AVAILABLE, SEARCH_FOR_NETWORK, FULL_SERVICE*)

The usage of each node will be described in Section 3.2

3.2 Management Operations

We have designed the management operations based on the DM tree defined in Section 3.1. There are three separate phases in the management operation: initialization, execution, and gathering phase. At the initialization phase, the DM Server checks whether the mobile device can support the RF signal monitoring or not. Also, it can create the RF MOs in the mobile device's DM tree if possible. At the execution

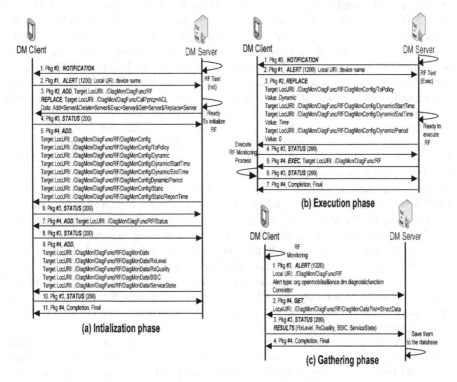

Fig. 2. Three phases of management operation for RF signal monitoring

phase, the DM Server sets the policy information related to the RF signal monitoring and executes it. At the gathering phase, the DM Server gathers the RF signal data from the DM Client when it notifies the low signal event.

By dividing the management operation into three phases as shown in Fig. 2, an efficient management operation can be achieved. For instance, *ADD* commands exist in the initialization phase except one *REPLACE* command for setting the *ACL* of *RF* node. First, each management phase consists of the same management commands. Hence, a single management command can process an operation of many MO addresses (Target *LocURIs*), which decreases the size of management package. Second, each phase can be independently used for its purposes. That is, to monitor the RF signal data, all three phases do not need to be repeated. Once the initialization is processed, it does not need to be repeated. Also, after the execution phase, there is no need to repeat it to process gathering, as long as the policy for collecting the data remains unchanged. Therefore, it is more efficient than processing all three phases to monitor. We will present the results of the performance evaluation to validate our proposed method in Section 5.

Fig. 2 (a) shows the initialization phase of the RF signal monitoring. When the DM Server wants to initialize the RF signal monitoring function, it needs to send the *NOTIFICATION* message [13] to the DM Client. When the DM Client receives the *NOTIFICATION* message, it sends the server-initiated *ALERT* command to the DM Server with the device name. Next, the DM Server sends the *ADD* command to initialize the RF signal monitoring function and the *REPLACE* command to set *ACL* for *RF as GET, DELETE,* and *EXEC.* For efficiency, as shown in the package *#4* of the sequences 5 and 9 in Fig. 2 (a), we have added many MOs by using one *ADD* command. If the mobile device supports the RF signal monitoring, then it can add *RF* node to its DM tree and send a successful *STATUS* command (200) to the DM Server. If the addition of the *RF* node is successful, then the DM Server adds *DiagMonConfig, Status,* and *DiagMonData* step by step. Finally, the DM Server sends a completion message to the DM Client to finish this management session. After the initialization phase, the mobile device is ready to execute the RF signal monitoring function.

Fig. 2 (b) shows the execution phase of the RF signal monitoring. When the DM Server wants to execute the RF signal monitoring function, it sends the *NOTIFICATION* message as in the initialization phase. Then the DM Client sends the server-initiated *ALERT* command to the DM Server. The DM Server sends the *REPLACE* command to set the policy information. Since we need the real time data for analyzing the RF signal data, the policy is *Dynamic* in order to get the data from *StartTime* to *EndTime* periodically. The *Period* is 0 in order to receive the RF event (low signal event) immediately. If the mobile device has initialized the RF signal monitoring function, then it sends the *STATUS* command as 200. Otherwise, it sends the *STATUS* command as a predefined error constant. Then, the DM Server sends the *EXEC* command to execute the RF signal monitoring function. The DM Client executes it. Finally, the DM Server sends the completion message to the DM Client and the management session is finished.

Fig. 2 (c) shows the gathering phase of the RF signal monitoring. When the signal is lower than the predefined threshold, the DM Client stores all relevant information to its DM tree. The threshold is set by the service provider or the network operator. When it is ready to report, it sends the generic *ALERT* command to the DM Server. If the DM Server needs to gather the information about this mobile device, it sends the *GET* command for the *DiagMonData* node to retrieve all data related to the RF signal, which saves it to the database. We can analyze this data on the GPS or the base station management server and find the shadow area.

4 System Development

We now present the system development based on the MO definition and management operations in Section 3.

4.1 Design

Our proposed system is composed of the DM Client and the DM Server as illustrated in Fig. 3. The DM Client uses WSP [24], OBEX [25], and HTTP [26] as the exchange protocol. It uses SyncML as the representation protocol. The major components of the DM Client as shown in Fig. 3 (a) are *DM Tree Handler* and *RF Monitoring Process*. *DM Tree Handler* manages the MOs for the RF signal monitoring by commands which the manager requests. The *RF Monitoring Process* notifies the state when the RSS is lower than the threshold. It also collects all relevant information and fills it in the RF DM tree. The DM Server uses same exchange and representation protocol as the DM Client. The major component of the DM Server as shown in Fig. 3 (b) is *RF Tester*, which runs the initialization phase and the execution phase on the user's request. When the DM Client notifies RF event, they run the gathering phase to retrieve the data and save it to the data storage.

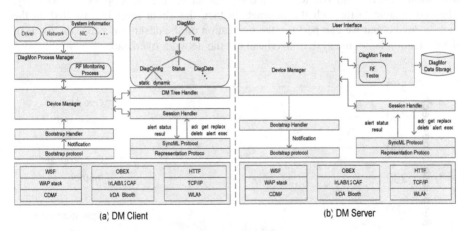

(a) DM Client   (b) DM Server

Fig. 3. System Functional Architecture Design

4.2 Implementation

Fig. 4 shows the screenshot of the RF Monitoring Client and the RF Monitoring Server. We have developed it based on the open source project called SyncML Conformance Test Suite [20]. Fig. 4 (a) shows the client system which has initialized the RF signal monitoring function. Fig. 4 (b) shows the server system which has gathered the device information and the RF signal data from the mobile device 1. The server saves all monitoring data to the database and share with the analysis server. In the future, we will improve our system to show the shadow area by using and analyzing this data integrated with any other map application such as Google Maps [22].

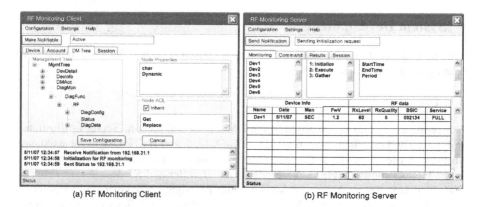

(a) RF Monitoring Client   (b) RF Monitoring Server

Fig. 4. Screenshot of RF Signal Monitoring System

5 Performance Evaluation

In this section, we present the results of performance evaluation. We installed the RF Monitoring Server and the RF Monitoring Client on the desktop PC individually. They communicate through the Internet. In fact, the client must be installed on the mobile device, but we can perform the evaluation on the desktop because the focus of the evaluation is not the system overhead but the network overhead.

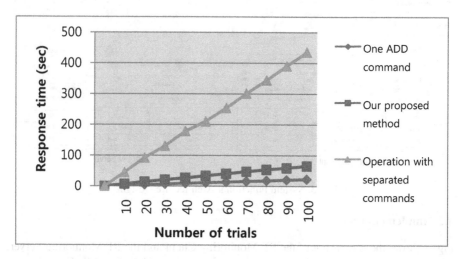

Fig. 5. Response time comparison of our proposed method and operation with separated commands

In the first experiment, we tested how to compose each phase of the management session. As we mentioned in Section 4.2, we designed each phase to send the same commands through one management session simultaneously. In the initialization phase, there are many *ADD* commands to enable the related information and function. Since each *ADD* command is transferred through its own management session, it requires heavy overhead of the network bandwidth and the long response time. Basically, the OMA DM protocol supports to transfer many commands with one management session. Hence, we considered this fact and designed the phase of the management operation. The bandwidth of the initialization phase when each command was transferred through each management session is 22529 bytes. The initialization phase has fifteen *ADD* commands and a *REPLACE* command. However, the bandwidth of the initialization phase by our proposed method is 3791 bytes. In the case of one *ADD* command, its bandwidth is 1336 bytes. Our proposed method spends the bandwidth as the bandwidth of three *ADD* commands. Fig. 5 shows the response time comparison. On the average, the response time of the initialization phase when each command was transferred through each management session is 4.68 seconds, but that of the initialization phase by our proposed method is 0.66 seconds. In the case of one *ADD* command, its response time is 0.23 seconds. This result shows that our proposed method is efficient.

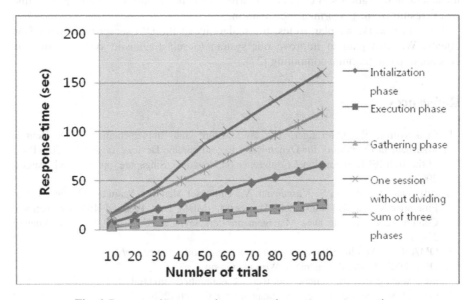

Fig. 6. Response time comparison among the management operations

The second experiment is to measure the bandwidth of the management operation with dividing into three phases and to compare it with that of the management operation without dividing. When we performed the management operation, we collected the generated OMA DM messages as a unit of a session. We measured the required bandwidth by the total bytes of the collected messages. We used an XML as the format [23]. We tested the management operation from 10 to 100 times. The bandwidth of the initialization phase is 3791 bytes, that of the execution phase is 2234 bytes, and that of the gathering phase is 1725 bytes. The management operation without dividing spends 7750 bytes. As shown in Fig. 6, we plotted the response time of each phase of the management operation based on the number of trials. On the average, the response time of the initialization phase is 0.66 seconds, that of the execution phase is 0.26 seconds, and that of the gathering phase is 0.28 seconds. The management operation without dividing in phases spends 1.61 seconds. As we have mentioned in Section 4.2, this result also shows that our proposed method for the design of the management operations, which divided the management operation into three phases, is efficient in the aspect of the bandwidth and the response time.

6 Concluding Remarks

The diagnostics and monitoring of the mobile device have become an important area in the mobile device management. In this paper, we proposed an efficient RF signal monitoring method of the mobile devices for the QoS improvement based on OMA DM. We defined the MOs for monitoring RF signal related data such as RSS. We also designed the management operation in three phases and presented that our proposed management operation was efficient in terms of the bandwidth and the response time by the results of the performance evaluation.

For future work, we plan to test the scalability of the DM server with many DM clients. We also plan to improve our system to self-diagnostic system using the concept of the autonomic computing [27].

References

1. Chakravorty, R., Ottevanger, H.: Architecture and Implementation of a Remote Management Framework for Dynamically Reconfigurable Devices. In: ICON 2002. Proc. of the 10th IEEE International Conference on Networks, Singapore, pp. 375–381 (August 2002)
2. Adwankar, S., Mohan, S., Vasudevan, V.: Universal Manager: Seamless Management of Enterprise Mobile and Non-Mobile Devices. In: MDM 2004. Proc. Of IEEE International Conference on Mobile Data Management, Berkeley, CA, USA, pp. 320–331 (January 2004)
3. OMA (Open Mobile Alliance), http://www.openmobilealliance.org/
4. OMA DM (Device Management) Working Group, http://www.openmobilealliance.org/tech/wg_committees/dm.html
5. OMA: OMA Device Management Standardized Objects (2007)
6. OMA: OMA Device Management Protocol (2007)
7. SyncML Forum: SyncML Device Management Protocol, http://www.syncml.org/
8. OMA: OMA DM Device Description Framework, Version 1.2 (2007)
9. OMA: OMA Device Management Bootstrap (2007)
10. OMA: OMA Device Management Tree and Description (2007)
11. IETF: Uniform Resource Identifiers (URI), RFC 2396 (1998)
12. Stallings, W.: SNMP, SNMPv2, SNMPv3 and RMON 1 and 2, 3rd edn. Addison-Wesley, Reading, MA (1999)

13. Case, J., Fedor, M., Schoffstall, M., Davin, J.: A Simple Network Management Protocol (SNMP). RFC 1157, http://www.ietf.org/rfc/rfc1157.txt
14. OMA: DiagMon (Diagnostics and Monitoring) Working Group
15. OMA: DiagMon Requirement draft version 1.0 (June 2006)
16. van Thanh, D.D., Jonvik, T., Vanem, E., van Tran, D., Audestad, J.A.: The Device Management Service. In: IN 2001. IEEE Intelligent Network Workshop 2001, Boston, MA, USA, pp. 199–211 (May 2001)
17. State, R., Festor, O., Zores, B.: An extensible agent toolkit for device management. In: NOMS 2004. IEEE/IFIP Network Operations and Management Symposium, Seoul, Korea, pp. 845–858 (April 2004)
18. Nokia, http://www.nokia.com/
19. Nokia Forum, http://forum.nokia.com/
20. SyncML Forum: SyncML Conformation Test Suite, http://sourceforge.net/projects/oma-scts/
21. Jiang, Y., Tham, C.K., Ko, C.C.: Challenges and approaches in providing QoS monitoring. Int. J. Network Mgmt. 10, 323–334 (2000)
22. Google Maps Service, http://maps.google.com/
23. W3C: Extensible Markup Language (XML), http://www.w3.org/XML/
24. WAP: (Wireless Application Protocol) WSP (Wireless Session Protocol), WAP Forum, http://www.wapforum.org/
25. OBEX: (OBject EXchange), Infrared Data Association, http://www.irda.org/
26. Fielding, R., Gettys, J., Mogul, J., Frystyk, H., Berners-Lee, T.: Hypertext Transfer Protocol – HTTP/1.1, RFC 2068 (1997)
27. IBM Corporation: An architectural blueprint for autonomic computing. White Paper (2003)

Online Control Techniques for Management of Shared Bandwidth in Multimedia Networks

K. Ravindran and M. Rabby

City College of CUNY and Graduate Center,
Department of Computer Science,
Convent Avenue at 138th Street,
New York, NY 10031, USA
ravi@cs.ccny.cuny.edu, mfrabby@yahoo.com

Abstract. In this paper, we provide an online monitor and control approach for adaptive bandwidth allocations in a QoS-aware multimedia network system. Accurate management of bandwidth allocations with a goal of maximizing the revenues is quite complex, due to the interactions among various data flows that dynamically share the network bandwidth. So, we adopt a heuristics-aided control that iteratively adjusts the bandwidth allocation based on the observed packet loss rate and delays. In terms of 'control theory', the bandwidth allocation and the packet loss rate constitute the system input and output respectively, with the heuristics-based bandwidth adjustment strategies incorporated in a controller along the feedback loop. A 'control-theoretic' treatment of the QoS adaptation problem allows studying the stability and convergence properties of the QoS delivered to the applications, while maximizing the connectivity service provider's revenues.

1 Introduction

The end-to-end data transfer in distributed multimedia applications may be viewed as a series of packet-level transport activities using a network service that offers QoS-enabled data connectivity between the end-points. The service provider (CSP) uses the shared resource pools maintained as part of its infrastructure, namely, the network capacity C available from a physical line provider (PLP), in offering the required logical connectivity between end-points. See Figure 1. The underlying network may, in one extreme, consist of the FIFO routers in a bandwidth-oblivious Internet and, in the other extreme, be the proxy nodes serving as packet forwarding points using UDP-based transport layer links.

The goal of CSP is to maximize its revenues by exercising just-enough bandwidth allocations that suffice to match the QoS needs of applications. This bandwidth allocation problem has two twists:

- Fuzziness in the bandwidth needs of an application-level data flow due to the inability to precisely characterize the traffic parameters;

D. Krishnaswamy, T. Pfeifer, and D. Raz (Eds.): MMNS 2007, LNCS 4787, pp. 88–100, 2007.

– Statistical sharing of the network capacity among many logical connections that attempts to reduce the bandwidth allocation.

Despite the above sources of inaccuracies in the bandwidth management process, the CSP needs to accomplish its revenue-oriented goal.

The management functions of the CSP employ 'feedback control' principles to overcome the problems that arise due to the fuzziness in the bandwidth

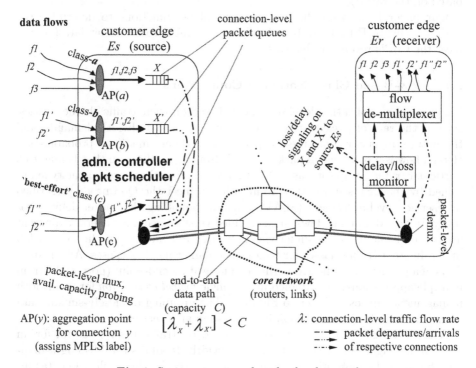

Fig. 1. System structure for edge-level control

estimation process. We employ certain widely applicable monotonicity properties of the bandwidth allocation process to derive our heuristics-based control strategies. For instance, an increase in the send rate of a bursty data flow by δ incurs an additional bandwidth allocation of δ' such that $0 < \delta' < \delta$. Based on such (macroscopic) intuitive properties, the management functions of the CSP may exercise bandwidth allocation control at various degrees of granularity and accuracy.

The paper is organized as follows. Section 2 provides a management view of QoS-adaptive data transfers between multimedia end-points. Section 3 introduces the monitor-and-control based allocation of bandwidth. Section 4 discusses the system latency incurred during bandwidth allocation steps. Section 5 studies our monitor-and-control approach by simulation. Section 6 concludes the paper.

2   Management View of QoS-Adaptive Data Transfers

The end-to-end connectivity service provider (CSP) allocates a portion B of the available capacity C for use in supporting data transfers that yield QoS-based revenues, where $B < C$. The left-over bandwidth $(C - B)$ is then taken by the non-revenue yielding 'best-effort connection' data. The bandwidth allocation B is itself realized by 'weighted fair queue' (WFQ) packet scheduling mechanisms, based on the ratio $\frac{B}{C}$.

Our paper focuses on the 'management plane' functions to determine the optimal value of B that can be suitably spread out across various data flows to meet the CSP's revenue objectives.

2.1   Flow-Based Classification of Connections

We group the application-level data flows based on their traffic characteristics: such as the rate of packet arrivals, the burstiness in bandwidth demands, and the nature of service guarantees expected (say, deterministic or probabilistic). Here, a flow is a sequence of packet arrivals from an application that belong to a particular traffic group (or class). A data flow exercises the shared capacity maintained by the CSP's infrastructure in order to meet the QoS needs prescribed in a service-level agreement (SLA) — such as bounding the packet delivery latency. Widely dissimilar flows, such as video versus voice, may exercise different amount of demands on the underlying network bandwidth — and hence may fall under different traffic classes for bandwidth management purposes. All the data flows of a particular traffic group that emanate at an end-point (potentially from multiple applications) are bundled into a single *logical connection* for bandwidth management purposes. Refer to Figure 1. The grouping of closely-similar data flows is a 'control plane' function in our system architecture.

A characterization of packet arrivals based on traffic loads is useful for an effective management of the network bandwidth. It allows establishing a mapping between the QoS-oriented guarantees expected by the applications (as incorporated into SLAs) and their usage of network bandwidth (internal to the service infrastructure) [4,5,6]. Based on the estimated bandwidth needs, a packet scheduler at the sending end moves the packets of various flows waiting in the connection queues over the data path maintained by the network infrastructure.

2.2   Exploiting Statistical Bandwidth Sharing Gains

Potentially, multiple classes of packet traffic may share a common network infrastructure maintained by the CSP. Given the bursty and random nature of most packet transfers (e.g., video), the CSP incorporates the gains accrued from statistical bandwidth sharing in its QoS management decisions.

Typically, a bandwidth allocated for the flows belonging to a class i can be used by the flows belonging to a class j when i does not have any demands in a certain time interval but j has demands. A statistical resource sharing method interweaves with the QoS delivery to the applications by making the guarantees probabilistic (instead of a deterministic). An example is to keep the 90-percentile response time of an application flow within a given tolerance limit. Since a probabilistic quality suffices for most real-time multimedia applications, the CSP's revenue goals can be met by a careful control of the degree of statistical sharing of network bandwidth. Our grouping of data flows at end-points towards this goal aligns architecturally (along the 'control plane') with the hose model of VPNs studied elsewhere [3].

Though statistical bandwidth sharing by itself is not a new concept, how the gains accrued from such a sharing can be quantified for incorporation into the CSP's QoS management decisions has not been studied so far. To realize this revenue-driven goal, we describe an online monitor-and-control approach next.

3   Online Control Procedures for Bandwidth Allocation

The problem of optimal bandwidth allocation is quite complex for two reasons: i) the CSP's desire to allocate just enough bandwidth in the presence of statistical multiplexing gains among bursty data flows — such as video, and ii) the absence of precise QoS-to-bandwidth mapping relations due to incomplete traffic specs. We deal with the complexity issue by incremental bandwidth allocations over multiple heuristics-aided control iterations.

3.1   Mapping of Flow Specs to Bandwidth Needs

We may view the flow specs of a multimedia data, specified as a tuple [peak_rate, average_rate,loss_tolerance], as being mapped onto the required amount of bandwidth (measured in bits/sec bps) to transport the data over a connection. The bandwidth needs of a QoS-controlled data connection may be denoted as a transfer function:

$$\text{bandwidth needed} = \mathcal{F}([n, f], e),$$

where f is the flow specs (such as data send rate and loss tolerance) and n is the number of flows multiplexed over the connection. The parameter e pertains to the external environment that is not under the control of the end-point users — such as the burstiness of data and the residual loss rate on a transport link. If the allocated bandwidth $B_v > \mathcal{F}([n, f], e)$, there is no noticeable packet loss; otherwise, the (per-flow) packet loss rate is proportional to the amount of under-allocation of bandwidth, namely, $\mathcal{F}([n, f], e) - B_v$.

The function $\mathcal{F}$, which is bound to a logical connection, satisfies the property of weak additivity across multiple flows carried over this connection, i.e., $\mathcal{F}([n+\delta n, f], e) - \mathcal{F}([n, f], e) < \mathcal{F}([\delta n, f], e)$. This property depicts the statistical multiplexing gains accrued by having the flows share the connection bandwidth.

The mapping function $\mathcal{F}$ is only coarse and approximate, due to the random and bursty arrival of data and the inability of a traffic specs method to capture comprehensive data flow characteristics. So, the mapping function $\mathcal{F}$ may not be known to the end-point management functions. The absence of knowledge about the mapping relation $\mathcal{F}$ in a closed-form forces the management station to determine the bandwidth needs using end-to-end monitoring techniques. Any analytical formulation of $\mathcal{F}$ (or a tabular representation of $\mathcal{F}$) that may coarsely be known is used to enhance the accuracy of bandwidth estimator $\mathcal{F}$.

Another source of inaccuracy is the potentially large dimensionality of the traffic meta-data. This is compounded by the inherent limitations in a flow specs language chosen to describe the data traffic. In a way, most of the traffic specs are only closed-form approximations to the real traffic descriptions. Consequently, a static estimate of the bandwidth allocation needs for a data flow may deviate significantly from the actual needs. Such inaccuracies can best be countered by resorting to an 'allocate-and-see-what-happens' approach. In this context, the hose resource provisioning model studied elsewhere [8] estimates the bandwidth needs from the traffic parameters using linear programming techniques. Such estimates can be iteratively refined further to a reasonable accuracy with our online monitor-and-control approach.

3.2   Procedural Realization of Monitor-and-Control

Figure 2 illustrates how a monitor-and-control paradigm can be realized for QoS adaptation. The agents S_C_Agent and R_C_Agent employ a heuristics-based control algorithm that adjusts the allocation B_v based on the monitored data loss rate, in order to determine the bandwidth needs. For this purpose, we characterize the multimedia transport system with the following properties:

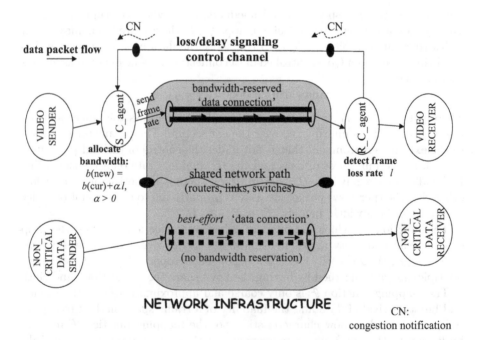

Fig. 2. Agent-based control of bandwidth allocation for video transport

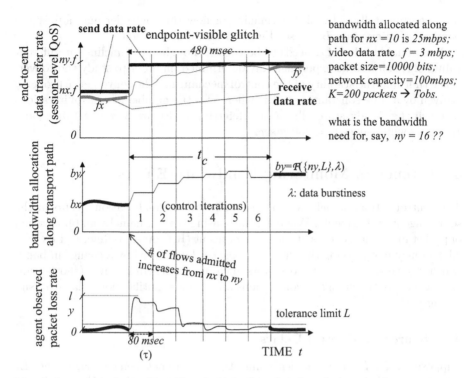

Fig. 3. An empirical time-line of bandwidth allocations based on packet loss monitoring

(i) When the bandwidth is increased from B_v to $B_v + \delta b$, it takes τ time units for the increase in bandwidth to have an observable effect on the data loss rate (due to the coupling between the BE and reserved connections that share a single network infrastructure);

(ii) The monitor observes K back-to-back packets in order to accurately determine the packet loss rate after a bandwidth allocation B_v occurs;

(iii) The control algorithm employs:
   - A multiplicative law that increases B_v in proportion to the observed loss rate, as given by: $B_v(\text{new}) = B_v(\text{cur}) + \alpha l$, where l is the packet loss rate and $\alpha > 0$ is a constant;
   - An additive law that decreases bandwidth by a fixed amount when no packet loss is observed, as given by: $B_v(\text{new}) = B_v(\text{cur}) - \beta$;
   the increase/decrease steps are taken in each control iteration;

(iv) The data receivers exhibit a small amount of tolerance to packet loss (L).

Suppose the send rate over the connection is increased due to the admission of new data flows at time = 0, thereby increasing the number of flows from n_x to n_y — say, 6 more data flows are added to the current level of 10 data flows. For the parameter values $\tau = 80\ msec$, $K = 200$, $\beta = 2 \times 10^5$ and $L = 2\%$, we can experimentally determine a timeline of how the controller may adjust the bandwidth reservation B_v — see Figure 3 for an illustration.

A reasonable value of α needs to be chosen though. The timeline for different values of α can also be experimentally determined, in order to study the convergence time and the stability of the control mechanism. The convergence property is given by a time constant: $t_c \approx R\tau$, where R is the number of control iterations to reach the steady state allocation. Referring to Figure 3, $\tau = 80\ msec$ and $R = 6$ — which gives $t_c = 480\ msec$.

4   Latency in Monitoring Bandwidth Effects

The control action, namely, a bandwidth allocation/de-allocation, occurs at the source agent (S_C_Agent). Whereas, the sensing action, namely, an observation of packet loss/delay, occurs at the receiver agent (R_C_Agent). Refer to Figure 2. The latency in observing the changes in packet loss caused by a change in bandwidth allocation arises due to factors such as the scheduler-level (short-term) cross-effects between logical connections and the loss notification delay over signaling paths.

4.1   Sources of Control Delays

Suppose X, X', X'' are the logical connections set up between customer edges E_s (source) and E_r (receiver) to carry distinct groups of data flows. E_r periodically sends a report to E_s indicating the packet loss rates observed on the bandwidth-reserved connections X and X' — note[1] that X'' is a 'best-effort' connection. See Figure 4. A network element in the data path may be a router in the core/access network or a overlay proxy node, forwarding the packets of connections X, X', X'' and any other unrelated cross-traffic through FIFO queues.

When a change in bandwidth allocation occurs, say, for connection X, how[2] long E_s should wait to assess the impact on packet loss depends on the following.

Forward propagation of scheduling effects:
A changed schedule of packet arrivals from E_s at a network element R is reflected in the packet departures from R only after all the packets currently queued up at R have departed. Given the FIFO packet queuing at R, the packet schedules generated at E_s transparently pass through R to the next element in the path. If $\bar{q}$ is the average queue length at R and $\bar{S}$ is the average packet size, a measure of the time taken for the packet departure schedule at R to change is $\frac{\bar{q}\bar{S}}{C_R}$, where C_R is the output capacity of R (note that $C_R \geq C$). Thus, the change in packet arrival schedule from E_s 'tunnels' through various network elements in the path until it reaches E_r, suffering a non-zero delay at each element — we denote the combined delay at all the elements as $t_{(s,r)}$.

---

[1] RTCP-like signaling protocols can be employed for the loss notification.

[2] A bandwidth increase of δb on connection X manifests as increasing the scheduling weight assigned to the packet queue for X by $\frac{\delta b}{C}$.

Steady observation of packet loss behavior:

To assess the impact of a bandwidth change (that occurred at E_s) on packet loss rate, E_r should receive K packets of connection X under the changed arrival

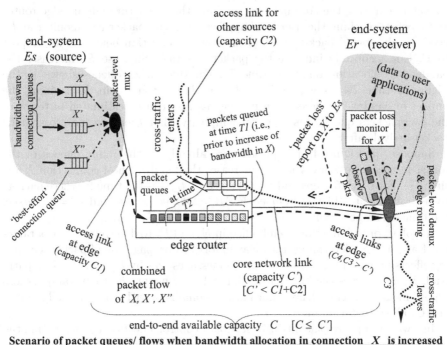

Scenario of packet queues/ flows when bandwidth allocation in connection X is increased

Fig. 4. Latency factors during a change in bandwidth allocation

schedule. This manifests as a delay of $\frac{K.\overline{S}}{C.w_X}$ after E_r receives the first packet of X under the changed schedule, where w_X is the weight assigned to X (on a normalized scale of 1.0) relative to the available capacity of data path from E_s to E_r. If T_l is the loss reporting interval, the number of back-to-back intervals that should elapse at E_r before the impact of a bandwidth change is fully captured in a loss report is: $\left\lceil \frac{t_{(s,r)} + \frac{K.\overline{S}}{C.w_X}}{T_l} \right\rceil$.

As can be seen, the system dynamics, as captured by the time-constant parameter τ, depends on the propagation of scheduling effects through network elements and the observation of resulting changes in packet arrivals at E_r.

4.2   Determination of System Time-Constant

Basically, E_s sends a time-stamped probe message over the data path, and E_r bounces this message back along the reverse path. The time elapsed between the send and return of the probe message at E_s gives the propagation delay $[t_{(s,r)} + t_{(r,s)}]$. The time-constant of the system, which is the time taken for the control point in E_s to observe the visible effects of a bandwidth change, is then given by: $\tau = t_{(s,r)} + t_{(r,s)} + T_l.[\lceil \frac{K.\overline{S}}{C.w_X.T_l} \rceil + 0.5]$.

Consider the data connections X, X', X'' set up from E_s to E_r — refer to Figure 4. The packets of these connections are sent through an edge router at E_s before entering the core network, and are then sent through an edge router at E_r before reaching the user-level applications. The packet loss monitor at E_r needs to observe K back-to-back packets of a connection before its loss report to E_s can accurately indicate the packet loss rate. Suppose E_s increases the bandwidth allocation on X at time T_1. For the packet queues shown in the Figure at time T_2 — where $T_2 > T_1$, the latency at E_s in determining the impact of bandwidth increase on packet loss rate can be estimated in terms of the two packets queues (assume, for simplicity, that there are no cross-traffic packet arrivals after T_2).

Suppose, in Figure 4, 100 packets are already in the input queues of the router in access network when E_s increases the bandwidth of connection X (at time T_1). For $C = 25$ $mbps$ and $\overline{S} = 10000$ $bits$, $t_{(s,r)}$ is the time for these packets to be drained out, which is 40 $msec$. For $K = 200$, $w_X = 0.6$, and $T_l = 250$ $msec$, the time-constant $\tau = 455$ $msec$ — assuming that $t_{(r,s)} = t_{(s,r)}$.

A global control function is embodied in E_s and E_r to determine the τ parameter. Basically, E_r determines the delay in forward propagation of packet scheduling effects based on time-stamped probe messages sent by E_s over the data path. And, E_s determines the loss notification delay by having E_r time-stamp its loss report messages. This delay information, combined with the knowledge of K and C, allows determining τ.

In a way, τ captures the intrinsic 'feedback control' effects occurring within the WFQ packet scheduler when a step increase/decrease in bandwidth allocation is exercised in one of the connections sharing the transport link. Whereas, t_c depicts the number of such allocation steps needed to accurately determine the bandwidth. We note here that the work in [7] employs modeling techniques primarily to determine τ. In contrast, our goal is to determine t_c, with the knowledge of τ needed therein obtained by the methods we discussed earlier.

5   Simulation Results

The simulation study is based on generating packet flows that closely approximate the video traffic traces of a *starwars* movie segment. These packet flows are then subjected to our bandwidth allocation scheme. The peak rate used in our study is 3.5 $mbps$. We do not use any apriori traffic analysis of the traces (such as estimating the burstiness and average rate parameters from the packet size distributions). Instead, we simply send the data traffic through the simulated model of our end-system.

Figure 5 gives our preliminary results on the adjustment of bandwidth allocation based on the monitored packet loss rate. The results are for the case of multiplicative increase in bandwidth. The transport network assumed is a physical link with a capacity of 100 $mbps$.

There are 10 video data flows initially, multiplexed over a single data connection. The initial combined bandwidth allocation is 30 *mbps* (i.e., 3.0 *mbps* per flow). Besides this candidate connection under study, two other connections carrying 8 and 6 flows respectively are also set up over the shared physical link (with approximately 25 *mbps* and 20 *mbps* allocated respectively). The latter is to incorporate the cross-coupling effects between multiple connections in our study. We then increase the number of flows from 10 to 16 on the connection being tested (i.e., apply a step increase in the input), and let the iterative control algorithm determine the new combined bandwidth needs. The result shows that it takes a little less than about 1.2 *sec* for a bandwidth adaptation procedure to complete successfully i.e., $t_c = 1.2$ *sec* — which is the time taken to determine the bandwidth allocation needs when the input traffic load is changed. There are about 6 control iterations, with each iteration taking about 200 *msec*. We have set 50 *msec* as the loss reporting interval.

We now include the additive decrease in bandwidth as well (when there is negligible packet loss) in the control algorithm, and then repeat the experiments. The results are shown in Figures 6 and 7, for different values of α and β. The dynamics of the packet scheduler is itself measured by the parameter $\tau \approx 225$ *msec*, which is the time taken for the loss rate to start decreasing (or increasing) after an additional bandwidth allocation (or a bandwidth de-allocation) has been

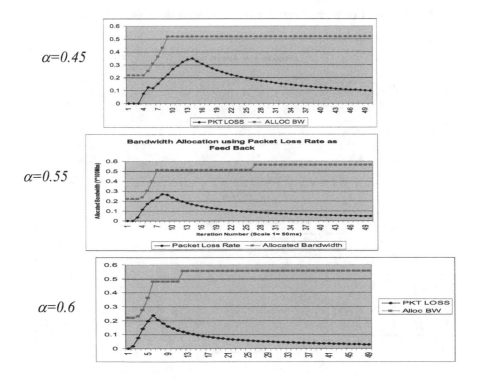

Fig. 5. Case of 'multiplicative increase' in bandwidth (with multiplexed video traffic)

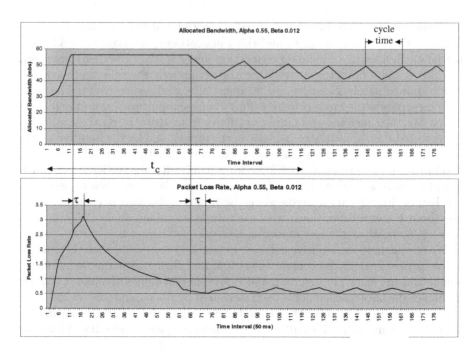

Fig. 6. Case 1 of 'multiplicative increase additive decrease' in bandwidth

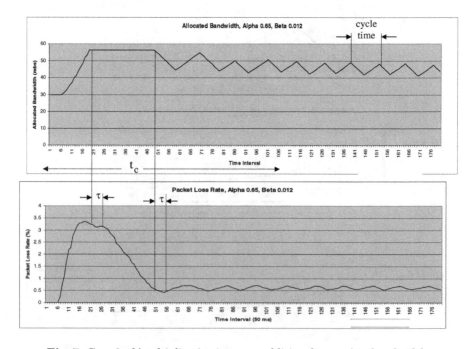

Fig. 7. Case 2 of 'multiplicative increase additive decrease' in bandwidth

made. A parameter value of $\beta = .012$ used in the experiments (with a scaling factor) corresponds to a bandwidth reduction of 1.2 $mbps$, whereas $\alpha = 0.55$ and $l = 0.1$ (depicting a 1% packet loss) corresponds to a bandwidth increase of 5.5 $mbps$ — with a bandwidth adjustment occurring potentially at every control iteration (which is of 50 $msec$ duration).

The time-constant of the overall system is: $t_c \approx 5.75\ sec$ for $[\alpha = 0.55, \beta = 0.012]$ (case 1) and $t_c \approx 5.25\ sec$ for $[\alpha = 0.65, \beta = 0.012]$ (case 2). The total time to determine the optimal bandwidth allocation is however considerably longer, taking many cycles of increase and decrease in bandwidths. The settling time is dependent on α and β. As can be seen, the cycle time in the steady state is about 750 $msec$ for case 1 and about 700 $msec$ for case 2. The bandwidth allocation settles down to about 45 $mbps$, which is about 2.8 $mbps$ per flow.

Figures 6 and 7 give some preliminary results on the dynamics of the packet scheduler, and at a macro-level, the dynamics of the overall QoS-adaptive bandwidth allocation.

For brevity, we have not attempted to determine the best allocation for various cases of bandwidth sharing and flow specs. Nevertheless, the results demonstrate the benefits of statistical bandwidth sharing among multiple video streams and the usefulness of heuristics-based control strategies in achieving a reasonably optimal steady-state allocation.

6   Conclusions

We described a model of MIAD-based bandwidth allocation for end-to-end QoS-controlled data connectivity. The model addresses the complex traffic management problem that involves bandwidth sharing across many applications over a data transport network: such as LAN/MANs, proxy-based overlay networks, and leased-line networks. Due to the complexity of interactions among the network components, a closed-form relationship does not exist to map the end-to-end QoS and the network resources. So, we resort to an on-line monitor-and-control approach that employs heuristics-based linear predictions to estimate the bandwidth needs. Using the observed packet loss/delays as indicative of the accuracy of bandwidth estimation, the controller adjusts the future bandwidth allocations.

We used video transport as a case study to illustrate the MIAD technique. We find that our technique scales quite well, is reasonably accurate, and does not require extensive management-level computations.

References

1. Erfani, S., Lawrence, V.B., Malek, M.: The Management Paradigm Shift: Challenges from Element Management to Service Management. Applications, Platforms, and Services, Bell Labs Technical Journal 5(3), 3–20 (2000)
2. Keshav, S.: Real-time Scheduling. In: An Engineering Approach to Computer Networking, Addison-Wesley Publ. Co., Reading (1996)

3. Duffield, N.G., Goyal, P., Greenberg, A., Mishra, P., Ramakrishnan, K.K., Merwe, J.E.V.: Resource Management with Hoses: Point-to-Cloud Services with Virtual Private Networks. In: IEEE/ACM Transactions on Networking, pp. 679–692 (October 2002)
4. Wang, Z., Zhu, X., Singhal, S.: Utilization and SLO-based Control for Dynamic Sizing of Resource Partitions. In: Schönwälder, J., Serrat, J. (eds.) DSOM 2005. LNCS, vol. 3775, pp. 133–144. Springer, Heidelberg (2005)
5. Lai, K., Rasmusson, L., Adar, E., Sorkin, S., Zhang, L., Huberman, B.A.: Tycoon: an Implementation of a Distributed Market-based Resource Allocation Systems. In: Technical Report, HP Labs, Palo Alto (November 2004)
6. Sahai, A., Graupner, S., Machiraju, V., Moorsel, A.V.: Specifying and Monitoring Guarantees in Commercial Grids through SLA. In: Technical Report (HPL-2002-324), HP Labs, Palo Alto (November 2002)
7. Li, B., Nahrstedt, K.: A Control-based Middleware Framework for Quality of Service Adaptations. IEEE Journal on Selected Areas in Communications 17(9) (September 1999)
8. Juttner, A., Szabo, I., Szentesi, A.: On Bandwidth Efficiency of the Hose Resource Management Model in Virtual Private Networks. In: proc. of INFOCOM 2003, pp.386–395 (March 2003)

Broadcasting in Multi-Radio
Multi-Channel and Multi-Hop Wireless Networks

Li Li, Bin Qin, and Chunyuan Zhang

School of Computer Science
National University of Defense Technology
Changsha, Hunan province, 410073, China
liligfkd@163.com, qbsn@tom.com, cyzhang@163.com

Abstract. Multi-radio multi-channel multi-hop wireless networks have recently received a substantial amount of interest. An important question in multi-radio multi-channel networks is how to perform efficient network-wide broadcast. However, currently almost all broadcasting protocols assume a single-radio single-channel network model. Simply using them in multi-channel environment without careful enhancement will result in unnecessary redundancy. In this paper, we propose a general model of the broadcasting problem under multi-channel environment and show the efficient broadcasting problem is NP-hard. Then we reduce the problem into the minimal strong connected dominating set problem of the *interface-extend* graph which extends the original network topology across interfaces. Using interface-extend graph, we describe our Multi-Channel Self-Pruning broadcast protocol and simulation shows that our protocol can significantly reduce the transmission cost.

1 Introduction

A fundamental obstacle to building large scale multi-hop networks is the insufficient network capacity when route lengths and network density increase due to the limited spectrum shared in the neighborhood [1]. The use of multiple radios which tuned to orthogonal channels can significantly improve the network capacity by employing concurrent transmissions under different channels, and that motivates the development of new protocols for multi-radio multi-channel (MR-MC) networks.

An important question in multi-radio multi-channel multi-hop networks which we attempt to address in this paper is how to perform efficient network-wide broadcast in such networks. Broadcasting is frequently used in multi-hop networks not only for data dissemination, but also for route discovery in reactive unicast routing protocols [2]. The presence of several multi-party applications—such as local content distribution and multimedia gaming—also imposes more capacity requirements to the broadcast protocol. However, naive broadcast scheme will generate an excessive amount of redundant traffic and exaggerates interference in the shared medium among neighboring nodes, which is called the broadcast storm problem [3]. A vast amount of broadcasting protocols such as probability-based methods, area-based methods, and neighbor-knowledge-based methods [4] have been proposed to mitigate the broadcast

D. Krishnaswamy, T. Pfeifer, and D. Raz (Eds.): MMNS 2007, LNCS 4787, pp. 101–112, 2007.
© IFIP International Federation for Information Processing 2007

storm problem. However, all of the above protocols assume a single-radio single-channel (SR-SC) model.

There exist large amount of research on channel assignment and protocol design for MR-MC networks, but the study on broadcasting is very limited. The use of multiple radios and multiple channels proposes new challenges to broadcast protocol design. Kyasanur [5] has hinted about some of the potential problems of broadcasting in MR-MC networks. In SR-SC networks with omni-directional antenna, a transmission by a node can be received by all neighboring nodes that lie within its communication range, and this is called 'wireless broadcast advantage' (WBA). However, when multiple channels are being used, a packet broadcast on a channel is received only by those nodes listening to that channel. Simply using the SR-SC broadcast protocols without careful enhancement will result in unnecessary redundancy. For example, in figure 1, node a initials a network-wide broadcast process. Under the SR-SC broadcast protocols which will only choose node b as the forward node, totally 4 transmissions are needed to cover all nodes. However, if we choose node b (use channel 1) and node f (use channel 4) to forward packets, only 3 transmissions are sufficient to complete the broadcast.

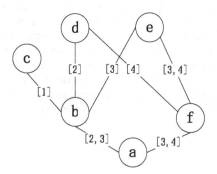

Fig. 1. A 6-node network with 4 available channels. The number in [] represents the assigned channel of the link.

In this paper, we consider to mitigate the broadcast storm problem in MR-MC networks. The objective is to achieve full coverage, and at the same time reduce the amount of redundant traffic. We show that the efficient broadcast problem in MR-MC environment can be reduced into the minimal strong connected dominating set problem of the interface-extend graph which extends the original network topology across interfaces. Using interface-extend graph, we describe our protocols called Multi-Channel Self-Pruning (MCSP) broadcast protocols, both in static (virtual backbone) and dynamic approach, extending the localized neighbor-knowledge-based broadcast protocols called self-pruning [6][7][8] in SR-SC environment. Our simulation results show that our MCSP protocol can significantly minimize redundant traffic. To the best our knowledge, our work is the first neighbor-knowledge-based broadcast scheme in this area.

The rest of the paper is organized as follows. Section 2 reviews existing broadcast schemes. Section 3 presents the network model and defines the efficient broadcasting problem in MR-MC wireless networks. In Section 4, we propose the *interface-extend* graph and describe the MCSP broadcast protocol and its properties. Simulation results are presented in Section 5, and Section 6 concludes this paper.

2 Related Works

Williams and Camp [4] divided broadcast techniques into four categories: simple flooding, probability-based methods, area-based methods, and neighbor-knowledge-based methods. Blind flooding may be the simplest form of broadcasting. In blind flooding, upon receipt of a new broadcast packet, a node simply sends it to all its neighbors. This, however, causes serious network congestion and collision. In probability-based and area-based methods, each node estimates its potential contribution to the overall broadcasting to make a decision whether or not to forward the packet. Though smaller forward node sets can be generated, they cannot ensure the full coverage. Neighbor-knowledge-based methods are based on the following idea: select a small set of nodes to form a connected dominating set (CDS) as virtual backbone to forward packet. A node set is a dominating set if every node in the network is either in the set or the neighbor of a node in the set. In [10], it is demonstrated that broadcast scheme based on a backbone of size proportional to the minimum connected dominating set guarantees a throughput within a constant factor of the broadcast capacity.

Neighbor-knowledge-based algorithms can be divided into neighbor-designating methods and self-pruning methods. In neighbor-designating methods [11][12][13], each forward node uses a greedy algorithm to selects a few 1-hop neighbors as new forward nodes to cover its 2-hop neighbors. The forward node list is piggybacked in the broadcast packet and each forward node in turn designates its own forward node list. In self-pruning methods, each node determines it own status (forward or non-forward) according the local topology information and broadcast routing history information. Wu and Li [7] proposed a marking process and *Rule k* which can make use of local topology and priority among nodes to determine a small CDS. Peng and Lu's SBA [6] uses a random backoff delay to discover more forwarded nodes, and then uses a neighbor elimination scheme to determine the forward status for each node. A generic self-pruning scheme was proposed by Wu and Dai [8] to unify all the above self pruning protocols. In [14][15][16], some schemes are proposed for broadcasting using directional antennas.

All of the aforementioned protocols assume a SR-SC model. Broadcasting in MR-MC networks is very limited in literature. Kyasanur and Vaidya [5] simply propose to transmit a copy of the broadcast packet on every channel or use a separate broadcast channel at the expense of a dedicated interface. Qadir and Chou [17] design a set of centralized algorithms to achieve minimum broadcasting latency in multi-radio multi-channel and multi-rate mesh networks. However, the centralized approach results in a nontrivial overhead to construct and maintain the broadcast tree.

3 Network Model and Problem Formulation

3.1 Network Model

We consider a multi-radio multi-channel multi-hop network in which all nodes communicate with one another based on the IEEE 802.11 MAC protocol. It's assumed that there are totally C non-overlapping orthogonal frequency channels in the system and each node v is equipped with $I(v)$ omni-directional radio interfaces, $I(v) \leq C$. The unit disk graph model is used to model the transmission. A channel assignment scheme A assigns each node v, $I(v)$ different channels denoted by the set:

$A(v) = \{a_1(v), ..., a_{I(v)}(v) \mid \forall i, 1 \leq a_i(v) \leq C; \forall i \neq j, a_i(v) \neq a_j(v)\}$, where $a_i(v)$ represents

the channel assigned to *ith* radio interface of node v. Generally speaking, the channel assignment scheme can be classified into static, dynamic, and hybrid approach [5]. However, in our work, we currently assume that the channel assignment is given independently from our broadcasting because the channel assignment strategy is influenced by many factors, such as the unicast traffic. We further assume the channel assignment is static during the process of broadcasting and can keep the networks connected. Recognizing that channel assignment in MR-MC networks plays an important part in the actual performance, we will jointly consider channel assignment and broadcasting in our future work.

Given a channel assignment scheme A, we can use an undirected graph $G = (V, E)$ to model the MR-MC network topology, where V is the set of vertices and E is the set of edges. A vertex in V corresponds to a wireless node in the network. An edge $e = (u, v, k)$, corresponding to a communication link between nodes u and v under channel k, is in the set E if and only if $k \in A(u) \bigcap A(v)$ and $d(u, v) \leq r$, where $d(u, v)$ is the Euclidean distance between u and v, and r is the communication range of the transmission. Note that G may be a multi-graph, with multiple edges between the same pair of nodes, when the node pair shares two or more channels.

For each node v, $N_k(v)$ denotes the set of neighbors of v that are using channel k, and $N(v) = N_1(v) \bigcup ... \bigcup N_c(v)$ is v's neighbor set. Note that a neighbor may appear in several $N_i(v)$.

3.2 Problem Formulation

In SR-SC networks, some nodes (called forward nodes) are selected to form connected dominating set (CDS) to relay the packet. There're two approaches that can be adopted: one is the static approach, i.e. the virtual backbone method, where the CDS is constructed based on the network topology, but irrelative to any broadcasting; another is the dynamic approach, where the CDS is constructed for a particular broadcast request, and dependent on the progress of the broadcast process. In MR-MC environment, we will consider both approaches.

First, we define the forward scheme, F, as a function on V, where $F(v)$ is the set of node v's forward channels, $F(v) \subseteq A(v)$. We use $B = \{v \mid v \in V, F(v) \neq \varnothing\}$ to denote the forward node set. For two nodes $u \in V$ and $v \in B$, we say u is reachable from v under forward scheme F, if $u = v$ or there exists a path P: $(v_1 = v, ..., v_l = u)$, satisfying $v_i \in B$ and $F(v_i) \cap A(v_{i+1}) \neq \varnothing$, $i = 1, ..., l-1$. For example, in figure 2, under forward scheme $F = \{a[3], b, c[2,3], d[1], e, f\}$ (which means node a uses channel 3, node c use channel 2 and 3, node d uses channel 1 as forward channels, and other nodes don't forward packets), node d can reach node f and b.

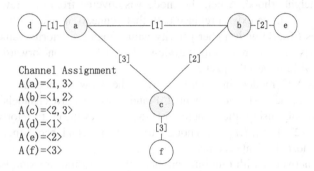

Channel Assignment
$A(a) = \langle 1, 3 \rangle$
$A(b) = \langle 1, 2 \rangle$
$A(c) = \langle 2, 3 \rangle$
$A(d) = \langle 1 \rangle$
$A(e) = \langle 2 \rangle$
$A(f) = \langle 3 \rangle$

Fig. 2. An example for illustration the problem formulation

In the static approach, we say a forward scheme F can form a virtual backbone if $\forall u \in V, \forall v \in B$, u is reachable from v under F. Obviously, for any broadcast process with source node $s \in B$, every other node can receive s' packets. For broadcast process with source node $s \in V - B$, there must exist a node $u \in B$ and $F(u) \cap A(s) \neq \varnothing$, so s can send data to node u, then to other nodes. Compared with the broadcasting with source node in B, only one more transmission is needed. For example, in figure 2, both forward schemes $F_1 = \{a[1], b[2], c[3], d, e, f\}$ and $F_2 = \{a[1,3], b[1,2], c[2,3], d, e, f\}$ can form virtual backbone.

In the dynamic approach for a particular broadcast with node s as source node, we say a forward scheme F achieves full delivery if $\forall u \in V$, u is reachable from node s. For example, in figure 2, forward scheme $F_1 = \{a[1], b[2], c[2,3], d, e, f\}$ can achieve full delivery for the broadcast process with source node f.

Our aim is to ensure cover every node, and at the same time reduce the amount of redundant traffic. Next we define the transmission cost of a forward scheme F as $|F| = \sum_{v \in B} |F(v)|$, where $|F(v)|$ is the number of forward channels of node v. So our efficient broadcasting problem in MR-MC networks can be defined as follows: given networks G under channel assignment scheme A, find the forward scheme F with minimum transmission cost $|F|$ that can form a virtual backbone in the static approach or achieve full delivery in the dynamic approach. Obviously, forward scheme $F = \{a[1], b[2], c[3], d, e, f\}$ can form a virtual backbone with minimum transmission cost in figure 2.

Efficient broadcasting in SR-SC networks is a special case of the above problem with $C = 1$. It is equal to find the minimal connected dominating set (MCDS) which is proved to be NP-complete [18]. So we can also conclude that it's NP-hard to find an efficient broadcasting scheme for a MR-MC network under a given channel assignment scheme.

4 Proposed Scheme

We first review the self-pruning protocol [8] under omni-directional SR-SC model as a trivial example solution to the above problem. In [8], each node computes the coverage of its neighborhood. A neighbor node v is covered from the view of node u if $\forall w \in N(u), w \neq v$, there exist a replace path that connects w and v via several intermediate nodes (if any) with higher priority values than the priority value of u. If all neighbor nodes are covered from the view of v, v has a non-forward node status, otherwise, it will forward the packet.

Under MR-MC model, in figure 2, from the view of node a, all neighbors are not covered, he will select channel 1 and 3 as forward channels to cover all neighbors. Simply using the scheme of [8] will result in the forward scheme $F = \{a[1,3], b[1,2], c[2,3], d, e, f\}$. Though forming a virtual backbone, F is apparently not the most efficient scheme.

In SR-SC networks with omni-directional antennas, a transmission by a node can be received by all neighboring nodes within its communication range. The 'wireless broadcast advantage' (WBA) makes broadcasting in SR-SC wireless networks fundamentally different from broadcasting in wired networks where the cost to reach two neighbors is generally the sum of the costs to reach them individually. This arise the shift in paradigm from the 'link-centric' nature of wired networks to the 'node centric' nature of wireless communications. However, when multiple radios and multiple channels are used, a packet broadcast on a channel is received only by those nodes listening to that channel. Motivated by the above example, we argue that we should shift the paradigm from the 'node centric' to 'channel/interface centric' in MR-MC environment. In this section, we will reduce the efficient broadcast problem in MR-MC environment into the minimal strong connected dominating set problem of the *interface-extend* graph which extends the original network topology across interfaces. Then we propose our Multi-Channel Self-Pruning (MCSP) broadcast protocol, both in static and dynamic approach and describe its property.

4.1 Extended Graph G Across Interface

In this subsection, we extend the original graph G into *interface-extend* graph G'. The basic idea here is to treat every interface of every node in MR-MC networks as a vertex of a directed graph. Using interface-extend graph, we will show the efficient broadcast problem in MR-MC environment can be reduced into the minimal strong connected dominating set problem of G'.

Definition 1: Interface-Extend Graph
For an undirected connected graph $G = (V, E)$, we construct a directed graph $G' = (V', E')$, where $V' = \{v_i \mid v \in V, i = 1, ..., I(v)\}$ is the set of vertices and

$E' = \{< v_i, u_j >| v = u \& i \neq j \ or \ v \neq u \& (v, u, a_i(v)) \in E\}$ is the set of directed edges. We call G' the interface-extend graph of G.

Figure 3 shows the interface-extend graph of figure 2.

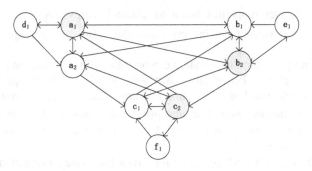

Fig. 3. Interface-extend graph of figure 2

Definition 2: Strong connected dominating set
In a strong connected directed graph $G' = (V', E')$, a set $S' \subseteq V'$ is a strong connected dominating set of G' if every vertex in $V' - S'$ is dominated by at least one vertex in S' (i.e. $\forall v' \in V' - S'$, $\exists u' \in S'$ satisfying $< u', v' > \in E'$) and the deduced graph $G'[S']$ is strong connected (i.e. $\forall u' \in S', \forall v' \in S'$, there exists a directed path in $G'[S']$ from u' to v'). For example, in figure 3, vertex a_1, b_2 and c_2 form a strong connected dominating set.

Next, we use the following theorem to reduce the broadcast problem in MR-MC networks G into the minimal strong connected dominating set problem.

Theorem 1. To find the virtual backbone with minimum transmission cost for a MR-MC network G is equivalent to find the minimal strong connected dominating set of the interface-extend graph G'.

Proof. Let $F^* = \{F \mid forward \ scheme \ F \ that \ can \ form \ a \ virtual \ backbone \ in \ G\}$, $D^* = \{D \mid D \ is \ a \ strong \ connected \ dominating \ set \ of \ G'\}$, and $g : F^* \to 2^{V'}$, $g(F) = \{v'_{i,m} \mid i \in B, a_m(i) \in F(i)\}$. From definition 2, we can prove $g(F) \in D^*$ and $|F| = |g(F)|$.

For $\forall D \in D^*$, we can construct a forward scheme F, $F(v_i) = \{m \mid v'_{i,m} \in D\}$, $\forall v_i \in V$. It's easy to verify that F forms a virtual backbone of G and $g(F) = D, |F| = |D|$.

We can also prove $\forall F_1, F_2, F_1 \neq F_2, g(F_1) \neq g(F_2)$. So g is a bijective mapping from F^* to D^* and $|F| = |g(F)|$. And the virtual backbone with minimum transmission cost in MR-MC networks G can be reduced into the minimal strong connected dominating set problem in directed graph G'. $\qquad \square$

4.2 Multi-Channel Self-Pruning (MCSP) Broadcast Protocol

Theorem 1 mplies that we can get the best forward scheme through seeking for the minimal strong connected dominating set of correspond interface-extend graph. The localized approximation algorithms for minimal strong connected dominating set have been studied in [9]. In this subsection, using the localized interface-extend graph, we propose our MCSP broadcast protocol, extending the self-pruning protocol in [8][9]. We redefine new priority among all interfaces using a combination of node ID and the interface/channel properties (such as channel degree $| N_k(v) |$, interface ID and so on). For other self-pruning protocols, they also can be adapted with some modification.

In MCSP, neighborhood information can be collected via exchanging "Hello" messages among neighbors. Periodically, each node broadcasts "Hello" packets on each channel. In the *kth* round of information exchange, the hello packet contains *(k – 1)*-hop neighbor's channel assignment and priority information. After *m* round of information exchange, where generally $m \leq 3$, each node can build its local *(m – 1)*-hop interface-extend graph.

Figure 4 shows the MCSP algorithm for virtual backbone construction in the static approach.

Algorithms MCSP (the static virtual backbone approach)
For each node v

1.   Calculate the uncovered interface set *Uncovered_Set$_i$*, for every interface v_i ,
     $i = 1,..., I(v)$ in the interface-extend graph G'

2. $Uncovered\_Set = \sum_{1 \leq i \leq I(v)} Uncovered\_Set_i$

3.   Calculate the uncovered node set from *Uncovered_Set*

4.   If *Uncovered_Set* $= \varnothing$, node v has a non-forward status, otherwise use greedy algorithm to compute the forward channels $F(v)$ that cover all the uncovered neighbors.

Fig. 4. MCSP algorithm in virtual backbone approach

Similar to the coverage condition of [8], we say an interface w is covered from the view of u if w is an out-neighbor of u , and for any u 's in-neighbor v , there exist a replace path that connects from v to w via several intermediate nodes (if any) with higher priority values than that of u . Note that here u , v and w are all interfaces of the interface-extend graph.

Every interface can make decision independently. However, interfaces on the same node can interact with each other without extra communication cost. So in the above algorithm, every interface first calculates its own uncovered neighbors, then we combine them and use greedy algorithms to reselect forward channels in order to save extra transmission. In the example of figure 2, if we use channel degree $N_k(v)$ as interface's priority, MCSP will mark the interface a_1 , b_2 and c_2 to forward, which form a minimal strong connected dominating set of figure 3.

We also present the MCSP algorithm in the dynamic approach in Figure 5.

In the dynamic approach, every node can use broadcast routing history to further eliminate the uncovered neighbors. Broadcast routing history can be piggyback in the packet. In the example of figure 1, when node a initials a broadcast process, it will use channel 3 to cover all its neighbors, and then node b will use channel 1, node f will use channel 4 to forward packets. Please note that the broadcast scheme of the dynamic approach sometimes can't form a virtual backbone. In figure 1, when node c initials a broadcast, the above forward scheme can't achieve full delivery.

Algorithms MCSP (the dynamic approach)

1. *For source node s, use greedy algorithm to compute the forward channels $F(s)$ that cover all neighbors*

2. *For other node v, when v fist receives a new packet*

   2.1. For each interface v_i of node v, compute the uncovered interface set

      2.1.1. Forward_Set$_i$ = all known forwarded interface

      2.1.2. Covered_Set$_i$ = Forward_Set$_i$ + { $N_{out}(v')$ | $v' \in$ Forward_Set }

      2.1.3. While there exists an interface $w' \in N_{out}(u')$, $u' \in$ Covered_Set and Priority (u') > Priority (v_i)

          Covered_Set$_i$ = Coverws_Set +{ w' },

      2.1.4. Uncovered_Set$_i$= $N_{out}(v_i)$ - Cover_Set$_i$

   2.2. Compute the forward channels

      2.2.1. Uncovered_Set = $\displaystyle\sum_{1 \le i \le I(v)}$ Uncovered_Set$_i$

      2.2.2. If Uncovered_Set $=\emptyset$, node v has a non-forward status, otherwise use greedy algorithm to compute the forward channels $F(v)$ that can cover all the uncovered neighbors.

Fig. 5. MCSP algorithm in the dynamic approach

Following theorem guarantees that the MCSP protocol in the dynamic approach can assure every node eventually receives the broadcast packet of the source node s.

Theorem 2. The forward scheme determined by MCSP in the dynamic approach achieves full delivery.

Proof. We use contradiction to conclude the theorem. Suppose there exists a non-empty node set $M \subseteq V$ that every node in M is not reachable from the source node s. Let $M' = \{v_i \mid v \in M, i = 1,...,I(v)\}$. So there must exist a non-empty interface set $U' \subseteq N_{in}(M') - M'$ in which every interface in U' is reachable from one interface of the source node s. Let $u_k = \max_{v_i \in U'}\{priority(v_i)\}$. Let $v' \in N_{out}(u_k) \cap M'$. u_k doesn't forward packet, so v' is covered from local view of u_k. However, according to 2.1.1-2.1.3, v' cannot be covered, because:

1. If v' is a known forwarded interface (2.1.1) or v' is a neighbor of a known forwarded interface (2.1.2), v' is reachable from one interface of the source node s, which contradicts the assumption that $v' \in M'$.

2. If v' is an out-neighbor of a covered interface w' and Priority (w') > Priority (u_k) (2.1.3), according to the loop of 2.1.3, there exists a path P: $(x', y_1', y_2',..., y_l', v')$ from a known forwarded interface x' to interface v',

where Priority (y_i') > Priority (u_k), $i=1,2,...,l$. Because $v' \in M'$, there is at least one interface y_j' in P that is reachable from one interface of s but $y_{j+1}' \in M', 1 \leq j \leq l$, so, $y_j' \in U'$, but Priority (y_j') > Priority(u_k), which contradicts the assumption that u_k is the interface in U' that has the highest priority.   □

5 Simulation

The proposed MCSP protocols have been implemented in ns-2. For comparison purpose, we implement a centralized broadcast algorithm (CBA) which is similar to what Das et al. [19] proposed. The centralized broadcast algorithm finds the forward scheme by growing a directed tree T in the interface-extend graph starting from an interface with the maximum channel degree, and adding new interface to T according to its effective channel degree (number of neighbors that are not covered). Then we can translate T to the resulting forward scheme. The centralized style makes the algorithm unpractical since it requires global information to compute the forward scheme. However, it can produce a near-optimal result. Here we use it as a substitution of the "perfect" algorithm that produces the optimal forward scheme. The original self-pruning protocols (OSP) [8] are also implemented for comparison. We evaluate the above 3 algorithms both in static and dynamic approach in terms of efficiency and reliability.

The simulated MR-MC network is deployed in a 1000m×1000m area with 20-110 nodes. Each node is equipped with four radios and twelve 2Mb/s channels are available in the system. The communication range for all nodes is 250m and the interference range is 500m. All nodes are randomly deployed and interfaces are randomly assigned with a constraint of full network connectivity. The "Hello" message interval is 1s and every node gathers 2-hop local topology and channel assignment information. 1-hop broadcasting routing history information is piggybacked in the broadcast packet. We use channel degree $| N_k(v) |$ followed by interface ID and node ID to break tie as interface's priority value.

Figure 6 and 7 present the comparison of CBA, OSP and MCSP in generated number of forward nodes and forward channels. Generally speaking, the static approach has a larger set of forward nodes and forward channels than dynamic approach. The centralized broadcast algorithm (CBA) has the smallest set of forward node set and forward channels. The OSP protocol have a little smaller forward nodes set than MCSP protocol, but has much more forward channels thus more transmission cost than MCSP protocol, especially when node number is large. When node number is larger than 60, MCSP can save 25-30% of OSP's transmission cost.

MCSP and other neighbor-knowledge-based broadcast protocol can cover all nodes. But because of the deficiency of the contention-based 802.11 MAC mechanism, collisions are likely to occur and cause some damage. Fig. 8 compares reliability in terms of delivery ratio. Flooding achieves almost 100 percent delivery in networks with more than 50 nodes. The delivery ratios of MCSP and OSP are less than that of flooding, but when the node number is larger than 100, they achieve almost the same level.

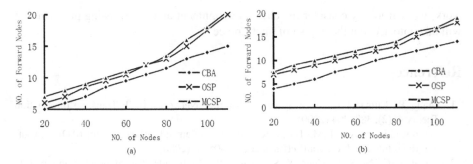

Fig. 6. Forward node number. (a) in static approach (b) in dynamic approach.

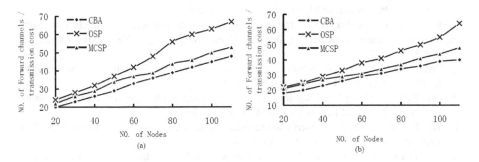

Fig. 7. Transmission cost. (a) in dynamic approach, (b) in static approach.

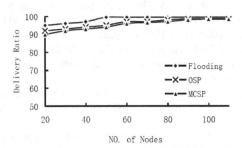

Fig. 8. Delivery ratio versus network size

6 Conclusion

This paper aims to provide a general model for broadcasting in multi-radio multi-channel multi-hop networks that uses self-pruning techniques to reduce the transmission cost. We reduce the efficient broadcast problem into the minimal strong connected dominating set of the interface-extend graph. We propose our MCSP protocol, both in virtual backbone approach and dynamic approach. The simulation result shows that our protocol can significantly reduce the transmission cost. In our future work, we will jointly consider the channel assignment and broadcasting problem that will take into account the impact of interference.

References

1. Gupta, P., Kumar, P.R.: The Capacity of Wireless Networks. IEEE Trans. on Information Theory 46(2), 388–404 (2000)
2. Perkins, C.E., Moyer, E.M., Das, S.R.: Ad hoc on-demand distance vector (AODV) routing, IETF Internet draft, draft-ietf-manet-aodv-05.txt (2000)
3. Tseng, Y.-C., Ni, S.-Y., Chen, Y.-S., Sheu, J.-P.: The broadcast storm problem in a mobile ad hoc network. Wireless Networks 8(2/3), 153–167 (2002)
4. Williams, B., Camp, T.: Comparison of broadcasting techniques for mobile ad hoc networks. In: Proceedings of MobiHoc, pp. 194–205 (2002)
5. Kyasanur, P., Vaidya, N.H.: Routing and interface assignment in multichannel multi-interface wireless networks. In: Wireless Communications and Networking Conference (2005)
6. Peng, W., Lu, X.: On the reduction of broadcast redundancy in mobile ad hoc networks. In: Proceedings MobiHoc, pp. 129–130 (2002)
7. Dai, F., Wu, J.: Distributed dominant pruning in ad hoc wireless networks. Florida Atlantic University, Technical Report TR-CSE-FAU-02-02 (2002)
8. Wu, J., Dai, F.: A generic distributed broadcast scheme in ad hoc wireless networks. IEEE Transactions on Computers (10), 1343–1354 (2004)
9. Wu, J.: Extended dominating-set-based routing in ad hoc wireless networks with unidirectional links. IEEE Transactions on Parallel and Distributed Computing (1-4), 327–340 (2002)
10. Keshavarz-Haddad, A., Ribeiro, V., Riedi, R.: Broadcast capacity in multi-hop wireless networks. In: Proc. of ACM MobiCom, ACM Press, New York (2006)
11. Peng, W., Lu, X.: AHBP: An efficient broadcast protocol for mobile ad hoc networks. Journal of Science and Technology, Beijing, China (2002)
12. Lim, H., Kim, C.: Multicast tree construction and flooding in wireless ad hoc networks. In: Proceedings of MSWiM (2000)
13. Qayyum, A., Viennot, L., Laouiti, L.: Multipoint relaying: An efficient technique for flooding in mobile wireless networks. INRIARapport de recherche, Tech. Rep. 3898 (2000)
14. Hu, C., Hong, Y., Hou, J.: On mitigating the broadcast storm problem with directional antennas. In: Proc. of IEEE ICC, IEEE Computer Society Press, Los Alamitos (2003)
15. Dai, F., Wu, J.: Efficient broadcasting in ad hoc wireless networks using directional antennas. IEEE Transactions on Parallel and Distributed Systems (4), 1–13 (2006)
16. Roy, S., Hu, Y.C., Peroulis, D., Li, X.-Y.: Minimum-Energy Broadcast Using Practical Directional Antennas in All-Wireless Networks. In: Proc. of IEEE InfoCom, IEEE Computer Society Press, Los Alamitos (2006)
17. Qadir, J., Chou, C.T., Misra, A.: Minimum Latency Broadcasting in Multi-Radio Multi-Channel Multi-Rate Wireless Mesh Networks. In: Proc. of IEEE SECON, IEEE Computer Society Press, Los Alamitos (2006)
18. Garey, M.L., Johnson, D.S.: Computers and Intractability: A Guide to the Theory of NP-Completeness. W.H. Freeman, San Francisco (1979)
19. Das, B., Sivakumar, R., Bharghavan, V.: Routing in ad-hoc networks using a spine. In: Proc. of IC3N (1997)

Network Planning for Multicast Using Partitioned Virtual User Domains*

Xuezhou Ma[1], Selcuk Cevher[1], M. Umit Uyar[1], Mariusz Fecko[2], John Sucec[2], and Sunil Samtani[2]

[1] The City College and Graduate Center of the City University of New York, NY, USA
{zxue00,scevher,uyar}@ccny.cuny.edu
[2] Applied Research, Telcordia Technologies Inc., Piscataway, NJ, USA
{mfecko,jsucec,ssamtani}@research.telcordia.com

Abstract. We introduce a new network planning approach for management of multicast communications in large data dissemination networks. Our approach, addressing *Channelization Problem*, considers both the common user interests and geographical dependencies while evaluating multicast configurations. We first perform *Global Similarity Classification* to partition users into virtual domains based on their characteristics within the same geographical vicinity. Second, based on the resource availability of a given network, *Localized Multicast Update* mechanism is used to evaluate the benefits of forming a new multicast group and the cost of the management overhead. We evaluate the performance of the proposed approach using our simulation software. Preliminary results show that, using two-stage planning, the performance of our approach is at least 40% better than the existing greedy approaches.

Keywords: Multicast, network planning, channelization.

1 Introduction

Multicast is the most efficient mechanism for information delivery in large scale data dissemination network (LSDDN) applications which require delivering a large number of information flows to many users. In management of such networks, multicast planning prior to network deployment is of particular importance. Moreover, properly planned multicast communications can assist in network management itself by disseminating management information.

The nature of LSDDN applications, such as multi-player online games [4], and distributed event notification systems [6], is such that individual users are

---

* This work has been prepared through collaborative participation in the Communications Networks Consortium sponsored by the U.S. Army Research Lab under the Collaborative Technology Alliance Program, Cooperative Agreement DAAD19-01-2-0011. The U.S. Government is authorized to reproduce and distribute reprints for Government purposes notwithstanding any copyright notation thereon. Copyright © 2007 The City University of New York and Telcordia Technologies, Inc. All rights reserved.

D. Krishnaswamy, T. Pfeifer, and D. Raz (Eds.): MMNS 2007, LNCS 4787, pp. 113–124, 2007.
© IFIP International Federation for Information Processing 2007

not interested in all information flows. Instead, users in the same geographical vicinity show common characteristics by having high similarity in their information flow interests, while users not in the same neighborhood do not have such characteristics. Each user receives all of the information flows mapped to the multicast groups to which it subscribed [2]. *Channelization problem* in multicasting is defined as finding an optimal mapping of information flows to the multicast groups, and an optimal subscription of users to the multicast groups so as to minimize the total bandwidth consumed. Fig. 1 shows the two components of channelization problem.

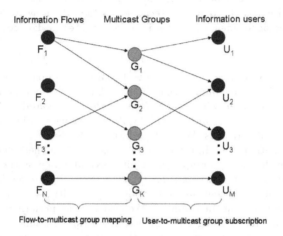

Fig. 1. Two components of channelization problem

Although it is desirable to use multicast for LSDDN to reduce the overall bandwidth demand, introduction of multicast groups requires configuration and management overhead [3] [1] (e.g., in terms of routing, determining the proper multicast route for each multicast group will consume additional bandwidth). Hence, there is a clear need for multicast group planning algorithms that provide a satisfactory balance between the unwanted traffic per user and multicast group management overhead, resulting in a near-optimal total bandwidth consumption. Specifically, the channelization problem addresses: *(i)* selection of the number of multicast groups to minimize total bandwidth consumption, *(ii)* update of multicast group planning in accordance with the network topology which dynamically changes due to user mobility, *(iii)* adaptation of the mapping algorithms to the networks with different characteristics (e.g., end-user tolerance to unwanted packets), and *(iv)* reduction of the computational complexity of the mapping algorithms.

In this paper, we provide a formal definition of channelization problem with respect to *no false exclusion* and *minimum false inclusion* requirements [1]. We consider the issues of homogeneous characteristics of the users within the same geographical boundary, routing overhead, total bandwidth consumption, and introduce a new multicast group planning approach which consists of two main components: *Global Similarity Classification* and *Localized Multicast Group Update*. We provide simulation results for comparing our approach with existing greedy algorithms with respect to the number of multicast groups and total bandwidth consumption.

2   Background

Based on the channelization problem structure shown in Fig. 1, a data dissemination system is defined as a triple (F, G, U) where $F = \{F_1, F_2, ..., F_N\}$ is the set of information flows with each flow F_i assigned a transmission rate λ_i, $G = \{G_1, G_2, ..., G_K\}$ is the set of multicast groups, and $U = \{U_1, U_2, ..., U_M\}$ is the set of users. In generalized channelization problem, the information flows (or users) might be mapped to more than one multicast groups. The user-flow interest matrix W, flow-to-multicast group mapping matrix X, and the subscription matrix Y are defined as follows [1]:

$$W = (w_{jm})_{M \times N}, \text{ where } j \in U, m \in F, M=| U |, N=| F |,$$

$$w_{jm} = \begin{cases} 1 \text{ user } j \text{ is interested in information flow } m \\ 0 \text{ otherwise} \end{cases}$$

$$X = (x_{im})_{N \times K}, \text{ where } i \in F, m \in G, N=| F |, K=| G |,$$

$$x_{im} = \begin{cases} 1 \text{ flow } i \text{ is assigned to multicast group } m \\ 0 \text{ otherwise} \end{cases}$$

$$Y = (y_{jm})_{M \times K}, \text{ where } j \in U, m \in G, M=| U |, K=| G |,$$

$$y_{jm} = \begin{cases} 1 \text{ user } j \text{ subscribes to multicast group } m \\ 0 \text{ otherwise} \end{cases}$$

Finding an optimal solution to the generalized channelization problem is NP-Complete [1]. However, some constrained polynomial-time instances can be considered since practical networking situations might not require the solution of the generalized form of channelization problem.

The existing solutions for channelization problem are either approximations using greedy approaches, such as User Based Merge (UBM) and Flow Based Merge (FBM) [1], or centralized control mechanisms such as Optimization-Based Congestion Control [3]. Since greedy approaches are based on a fixed number of multicast groups, they may not be appropriate for mobile networks. Also, such greedy approaches can be computationally inefficient since the flow-to-multicast group mapping and user-to-multicast group subscription have to be recalculated even for small amount of changes in network topology. On the other hand, centralized control mechanisms can be tuned to provide an acceptable level of total bandwidth consumption. However, they have to process feedback from all users leading to an unscalable multicast protocol overhead.

In general, the existing solutions need two improvements: *(i)* the benefits to the algorithms must be evaluated due to possible common interests of users residing in the same vicinity (compared to the users in different geographical locations), *(ii)* a more efficient solution may emerge if the number of multicast groups is a result of diversity of user flow interests as opposed to a fixed number.

The first direction mentioned above can reduce the hardness of the channelization problem to a polynomial solution since the similarity consideration. Similarly, the second improvement will remedy the typical cases where the tolerance to routing overhead in the network is limited.

3   Our Approach

In channelization problem, the flow-to-multicast group and user-to-multicast group mappings must be such that: *(i)* all data needed by a user is mapped to one or more multicast groups to which the user either subscribes or is designated as the data recipient (no false exclusion), *(ii)* the amount of unneeded data received by users belonging to various multicast groups carrying the needed data is minimized (minimum false inclusion).

Additionally, the total bandwidth consumption should be taken into consideration while determining the mappings. Furthermore, any increase in the number of multicast groups requires additional routing overhead to determine the proper multicast routes. Since multicast groups is a limited resource, the number of multicast groups should be determined based on a design tradeoff involving all of the issues just described (i.e., minimum false inclusion, no false exclusion, total bandwidth consumed, and routing overhead).

3.1   Global Similarity Classification

Although both constrained and generalized channelization problems are NP-Complete, in real LSDDN applications (e.g., hierarchical army networks, large wireless ad-hoc networks [5], online soccer games [4]), if the users can be partitioned into virtual domains at the planning stage based on their common characteristics and the geographical vicinity, the problems' computational complexity can be reduced to polynomial-time as described below.

Partitioning the users into virtual domains has three key benefits:

- It reduces the network layer protocol overhead. In most routing protocols, for example, the aggregate route update overhead grows as $O(n^2)$, where n is the number of routers in a routing domain [5]. Therefore, using the concept of virtual domains instead of considering all users as one single group reduces overall maintenance complexity for routing.
- If the virtual domains are well chosen, homogeneous characteristics among the users in the same domain will make channelization problem much easier. For example, in the context of Optimal Configuration Approach [1], when the number of virtual domains equals to the expected number of multicast groups, the partitioned result will independently work as a near-optimal configuration without any further consideration.
- Virtual user domain concept can fit to mobile networks characterized by highly dynamic arrival and departure of users.

Typically, the users in the same vicinity have common information flow interests with a higher probability than the ones in different geographical regions. For global similarity classification, we propose an interest-aware algorithm inspired by *overlap matrix technique* [2] to partition the users into virtual domains based on their common interests and geographical dependencies.

Let us first define similarity indicator $\delta_i(j_1, j_2)$ of users U_{j_1} and U_{j_2} as:

$$\delta_i(j_1, j_2) = \begin{cases} 1 \text{ if } w_{j_1,i} \oplus w_{j_2,i} = 0 \\ 0 \text{ if } w_{j_1,i} \oplus w_{j_2,i} = 1 \end{cases}$$

where $w_{j_1,i}$, $w_{j_2,i}$ represent the flow interests of the users U_{j_1} and U_{j_2} regarding information flow F_i, respectively. We maintain an $M \times M$ $(M=|U|)$ *similarity table* to store the similarity rates. Each entry k_{j_1,j_2} of the similarity table represents the similarity rate for the user pair of (U_{j_1}, U_{j_2}):

$$k_{j_1,j_2} = c_{j_1,j_2}\left(\frac{\sum\limits_{i \in F} \delta_i(j_1, j_2)}{\sum\limits_{i \in F}(1 - \delta_i(j_1, j_2))}\right) \tag{1}$$

where c_{j_1,j_2} is a proximity dependent coefficient $(0 < c_{j_1,j_2} < 1)$ where $c_{j_1,j_2} = 0$ if the users are far from each other, $c_{j_1,j_2} = 1$ if they are in the same vicinity, and between 0 and 1 depending on their distance. When $\sum\limits_{i \in F}(1 - \delta_i(j_1, j_2)) = 0$, we set k_{j_1,j_2} as ∞, which indicates the highest value.

We introduce Algorithm 1 as shown in Fig. 2 which uses global similarity classification to find a set of virtual domains based on the similarity rates in similarity table. In the *for* loop in Fig. 2 (lines 1 through 10), the exclusive-or operator shown as $\oplus$ in line 3 checks if the users U_{j_1} and U_{j_2} have common interest on information flow F_i ($\oplus$ operator results in 0 if $w_{j_1,i}$ and $w_{j_2,i}$ are the same, and 1 otherwise). The counter called *overlap* is incremented if there is a common interest (line 5), otherwise, the counter *non-overlap* is incremented (line 7). In each iteration of the *while* loop (lines 11 through 13), the user (or group) pair of (j_1, j_2) with the highest similarity rate k_{j_1,j_2} is selected among the unselected pairs. If neither of the users U_{j_1} and U_{j_2} belongs to any virtual domains created before, a new virtual domain is created for them. If one of the users U_{j_1} or U_{j_2} is already a member of a virtual domain, the user currently not in this domain will be added to the domain.

As can be seen in Fig. 2, global similarity classification reduces the computational complexity of the channelization problem. Moreover, if used after network deployment, Algorithm 1 does not have to run for all user pairs each time a user arrives in the network since the only decision to make in Algorithm 1 is either to assign a new virtual domain to the new user or include it in one of the existing domains, while greedy approaches such as FBM may require a computation with $O(N^2M + (N - K)^2M)$ running time to recover from such changes in the network topology.

Algorithm 1. Global Similarity Classification

Input : U (set of users in the network), F (set of information flows), W (user-flow interest matrix), and C (boundary dependent coefficients)
Output : Partitioned virtual user domains

PARTITION (W, F, U, C)

```
 1   for all possible user pairs (U_{j_1}, U_{j_2})
 2       do for m ← 1 to N                    /*N is the number of flows*/
 3          if (w_{j_1 m} ⊕ w_{j_2 m}) = 0
 4             then
 5                   overlap ← overlap +1
 6             else
 7                   non-overlap ← non-overlap +1
 8
 9          k_{j_1, j_2} ← c_{j_1, j_2}(overlap ÷ non-overlap)
10
11   while there is any user not partitioned to a virtual domain
12       do select the maximum similarity rate k_{j_1, j_2} and put
13           corresponding (U_{j_1}, U_{j_2}) into the same virtual domain.
```

Fig. 2. Algorithm for global similarity classification

Virtual domains can be represented as an undirected graph $G_N=(V,E)$ named *User Neighborhood Graph*, where V is the set of vertices (i.e., network users), and E is the set of edges among the vertices. There is an edge between any user pair (U_i, U_j) as long as the users U_i and U_j are in the same neighborhood. Since each user can belong to only one neighborhood, $G_N=(V,E)$ is naturally *disconnected*, and consists of *complete* subgraphs. Hence:

$$G_N = (V, E) \begin{cases} \text{V}=\{u : u \text{ is a network user}\} \\ \text{E}=\{(u,v) : u \text{ and } v \text{ are in the same neighborhood}\} \end{cases}$$

Fig. 3a depicts an example network in which black vertices represent information flows while gray vertices are for network users, and lines between vertices represent the communication links. Vertices in the same neighborhood are connected to each other with solid edges whereas dotted edges connect vertices in different neighborhoods. Fig. 3b shows G_N for the example network in Fig. 3a.

3.2   Constrained Channelization Problem

The cost C_{sub} of user-to-multicast group subscription of channelization problem is computed based on X and Y matrices, as defined in Section II, as follows:

$$C_{sub} = \sum_{i \in F}\sum_{j \in U}\sum_{m \in G} x_{im} y_{jm} \lambda_i \qquad (2)$$

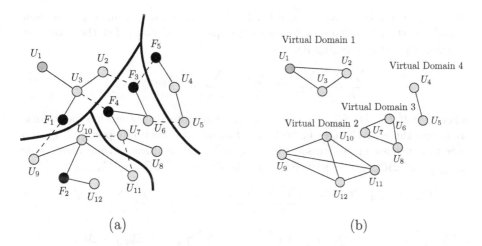

Fig. 3. Example of global similarity classification

where x_{im}, y_{jm} are the members of X and Y matrices, F, U, G are the sets of information flows, multicast groups, and users, respectively, and λ_i is the transmission rate of the corresponding information flow F_i. The cost C_{map} of flow-to-multicast group mapping is computed based on X matrix as follows:

$$C_{map} = \sum_{i \in F} \sum_{m \in G} x_{im} \lambda_i \tag{3}$$

Hence, the total cost C_c of channelization problem is the sum of Eqs. (2) and (3):

$$C_c = C_{sub} + C_{map} = w_1 \sum_{i \in F} \sum_{j \in U} \sum_{m \in G} x_{im} y_{jm} \lambda_i + w_2 \sum_{i \in F} \sum_{m \in G} x_{im} \lambda_i \tag{4}$$

where w_1 and w_2 are introduced to provide relative weights to the costs of subscription and mapping, respectively. Considering the costs of both channelization problem C_c and routing management C_r (i.e., setting up and maintaining the multicast routes), the total cost C_{tot} of multicasting is defined as follows :

$$C_{tot} = C_c + C_r = w_1 \sum_{i \in F} \sum_{j \in U} \sum_{m \in G} x_{im} y_{jm} \lambda_i + w_2 \sum_{i \in F} \sum_{m \in G} x_{im} \lambda_i + w_3 C_r \tag{5}$$

where w_3 is the corresponding relative weight for C_r. For simplicity, without loss of generality, we evaluate C_{tot} with the following approximations: *(i)* the cost of routing management increases linearly with the number of multicast groups, *(ii)* $w_1 = w_2 = w_3$ so that they can be ignored in the computation, *(iii)* one user subscribes to only one multicast group. Now, C_{tot} becomes:

$$C_{tot} = \sum_{i \in F} \sum_{j \in U} \sum_{m \in G} x_{im} y_{jm} \lambda_i + \sum_{i \in F} \sum_{m \in G} x_{im} \lambda_i + \sum_{m \in G} \gamma_m \tag{6}$$

where γ_m represents routing overhead for the multicast group G_m. We now consider cost of merging two multicast groups G_k and G_{k+1}. Let the total cost function C'_{tot} after merging be:

$$C'_{tot} = \sum_{i \in F'} \sum_{j \in U'} \sum_{m \in G'} x'_{im} y'_{jm} \lambda_i + \sum_{i \in F'} \sum_{m \in G'} x'_{im} \lambda_i + \sum_{m \in G'} \gamma'_m \quad (7)$$

where $F'=F$, $U'=U$, $|G'|=|G|-1$. Under the constrained subscription framework, we define the cost changes in both flow-to-multicast group mapping C_{map} and user-to-multicast group subscription C_{sub} after the multicast group merging as ΔC_{map} and ΔC_{sub}, respectively. Thus, the difference ΔC_{tot} of C_{tot} and C'_{tot} is:

$$\Delta C_{tot} = C_{tot} - C'_{tot} = \lambda_i \left(\sum_{i \in F} \sum_{j \in U} \sum_{m \in G} x_{im} y_{jm} - \sum_{i \in F'} \sum_{j \in U'} \sum_{m \in G'} x'_{im} y'_{jm} \right) +$$

$$\lambda_i \left(\sum_{i \in F} \sum_{m \in G} x_{im} - \sum_{i \in F'} \sum_{m \in G'} x'_{im} \right) + \left(\sum_{m \in G} \gamma_m - \sum_{m \in G'} \gamma'_m \right) = \Delta C_{map} + \Delta C_{sub} + \Delta C_r$$

$$(8)$$

where ΔC_{map} is determined based on three different cases: *(i)* if the flow is not sent to any multicast groups which have been merged, $\Delta C_{map} = 0$, *(ii)* if the flow is sent to only one of the multicast groups which have been merged, $\Delta C_{map} = 0$ *(iii)* if the flow is sent to both multicast groups which have been merged, $\Delta C_{map} = \sum_{i \in F} \delta_i \lambda_i$, where $\delta_i = 1$ if $w_{ji} \times w_{j'i} \neq 0$, and 0 otherwise. In the same way, ΔC_{sub} is determined as: *(i)* if the user is not subscribed to any multicast groups which have been merged, $\Delta C_{sub} = 0$, *(ii)* if the user is subscribed to only one of the multicast groups which have been merged, $\Delta C_{sub} = -\sum_{i \in F} \delta'_i \lambda_i$ where $\delta'_i = 1$ if $w_{ji} \oplus w_{j'i} = 1$, and 0 otherwise. Therefore, the total difference of cost functions before and after merging is:

$$\Delta C_{tot} = \left(\sum_{i \in F} \delta_i \lambda_i - \sum_{i \in F} \delta'_i \lambda_i \right) + \left(\sum_{m \in G} \gamma_m - \sum_{m \in G'} \gamma'_m \right) \quad (9)$$

An example exhibiting flow-to-multicast group mapping and user-to-multicast group subscription before and after multicast group merging is shown in Fig. 4a and Fig. 4b, respectively. Both users U_j and U_{j+1} are interested in the information flows F_i and F_{i+1}. The user U_{j+2} is interested in the information flows F_{i+1} and F_{i+2}. In Fig. 4a, which shows the multicast group configuration before merging, information flow F_{i+1} is sent to both multicast groups MG_k and MG_{k+1}, which makes the cost C_{map} of the flow-to-multicast group mapping equal to 235 and the cost C_{sub} of the user-to-multicast group subscription equal to 360. In Fig. 4b, the two multicast groups are merged into the new multicast group MG_{new}. The benefit after the merging is that F_{i+1} need to be sent only to one multicast group now which makes the cost C'_{map} of the flow-to-multicast group mapping reduce to 160. On the other hand, the cost C'_{sub} of the user-to-multicast group subscription increases to 480 due to the unwanted traffic generated since all of the three users are the members of a single multicast group now.

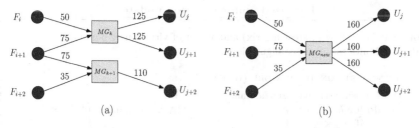

Fig. 4. An example for multicast group merging

3.3 Localized Multicast Group Update

In `resource-rich` networks (e.g., multi-player online games) are defined as networks whose users assign a greater weight to the cost of flow delivery than multicast routing overhead. In resource-rich networks, the users may tolerate very small amount of unwanted traffic, which requires the assignment of a separate multicast group for each user group even if it may not be a good choice for routing management. In some other networks, called `resource-constrained` networks, users may quickly recover from large amounts of unwanted traffic while they wait for a long time for the multicast tree maintenance. In resource-constrained networks, groups should be merged to reduce routing management as much as possible. In resource-constrained networks, if the pairwise merging cost ΔC_{tot} for any possible virtual domain pair (V_i, V_j) is positive, we may need to further reduce the number of multicast groups by merging this virtual domain pair in our localized multicast group update.

In resource-rich networks, starting with M multicast groups, we create one multicast group for each user, and apply our localized multicast group update inside of each virtual domain simultaneously. The user pairs with minimium merging costs inside of each virtual domain will be merged during each iteration of update until the amount of end-user unwanted traffic for one user is over the expected value. Fig. 5 shows the localized multicast group update algorithm, which first the merges the multicast group pairs that have the least merging cost. It is applied among all virtual user domains for resource-constrained networks, and inside each virtual domain for resource-rich networks. The output of the algorithm is the final multicast group configuration which is both suitable to user groups' homogeneous characteristics and to each end user's unique characteristic.

An example for user-flow-interest matrix is shown in Table 1. Without loss of generality, we set the transmission rate λ_i for F_i as one of two values 1 and 10. To show the implementation of ΔC_{tot} from Eq. (9) into a user-flow-interest matrix, we define Δ_{C_c} as:

$$\Delta C_c(U_i, U_j) = \Delta C_{map}(U_i, U_j) + \Delta C_{sub}(U_i, U_j) \tag{10}$$

Because $\Delta_{C_c}(U_1, U_2)$ and $\Delta_{C_c}(U_3, U_4)$ have the same maximum positive cost changes among all user pairs, we decide to merge the user pairs of (U_1, U_2) and (U_3, U_4), as shown in Table 2. Similarly, we will merge user pairs $(U_{1,2}, U_5)$

Localized multicast group update

Input : W (user-flow interest matrix) and V (set of virtual user domains)
Output : Multicast group configuration

RESOURCE-CONSTRAINED NETWORK (W, V)

1   **for** *all* possible virtual user domain pairs (V_i, V_j)
2   **do for** $h \leftarrow 1$ **to** N /*N is the number of flows*/
3   **if** $w_{ih} \times w_{jh} = 1$
4   **then**
5                    $overlap \leftarrow overlap + \lambda_h$
6   **else if** $w_{ih} \oplus w_{jh} = 1$
7                    $non\text{-}overlap \leftarrow non\text{-}overlap + \lambda_h$
8
9        $\Delta_{C_c}(V_i, V_j) \leftarrow overlap - non\text{-}overlap$
10
11    $\Delta_{tot}(V_i, V_j) \leftarrow \Delta_{C_c}(V_i, V_j) + \Delta_{C_r}(V_i, V_j)$
12   **Create** multicast groups by merging the virtual user domains
        v_i and v_j with the maximum $\Delta_{tot}(V_i, V_j)$ value into the same group

RESOURCE-RICH NETWORK (W, V)

1   **for** *all* possible user pairs (U_i, U_j) in each virtual domain V_k
2   **do for** $h \leftarrow 1$ **to** N
3   **if** $w_{ih} \times w_{jh} = 1$
4   **then**
5                    $overlap \leftarrow overlap + \lambda_h$
6   **else if** $w_{ih} \oplus w_{jh} = 1$
7                    $non\text{-}overlap \leftarrow non\text{-}overlap + \lambda_h$
8
9        $\Delta C_c(U_i, U_j) \leftarrow overlap - non\text{-}overlap$
10
11    $\Delta_{tot}(U_i, U_j) \leftarrow \Delta C_c(U_i, U_j) + \Delta C_r(U_i, U_j)$
12   **Create** multicast groups by merging the user pair with the maximum
        $\Delta_{tot}(U_i, U_j)$ value into the same group inside of virtual domain V_k

---

Fig. 5. Algorithm for multicast group update

Table 1. Example for 5 users and 5 flows user-flow-interest matrix

	F_1	F_2	F_3	F_4	F_5
	$(\lambda_1 = 1)$	$(\lambda_2 = 1)$	$(\lambda_3 = 10)$	$(\lambda_4 = 10)$	$(\lambda_5 = 10)$
U_1	1	0	0	10	10
U_2	0	1	0	10	10
U_3	1	0	10	0	10
U_4	0	1	10	0	10
U_5	1	1	0	0	10

$$\Delta_{C_c}(U_1, U_2) = 10 + 10 - 1 - 1 = 18$$
$$\Delta_{C_c}(U_3, U_4) = 10 + 10 - 1 - 1 = 18$$

Table 2. User-flow-interest Matrix after merging the user pairs (U_1, U_2) and (U_3, U_4)

	F_1	F_2	F_3	F_4	F_5
	$(\lambda_1 = 1)$	$(\lambda_2 = 1)$	$(\lambda_3 = 10)$	$(\lambda_4 = 10)$	$(\lambda_5 = 10)$
$U_{1,2}$	1	1	0	10	10
$U_{3,4}$	1	1	10	0	10
U_5	1	1	0	0	10

$$\Delta_{C_c}(U_{1,2}, U_5) = 12 - 10 = 2$$
$$\Delta_{C_c}(U_{3,4}, U_5) = 12 - 10 = 2$$
$$\Delta_{C_c}(U_{1,2,5}, U_{3,4}) = 12 - 30 - 20 = -38$$

based on $\Delta_{C_c}(U_{1,2}, U_5)$. Further, if Δ_{C_r} is greater than pairwise merging cost $\Delta_{C_c}(U_{1,2,5}, U_{3,4})$, we may merge $U_{1,2,5}$ and $U_{3,4}$ in next iteration to reduce C_{tot}.

4 Simulation Results

To study the effectiveness of our approach, we implemented Algorithms 1 and 2 in Figs. 2 and 5, respectively, in C++. The simulation parameters are set as follows: *(i)* each information flow F_i, once created, is assigned a transmission rate λ_i, which takes one of the following values $\lambda_h=100$, $\lambda_l=10$, with the equal probability; *(ii)* F_i is either popular or unpopular for users in its vicinity, with the probabilities of μ_p and μ_{up}, respectively; *(iii)* each user, once created, is assigned to one of the user groups with equal probability; *(iv)* resource-rich networks with more multicast groups are available to reduce unwanted traffic, and resource-constrained networks where more unwanted traffic is tolerated to reduce the expense for multicast group routing and management overhead.

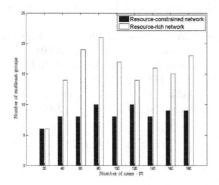 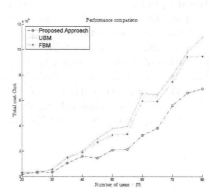

Fig. 6. (a) Effect of number of multicast groups for different networks for $|F| = 100$, $|U|=100$, $\lambda_h=100$, $\lambda_l=10$, $\mu_p=0.9$, $\mu_{up}=0.05$) (b) C_{tot} for our algorithm, FBM, and UBM

Our approach yields 10.3 and 5.6 as the average number of multicast groups for resource-rich networks and the resource-constrained networks, respectively (Fig. 6.(a)). This result implies that our approach is flexible enough to handle different network conditions for multicast group assignments as demonstrated by the smaller number of average multicast groups for constrained networks compared to the resource-rich networks. We also evaluated the cost of C_{tot} for different approaches when number of multicast groups k is pre-determined for the network of Fig. 6.(a) (except for the different (un)popularity rates of $\mu_{up} = 0.1, \mu_p = 0.85$). Fig. 6.(b) shows that our proposed approach achieves at least 40% better performance than UBM and FBM in spite of the fact that a k is available (which is supposed to enhance the performance of UBM and FBM).

5   Conclusions

[1]We introduced a new multicast group planning approach for channelization problem in management of large data dissemination networks. First, we propose a classification algorithm, which forms virtual user domains by considering both common interests and geographical dependency characteristics among users. Then we apply a greedy merging algorithm to reduce total consumed bandwidth, unwanted traffic and multicast group management overhead depending on the availability of network resources. Simulation experiments have validated that the performance of our algorithm is better than existing algorithms.

References

1. Adler, M., Ge, Z., Kurose, J.F., Towsley, D., Zabele, S.: Channelization Proble. In: Large Scale Data Dissemination, ICNP (2001)
2. Papaemmanouil, O., Cetintemel, U.: SemCast: Semantic Multicast for Content-Based Data Dissemination. In: ICDE (2005)
3. Shapiro, J.K., Towsley, D., Kurose, J.: Optimization-Based Congestion Control for Multicast Communication. In: ICDE (2002)
4. Levine, B.N., Crowcroft, J., Diot, C., Garcia-Luna-Aceves, J.J., Kurose, J.F.: Consideration of Receiver Interest for IP Multicast Delivery. In: Infocom (2000)
5. Galli, S., Luss, H., Sucec, J., McAuley, A., Samtani, S.: A Novel Approach to OSPF-Area Design for Large Wireless Ad-Hoc Networks, IEEE ICC (2005)
6. Carzaniga, A., Rosenblum, D.S., Wolf, A.L.: Achieving Scalability and Expressiveness in an Internet-scale Event Notification Service. In: ACM PODC (2000)

---

[1] The views and conclusions contained in this document are those of the authors and should not be interpreted as representing the official policies, either expressed or implied, of the Army Research Lab or the U.S. Government.

Empirical Effective Bandwidth Estimation for IPTV Admission Control

Alan Davy, Dmitri Botvich, and Brendan Jennings

Telecommunications Software & Systems Group,
Waterford Institute of Technology
Cork Rd., Waterford, Ireland
{adavy, dbotvich, bjennings}@tssg.org

Abstract. We propose an admission control approach for IPTV in which decisions to admit new flows are based on effective bandwidth estimates calculated using empirical traffic measurement. We describe our approach to estimate the effective bandwidth required to satisfy given Quality-of-Service constraints on traffic and specify a simple admission control algorithm which uses this estimation to manage flow admissions. We present the results of a simulation study, employing real traffic traces for long-lived flows, which indicate that our algorithm ensures that an adequate, but not overly generous, amount of bandwidth is allocated to ensure that Quality-of-Service targets for accepted flows will be met. We also compare our algorithm with alternative approaches based on analytical estimation of effective bandwidth; we demonstrate that these approaches are weak at taking into account related Quality of Service constraints and thus reserve inappropriate amounts of bandwidth, leading to either increased QoS target violations, or underutilisation of resources.

Keywords: IPTV, admission control, effective bandwidth estimation, Quality of Service.

1 Introduction

Admission control is a technique used by service providers to ensure customers' traffic flows are allocated sufficient bandwidth to ensure service level agreements relating to packet-level Quality-of-Service (QoS) are maintained during periods of network congestion. The goal of the service provider is to guarantee QoS for accepted traffic flows while maximising bandwidth available for newly arriving flows. In the context of IPTV service delivery, admission control plays a vital role, as flows (streaming movies and TV programmes) are typically high-bandwidth and must meet stringent QoS targets, so bad admission decisions can significantly degrade QoS for all accepted flows.

A key characteristic of any admission control algorithm how well it predicts the level of resources a new flow requires so that its QoS targets can be met. If a new flow request is accepted, the outlined packet level QoS must be guaranteed on the

D. Krishnaswamy, T. Pfeifer, and D. Raz (Eds.): MMNS 2007, LNCS 4787, pp. 125–137, 2007.

new request, without affecting QoS of already admitted flows. Fundamental to this process is the prediction of required *effective bandwidth* (the minimum amount of bandwidth required by a traffic stream to maintain specified QoS related targets [1]) of the aggregated traffic *following* admission of the new flow. If the admission control algorthim predicts that aggregated effective bandwidth should the flow be accepted will be greater than the available bandwidth, the flow must be rejected. Clearly, the more accurate the estimation of effective bandwidth, the more effective the admission control algorithm operates as a whole. Current effective bandwidth estimation approaches are typically based on theoretical analyses of traffic properties (see for example [1, 2, 3]), based on simplyfying assumptions such as constant packet sizes and inter-arrival times.

In this paper we propose an admission control algorithm based on an *empirical estimation* of effective bandwidth, or empirical admission control (EAC). This technique enables the admission control algorithm to predict more accurately the required amount of bandwidth needed to ensure admitted aggregated traffic flows will maintain agreed packet-level QoS targets. The paper is organised as follows: §2 discusses background to effective bandwidth estimation and admission control techniques; §3 defines the admission control framework, outlining the effective bandwidth estimation and admission control algorithm. It also details four admission control algorithms for comparison: Parameter Based Admission Control (PBAC) [4]; Experience based Admission Control (EBAC) [5]; Measurement and Traffic Descriptor based Admission Control (MTAC) [6]; and the ideal admission control algorithm. §4 defines the IPTV architecture studied, discussing topology settings and limitations imposed on the service provider with regards to IPTV service delivery. In §5 we evaluate the performance of our algorithm to the aforementioned admission control algorithms and show that our empirical approach to estimation of effective bandwidth supplies the admission control algorithm with adequate information to make well informed decisions on whether to admit additional services to the admitted aggregate traffic or not. §6 draws conclusions and outlines areas for future work.

2 Background and Related Work

Effective bandwidth is defined as the minimum amount of bandwidth required by a traffic stream to maintain specified QoS related targets [1]. There are many methods of theoretically estimating this value for different traffic models, see for example [1, 2, 3]. These approaches depend on statistical representation of traffic sources, and use limited constraints on traffic properties such as constant packet size and inter arrival times. As this is an unrealistic representation of real traffic, we adopt an empirical approach based on packet trace analysis that is similar to those outlined in [7, 8]. We believe empirical estimation of effective bandwidth can improve accuracy and thus improve admission control decisions over admission control algorithms dependent on theoretical estimation.

Admission control approaches can be broadly divided into two groups, namely: parameter based admission control, and measurement based admission control. Parameter based admission control (PBAC) [4] is based on the assumption that *a priori* knowledge of the bandwidth requirements of each traffic source. This technique also requires exact knowledge of currently admitted requests and current available bandwidth. PBAC describes service requests via sets of traffic descriptors; a disadvantage of this approach is that *a priori* knowledge of the service request can not always be established (for example, often only the peak or mean rate of the service is known).

Measurement based admission control (MBAC) [9] is an approach where the admission control scheme makes decisions based on measurements taken in real time from the network. The approach attempts to learn the characteristics and requirements of flows admitted and bases future decisions on this knowledge. The advantage of this approach is that estimation of required effective bandwidth from aggregate flows can be predicted with greater accuracy, and no a priori knowledge of service requests is required. In general measurements such as mean throughput and variance of traffic aggregate are collected and used as input to analytic techniques for estimating effective bandwidth. The major disadvantage of this technique is that it is susceptible to measurement inaccuracies that lead to inaccurate traffic predictions.

Hybrid approaches have been developed to address the problems highlighted with PBAC and MBAC approaches. Examples include Experience Based Admission Control (EBAC) [5] and Measurement Based and *a priori* Traffic Descriptor Admission Control (MTAC) [6]. These hybrid techniques use both measurements taken from the network and knowledge of submitted traffic descriptors to predict future bandwidth requirements of services. The algorithm we propose can also be considered as a hybrid approach: we directly estimate effective bandwidth from available traces (without use of complex traffic models), and use these estimates in conjunction with peak rate values (a traffic descriptor) in the admission decision process. For evaluation purposes we evaluate our algorithm against the MTAC and EBAC algorithms.

3 Admission Control Framework

Our admission control framework uses an approach to estimating the effective bandwidth of traffic by analysis of collected packet traces. A set of directly measured effective bandwidth levels are taken for the admitted aggregate traffic over a number of time intervals. Based on this collection we predict the required effective bandwidth for the following interval. Admission of a new service request is based on the addition of the predicted effective bandwidth and the peak throughput of the service request taken from the supplied traffic descriptor.

3.1 Empirical Estimation of Effective Bandwidth

Effective bandwidth can be defined for different types of QoS targets; for example: delay targets, loss targets, or both delay and loss targets combined. Our effective bandwidth estimation process (introduced in [10]) can be applied to all types of QoS targets; however in this paper we address delay targets only. A delay target specifies both the nominal maximum delay experienced on the network and the proportion of traffic that is allowed exceed this maximum delay. A typical example of a QoS delay target is (50ms, 0.001) which means that only 0.1% of traffic is allowed to be delayed by more than 50ms. As effective bandwidth depends on the QoS target, for different QoS targets the effective bandwidth will vary.

Our effective bandwidth estimation algorithm is defined as follows. Let $delay_{max}$ be the nominal maximum delay and let p_{delay} be the percentage of traffic which can exhibit delay greater than $delay_{max}$. We define effective bandwidth R_{eff} of a traffic source for delay QoS target $(delay_{max}, p_{delay})$ as the minimal rate R such that if we simulate a FIFO queue with unlimited buffer and processing rate R, the percentage of traffic which will exhibit delay greater than $delay_{max}$ will be less than p_{delay}. To estimate the effective bandwidth of a particular traffic source on the network, we take a recorded packet trace of that source. We observe that if we simulate a FIFO queue (initially assumed to be empty) with the same inputted traffic trace for different queue rates $R_1 > R_2$ and estimate the percentages p_1 and p_2 of traffic delayed more than $delay_{max}$ for different rates respectively, then $p_1 \leq p_2$. This means that the percentage of traffic, p, delayed more than $delay_{max}$ is a monotonically decreasing function of processing rate R. Using this observation it is straight forward to design, for example, a simple bisection algorithm for a recorded packet trace to find the minimal value of a queue rate such that the percentage of traffic delayed more than $delay_{max}$ is less than p_{delay}. We use this process to estimate the effective bandwidth R_{eff} of a collected trace, assuming all traffic within the trace is of the same traffic class, with a common QoS delay target. Note that we assume that all IPTV traffic for a given service provider will be subject to the same QoS targets and will therefore be assigned to the same traffic class.

3.2 Admission Control Logic

We assume that through provisioning and traffic engineering, C_{total} bandwidth is available edge-to-edge for the traffic aggregate. When a new flow f_{new} arrives it requests for a peak rate R_{fnew}. If (1) holds, admission is granted to f_{new}, otherwise the flow is rejected (2).

$$If \left(R_{f_{new}} + R_{eff\,predict} \right) \leq C_{total}, accept \tag{1}$$

$$If \left(R_{f_{new}} + R_{eff\,predict} \right) > C_{total}, reject \tag{2}$$

The algorithm adds the requested flow peak rate to the predicted effective bandwidth of the already admitted traffic to establish if there is adequate bandwidth available for the service, while guaranteeing QoS targets on admitted traffic are maintained. The process of predicting the required effective bandwidth $R_{eff\,predict}$ for the interval is as follows. Using the empirical effective bandwidth estimation algorithm and specified QoS target on packet delay, recorded packet traces are processed to find the adequate FIFO queue service rate that satisfies the QoS targets. The measured service rate or effective bandwidth R_{eff} is recorded for a number of N intervals within a set $\{R_{eff}\}$, where $N = \#\{R_{eff}\}$. From this set, the algorithm will choose the worst case effective bandwidth measurement to ensure a conservative prediction for the next interval.

$$R_{eff\,predict} = MAX\{R_{eff}\} \tag{3}$$

The decision on taking the worst effective bandwidth estimate out of N estimated values is to ensure the algorithm operates conservatively. Alternative approaches could be employed to predict an appropriate effective bandwidth value, such as using a simple moving average, exponentially weighted moving average, or a time exponentially weighted moving average [11]. All these approaches can lead the algorithm to be less conservative, although the memory of the latter two approaches can be configured to lead to more conservative behaviour.

3.3 Experience Based Admission Control Algorithm

We compare the performance of our admission control algorithm to that of the Experience Based Admission Control (EBAC) [5]. EBAC operates by taking into consideration a measured peak to mean ratio of previous admitted traffic. Based on a collection of these measurements, the algorithm chooses an appropriate up to date reciprocal of this ratio $\varphi(t)$, known as the over provisioning factor, suitable for inclusion in its admission control logic. The peak measurements used within the algorithm are explicit peak rate traffic descriptors supplied by the service request.

To take QoS into consideration, the algorithm uses a limited approach of representing traffic as a maximum link utilisation threshold ρ_{max}. This threshold is calculated using a well known queuing system method of estimating effective bandwidth [3] of traffic with constant packet size, and constant inter arrival times. Taking these considerations into account, the admission control algorithm is as follows. If

$$r_{f_{new}} + \sum_{f \in F(t)} r_f \le c_l \cdot \varphi(t) \cdot \rho_{max} \tag{4}$$

holds, admission is granted and f_{new} joins $F(t)$. r_f represents the peak rate of the newly arrived flow f_{new}. $F(t)$ are the set of all admitted flows at time t. c_l is the limit capacity or the maximum provisioned bandwidth. The algorithm gains experience by using a complex approach to estimating the current over provisioning factor. Previous peak to mean ratios are calculated and stored in a time exponentially weighted moving histogram. By choosing the 95th percentile of this histogram, the most up to date over provisioning factor can be calculated.

3.4 Measurement and Traffic Descriptor-Based Admission Control

We also compare the performance of our proposed algorithm to that of the MTAC algorithm [6]. MTAC estimates the required effective bandwidth of traffic based on the assumption that traffic arriving at the admission point follows Gaussian characteristics. Equation (5) defines a method of estimating the required effective bandwidth of the currently admitted traffic, where m is the mean aggregate bit rate, σ

is the standard deviation of the aggregate bit rate and ε is the upper bound on allowed queue overflow probability.

$$C = m + a'\sigma \quad \text{with} \quad a' = \sqrt{-2\ln(\varepsilon) - \ln(2\pi)} \tag{5}$$

The algorithm also specifies a precaution factor used to ensure the algorithm behaves more conservatively as the network approaches congestion; this factor is calculated as follows. A single reference flow is defined by a reference mean m_{ref} and reference standard deviation σ_{ref}. For the total link capacity C_{total}, the total number of reference flows T_{ref} that can be simultaneously admitted for a given target bound on ε (the Packet Loss Ratio), is calculated. Using mean and standard deviation measurements collected, the total number of reference flows N_{ref} within the admitted traffic is calculated. The precaution factor defines the relationship between estimated number of reference flows N_{ref} within the measured traffic, and the total number of reference flows T_{ref} allowed within the total link capacity C_{total}. In [8] the precaution factor also takes into consideration traffic with different QoS requirements than the reference flow; however, as all traffic within our scenario has common QoS requirements, we use a simplified precaution factor formula.

$$PF = \left(N_{ref} / T_{ref} \right) \tag{6}$$

Admission is simply based on whether the estimated bandwidth multiplied by the precaution factor is less than the total available bandwidth; if not, the flow is rejected.

$$\begin{aligned} &\text{If } \left(C_{est} \times PF \right) \leq C_{total}, \quad admit \\ &\text{If } \left(C_{est} \times PF \right) > C_{total}, \quad reject \end{aligned} \tag{7}$$

3.5 Parameter Based Admission Control

As a comparison to the worst case scenario, we model a PBAC [4] algorithm. The algorithms decision depends completely on the peak rate of services, supplied by the traffic descriptor. No measurement is involved in this process. On receiving a service request, the algorithm decides on admission if the following holds:

$$r_{f_{new}} + \sum_{f \in F(t)} r_f \leq c_l \tag{8}$$

r_f is the peak rate of a requesting flow. $F(t)$ holds a set of all admitted flows. The algorithm tests whether the sum of all admitted flows plus the new requesting flow, is less than the level of reservable bandwidth c_l.

3.6 Ideal Admission Control

We additionally model an ideal admission control algorithm having complete access to network measurements and precise knowledge of traffic descriptors. On receiving a service request the ideal admission control is able to predict exactly the required resources of the aggregate if the service was admitted; using this knowledge it can decide whether admission is possible or not.

4 IPTV Service Delivery Scenario

The scenario we use to evaluate our admission control algorithm is IPTV, which is defined as delivery of television related services over an IP network. We first discuss the relationships between business entities in the delivery of IPTV services. From the admission control perspective, the entities we are interested in are the customer, the service provider and the network operator. There have been a number of projects that have proposed business related scenarios [12, 13, 14] for delivery of video-on-demand service over QoS enabled IP networks. Within these projects, the concept of wholesale bandwidth is used to describe the arrangement where the service provider leases QoS guaranteed bandwidth from the network operator, as governed by an agreed Service Level Agreement (SLA). In turn, the service provider delivers QoS guaranteed services to its subscribed customers, as governed by a service provider to customer Service Level Agreement (constrained by the limits of its own agreement with the network provider). Failure to meet these SLA targets usually results in loss of revenue through discounting. We define packet level QoS targets related to these agreements within our IPTV scenario and focus on how the service provider ensures its customers receive guaranteed QoS on traffic in line with outlined SLAs.

The service provider has a maximum amount of bandwidth available at its disposal. We assume that within this limit, traffic will be guaranteed QoS on packet delay as specified by the service provider to network operator SLA. For our scenario the service provider leases bandwidth from the network operator assuming that at peak times, 20% of its customer base will be using offered services, in particular unicast video-on-demand. As delivery of this service can consume a large quantity of bandwidth, if the assumed peak in service access is exceeded without adequate management of bandwidth access there will be degradation in QoS experienced by *all* customers, resulting in significant revenue loss. In times of increasing network load, routers employ techniques such as Random Early Detection (RED), or Weighted Random Early Detection (WRED), which, when throughput reaches a particular threshold within a traffic class, drop packets randomly to avoid congestion. Packets are dropped randomly within the traffic aggregate; therefore, since users are not distinguished between within the traffic aggregate, all users' flows will experience degraded QoS. This potential problem is particularly relevant for IPTV, given the relatively strict QoS targets – for example, a packet loss ratio of 1×10^{-7} is specified by the DSL Forum [15]. The service provider therefore employs an admission control strategy to curb these losses, and maximise resource utilisation.

4.1 Simulation Model

Fig. 1 depicts a service provider, a network operator and a number of connected customers. Each customer is connected to the network through xDSL with a downstream maximum throughput of 24Mbps. The service provider has a single point of connection to the network, through which all service traffic is aggregated. It is at this ingress point that the effective bandwidth of aggregated traffic is measured, and the service provider performs admission control on service requests. All traffic measurement is also performed at this point and we assume that the required network dimensioning and traffic engineering has been performed by the network operator to

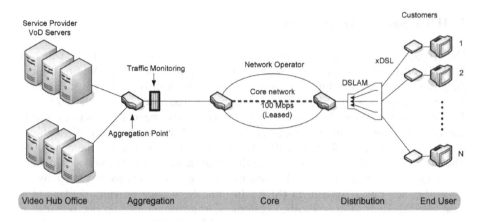

Fig. 1. IPTV Service Delivery Scenario

ensure that traffic within the service providers leased bandwidth capacity will be delivered within agreed SLAs. The service provider leases 100 Mbps of bandwidth from the network operator. The service provider wishes to perform admission control on bandwidth up to 90% of this link to ensure there is a 10% margin of precautionary bandwidth available. To ensure all video traffic is treated with common QoS targets, they are aggregated into common traffic classes (we assume the DiffServ Code Point is used for this purpose).

We use a number of the video frame traces available at [16]. These traces are imported into OPNET™ and streamed across our simulated topology. These frame traces have been generated from several video sequences of typically 60 minutes length each. For the measurement of peak throughput per video, we use a precision of 0.05 seconds as this is approximately within the range of the QoS delay targets being imposed on the traffic. If larger precision were to be used, an inaccurate value may be calculated per flow, losing appropriate precision. For more information regarding the traces used, please refer to [17]. Table 1 shows the content (films) available for the customer to select from. A new service request (to view a film) is selected every 300 seconds, with each film having an equal probability of selection.

5   Experimental Evaluation

We argue that by using our approach for empirical estimation of effective bandwidth, our admission control algorithm does not require the use of complex over booking or precaution factors. The following experiments intend to evaluate our algorithm's performance with regard to QoS target violations and bandwidth utilisation in comparison to the PBAC, EBAC and MTAC and ideal admission control algorithms.

5.1   Scenario Settings

Films are chosen at random from the set of films offered by the service provider to its customers. Each film has a common Quality of Service target on packet delay of

(0.01s, 0.0001) which outlines that only 0.0001 proportion of total traffic sent can be delayed by 10 ms or more. We look at the affect the admission control algorithms have on both traffic violations and bandwidth utilisation as service requests are submitted and accepted/rejected. For EBAC we need to set an appropriate maximum link utilisation threshold: in [3] the authors suggest setting a conservative and constant threshold value of 0.95, which ensures that during congestion a maximum utilisation of 95% of the link is used. MTAC controls QoS through a Packet Loss Ratio (PLR) parameter; we specify a PLR of 0.0001, which matches our QoS target.

5.2 Experimental Evaluation of Admission Control Algorithms

Fig. 2 demonstrates the ratio between predicted required bandwidth and mean throughput for EAC in comparison to the MTAC, EBAC and PBAC algorithms. The relationship depicts how each algorithm reacts to the addition of multiple admitted flows. As flows are admitted, the empirical estimation diverges from a ratio of ~12 for one admitted, to 2 from multiple flows greater then 10. On the other hand, the EBAC estimation demonstrates a linear relationship as flows increase, as does the PBAC. This will results in under estimation of required bandwidth for smaller numbers of admitted flows, and in the case of PBAC, over estimation for higher numbers of flows. The MTAC algorithm actually increases demand requirements in proportion to measured mean, this is a result of the precaution factor that enables the algorithm to be more conservative as it approaches congestion.

Fig. 3 depicts the predicted effective bandwidth requirements for each admission control algorithm upon which it bases its admission decisions. Each vertical line within the graph represents a new service request arrival every 300 seconds. Table 2 shows the mean bandwidth utilisation and number of admitted flows, once AC algorithms reach their rejection threshold. We analyse the performance of each admission control algorithm through inspection of the results in Fig. 3 and Table 2:

- The Ideal admission control algorithm shows us that a maximum of 21 service requests can be admitted with a bandwidth utilisation of 47.99 Mbps, without experiencing QoS violations. It reaches its rejection threshold at 6000s.
- PBAC algorithm reaches its rejection threshold first, since the summation of peak service rates reach 90Mbps relatively quick (1800s). The algorithm results in a maximum bandwidth utilisation of 12.4 Mbps and 6 admitted service requests in total. This has a relative error of 74% in comparison to the ideal. Whilst there are no QoS violations there is an unacceptable under utilisation of bandwidth.

Table 1. Characteristics of Video Traces

Film	Peak Throughput (Mbps)
Jurassic Park	19.47
Mr Bean	18.23
First Contact	12.60
From Dusk till Dawn	18.96
The Firm	11.48
Die Hard III	21.97
Aladdin	21.27

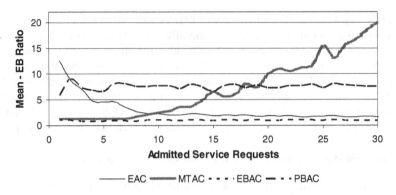

Fig. 2. Mean / estimated effective bandwidth ratios for aggregate traffic

- MTAC reaches its rejection threshold next, since the precaution factor bares an impact on predicted bandwidth requirements at 3000s. Once the request at this point is accepted, the algorithm begins to become conservative allowing 12 service requests to be admitted. It too under utilises bandwidth at an average bandwidth utilisation of 22.67 Mbps and error relative to the ideal of 52%.
- EAC allows more services than MTAC to be admitted before reaching its rejection threshold at 4800s, whilst remaining free of any QoS violations on packet delay. This leads to a higher utilisation of bandwidth of 38.75 Mbps and error relative to the ideal of ~20%, whilst still remaining relatively conservative with regards to QoS violations.

We note from Table 2 that the EBAC demonstrates the highest bandwidth utilisation of 77.33 Mbps, however as we see in Fig. 4 this is at a cost of incurring heavy QoS violations on traffic. EBAC, for our analysis scenario, is the only admission control algorithm that experiences QoS violations. Indeed, it performs the same as if no admission control algorithm was used. As the goal of the service

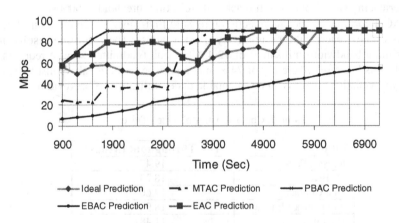

Fig. 3. Predicted required bandwidth for each admission control algorithm

Table 2. Accepted Admissions for each Algorithm

	Accepted Service Requests	Bandwidth Utilisation
Ideal Admission	21	47.99Mbps
EAC Admission	15	38.75Mbps
MTAC Admission	12	22.67Mbps
PBAC Admission	6	12.40Mbps
EBAC Admission	30	73.33Mbps
No Admission Control	30	73.33Mbps

provider is to maximise bandwidth utilisation while maintaining QoS targets, this algorithm falls considerably short in this scenario. QoS for this algorithm is controlled by the maximum bandwidth utilisation factor; the results here demonstrate that the value of 0.95 (as used for this simulation) is not sufficently conservative in relation to our QoS targets. If this algorithm were to take advantage of our proposed empirical approach to estimating effective bandwidth, we can see that the maximum link utilisation is 47.99 Mbps of the 90 Mbps (ideal AC), which in turn would set the threshold value to 0.53, significantly less than the proposed value of 0.95.

Based on these results we conclude that the EAC algorithm is most successful in addressing the service provider's goal of maximising bandwidth utilisation whilst minimising QoS violations. Table 2 indicates that our algorithm is quite close in performance to the ideal admission control solution: the difference in admissions averages approximately 20%, which we believe is a reasonable degree of error. One significant advantage is that the algorithm is conservative in its predictions, so in times of congestion, the algorithm will not under provision services.

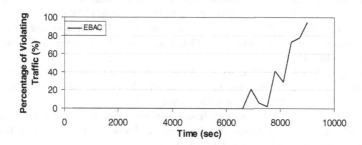

Fig. 4. QoS Violations after Admission Control for EBAC Algorithm

6   Conclusions

We have presented an admission control algorithm based on prediction of resources requirements using empirical estimation of effective bandwidth. We evaluated the algorithm through the use of an IPTV scenario with appropriate QoS targets on packet delay. IPTV was chosen as the basis of our study since the growing popularity of high bandwidth services like IPTV, which have strict QoS targets on packet loss and in turn delay, mean that effective QoS provisioning becomes ever more critical.

Preliminary results demonstrate that our algorithm, EAC, is relatively accurate in predicting required effective bandwidth for admission control. It tends to be conservative in that it over estimates predicted effective bandwidth for the new aggregate in comparison to the ideal. We have also demonstrated our algorithm performs conservatively in comparison to the EBAC estimation algorithm, but EBAC incurs QoS violations due to underestimation of the required effective bandwidth on aggregate traffic. On the other hand, in comparison to a strict PBAC and MTAC, EAC utilises bandwidth more efficiently while remaining QoS violation free.

It is important that an admission control algorithm can react to varying degrees of QoS targets imposed on traffic. In future work we plan to evaluate the proposed algorithm with respect to varying QoS targets. We also wish to extent the algorithm with respect to IPTV services, by enhancing the decision process to incorporate IPTV related service information such as cost and duration of film content.

Acknowledgements

This work has received support from Science Foundation Ireland via the Autonomic Management of Communications Networks and Services programme (grant no. 04/IN3/I4040C) and the 2005 Research Frontiers project Accounting for Dynamically Composed Services (grant no. CMS006).

References

1. Kelly, F.: Notes on Effective Bandwidth, in Stochastic Networks: Theory and Application. In: Kelly, F.P., Zachary, S., Ziedins, I.B. (eds.) Royal Statistical Society Lecture Notes Series, vol. 4, pp. 141–168. Oxford University Press, Oxford (1996)
2. Norros, I., Roberts, J.W., Simonian, A., Virtamo, J.T.: The superposition of variable bit rate sources in an ATM multiplexer. IEEE Journal on Selected Areas in Communications 9(3), 378–387 (1991)
3. Roberts, J., Mocci, U., Vritamo, J.: Broadband Network Teletraffic – Final report of Action COST 242. In: Roberts, J., Virtamo, J.T., Mocci, U. (eds.) Broadband Network Traffic. LNCS, vol. 1155, Springer, Heidelberg (1996)
4. Fidler, M., Sander, V.: A Parameter Based Admission Control for Differentiated Services Networks. Computer Networks: The International Journal of Computer and Telecommunication Networking 44(4), 463–479 (2004)
5. Milbrandt, J., Menth, M., Junker, J.: Experience-Based Admission Control in the Presence of Traffic Changes. Academic Publisher, Journal of Communications 2(1), 1796–2021 (2007)
6. Georgoulas, S., Trimintzios, P., Pavlou, G.: Joint Measurement- and Traffic Descriptor-based Admisión Control at Real-Time Traffic Aggregation Points. In: ICC 2004. IEEE International Conference on Communications, vol. 4, pp. 1841–1845. IEEE Computer Society Press, Los Alamitos (2004)
7. Botvich, D.D., Duffield, N.: Large deviations, the shape of the loss curve, and economies of scale in large multiplexers. Queueing Systems 20, 293–320 (1995)
8. Baras, J.S., Liu, N.X.: Measurement and simulation based effective bandwidth estimation. IEEE Global Telecommunications Conference GLOBECOM 2004 4, 2108–2112 (2004)

9. Lima, S.R., Carvalho, P., Freitas, V.: Distribution Admission Control for QoS and SLS Management. Journal of Network and Systems, Special Issue on Distributed Management 12(3), 397–426 (2004)

10. Davy, A., Botvich, D.D., Jennings, B.: On The Use of Accounting Data for QoS-Aware IP Network Planning. In: Mason, L., Drwiega, T. (eds.) ITC-20. LNCS, vol. 4516-0348, pp. 348–360. Springer, Heidelberg (2007)

11. Martin, R., Menth, M.: Improving the Timeless of Rate Measurements. In: PGTS. Proc of GI/ITG Conference on Measuring, Modelling and Evaluation of Computer and Communication Systems, pp. 145–154, ISBN 3-8007-2851-6, VDE Verlag (September 2004)

12. NetQoS, Policy Based Management of Heterogeneous Networks for Guaranteed QoS, Specific Targeted Research Project (STREP) from the 5th call of IST FP6 framework (June 18, 2007), last accessed www.netqos.eu

13. EuQoS, End-to-end Quality of Service support over heterogeneous networks, site last accessed (June 18, 2007), www.euqos.eu

14. MUSE, Multi Service Access Everywhere, IST 6th Framework Programme, site last accessed (June 18, 2007), www.ist-muse.org

15. DSL-Forum, Triple-play Services Quality of Experience (QoE) Requirements, Technical Report TR-126, Architecture & Transport Working Group, Rahrer, T., Faindra, R., Wright, S. (eds.) (December 2006)

16. Telecommunications Networks Group, Technical University of Berlin, MPEG-4 and H.263 Video Traces for Network Performance Evaluation, site last accessed (June 18, 2007), www.tkn.tu-berlin.de/research/trace/trace.html

17. Fitzek, F.H.P., Reisslein, M.: MPEG-4 and H.263 Video Traces for Network Performance Evaluation (Extended Version). TU Berlin, Dept. of Engineering, Telecommunication Networks Group, Technical Report: TKN-00-06, (October 2000)

Using Context Information for Tailoring Multimedia Services to User's Resources

José M. Oliveira[1] and Eurico M. Carrapatoso[2]

[1] INESC Porto, Faculdade de Economia, Universidade do Porto,
[2] INESC Porto, Faculdade de Engenharia, Universidade do Porto,
rua Dr. Roberto Frias, 378, 4200-465 Porto, Portugal
{jmo,emc}@inescporto.pt

Abstract. The integration of multiple network access technologies in the terminal is one of the most important trends in 4G networks. This integration places telecommunications service providers, and in particular operators, under the significant challenge of being able to transform their services in order to adapt them to a great variety of delivery contexts. This paper describes a generic methodology for the adaptation of telecommunications services provided in the context of an operator. A number of scenarios are examined which show how Parlay middleware can be used by trusted service providers to easily access network resources and context information for enhancing location-based and adaptable multimedia telecommunications services.

Keywords: Seamless Service Provisioning, Parlay Middleware, Context Gathering, Multimedia Adaptation.

1 Introduction

In the recent years, telecommunications have evolved to a new and highly competitive environment, especially for communications service providers. Factors such as the convergence between fixed and mobile networks, between broadcast and communications, and between mobile and Internet led to the need of seamless service provision across different types of networks and totally independent of terminal technologies. This independence requirement gains particular importance in the provision of next generation services, characterized not only by location based features, but also by context-aware features, multimedia contents and user mobility. The acceptability of new services will only be effective if the user has the possibility to access them anywhere, in any technological circumstances, even in roaming scenarios. This user requirement places multimedia service providers under the significant challenge of being able to transform their services in order to adapt them to a great variety of delivery contexts.

This paper presents a generic adaptation methodology suitable to adapt telecommunications services to different access mechanisms and connectivity capabilities. The adaptation methodology, introduced in the following section, is based mainly on two fundamental constructions: the *Multimedia Presentation*

D. Krishnaswamy, T. Pfeifer, and D. Raz (Eds.): MMNS 2007, LNCS 4787, pp. 138–148, 2007.
© IFIP International Federation for Information Processing 2007

Model (*MModel*) and *media adapters*. The former enables a device independent specification of the user interface, including the modelization of time-based features. *Media adapters* basically enable the materialization of the user interface specification in the most suitable format for a particular user context.

The integration of context information in telecommunications services and the development of context-sensitive applications have grown enormously in the present decade, mainly due to the increase mobility of users and to the research activities on ubiquitous and pervasive computing. We follow the approach of directly accessing user context information managed by network operators, using the open middleware offered by Parlay. Parlay APIs and Web services are designed to enable the creation of telecommunications applications outside the traditional network space and business model. Network operators consider Parlay a promising architecture to stimulate the development of Web service applications by third party providers, which may not necessarily be experts in telecommunications. This approach is currently promoted in the telecommunications field, namely by the 3GPP IP Multimedia Subsystem (IMS) standardization effort [1].

To explore the advantages of the adaptation methodology to produce multimedia services adapted to the user context, the paper presents in Section 3 a *media adapter* targeted to the SMIL language. In Section 4 we evaluate the proposed adaptation methodology using a case study service. We detail in several scenarios how this service uses the Parlay middleware to easily access network resources and information. In Section 5 we compare our approach for the dynamic adaptation of multimedia services with some related work. The paper finalizes reporting the main conclusions in Section 6.

2   A Methodology for the Adaptation of Telecommunications Services

The adaptation methodology presented in this section is based on the *MModel*, an abstract construction that holds an XML description of the user interface, including the complete list of available user interactions [2]. The objective is to create a mediator (the *Adaptation System*), between the service and the user, to manage all user interactions with the service. According to the actual service session parameters, the conversion of the *MModel* to a specific format and the adaptation of service contents to the right media type is achieved through specific implementations of the *media adapter* entity.

Fig. 1 places the *Adaptation System* into the IMS layer architecture. The *Adaptation System* and the Parlay Gateway, both positioned in the middleware layer, help applications, seen in this context as telecommunications services, to abstract from the below network infrastructure, which can involve completely different access technologies, such as WLAN, UMTS or circuit-switched networks. During the service adaptation process, the *Adaptation System* interacts with the Parlay Gateway, taking advantage of the functionalities offered by the Parlay APIs and Web services, as will be described later in Section 4.

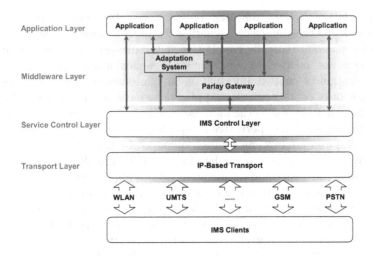

Fig. 1. IMS layer architecture

Each *Adaptation Session* is composed by two objects: the *MModel*, which can be seen as the representation of a service on the *adaptation system* side; and the *Interpreter*, which can be seen as a mediator between the *Media Adapter* and the *Service Listener*.

The user, after accessing his service provider, interacts with the portal application and chooses to use a service that he has previously subscribed. This interaction is transmitted to the *Portal Listener*, which triggers the creation of a new service session manager on the *adaptation system* side. This service session manager communicates with the service provider that offers the chosen service so that a service session manager on the service provider side and the associated listener can be also created (see Fig. 2).

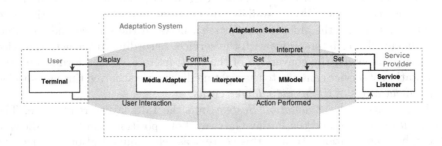

Fig. 2. Service adaptation cycle

The *Service Listener* is responsible for filling the *MModel* object with the user interface specification. This specification is usually divided into several parts, corresponding to the several views of the user interface. With the *MModel* set on the *adaptation system*, the service adaptation process starts, following a cycle approach (see Fig. 2). In each step, the adaptation is only carried out over one of the *MModel* parts. For that, the *Service Listener* sets the focus on the *MModel* part that should be adapted before it requests the Interpreter to interpret this part.

When the user receives a new interface in the terminal device, he has the opportunity to interact with it, leading the service to evolve to a new state. Each user interaction is characterized by the possible inputs introduced by the user and the order to go to a new state, typically represented by the reference of the interaction element. The *Interpreter* is the object that communicates the interaction description to the *Service Listener*. Using a parser, the *Service Listener* decodes the interaction and routes it to the right method of the service logic, which will process it and trigger the appropriate internal actions to answer the user interaction. Independently of the service, these changes in the service state will lead to an update of the *MModel* object, integrating the changes in the service state. The *Service Listener* sends a new user interface specification to the *MModel* and set the focus on the *MModel* part that it wants to be active.

3   The SMIL Adapter

This section presents a *media adapter* prototype specifically designed to enable the introduction of multimedia contents and to support time-based features in telecommunications services [3]. The objective was to specify and develop a *media adapter* that should produce a final form user interface from an input interface specification defined using the *MModel* format. In what concerns the output format, the *media adapter* should produce information in an interactive multimedia format, targeted to the Web. We chose SMIL, a language defined by the World Wide Web consortium (W3C), which enables the specification of multimedia presentations for delivery over the Web [4]. The choice of SMIL had the additional advantage of allow an easy mapping with the *MModel* due to its XML-based structure.

The adaptation methodology proposed by us prescribes the definition of the user interface structure as the initial point of the adaptation process, corresponding to the instantiation of the *MModel* object. Then, the interface structure is maintained stable during the different methodology phases, having no influence on the dynamic change of the user interface during the service session lifetime. External factors, such as the device characteristics, the network bandwidth conditions or the user available time, have a much more active role in the user interface dynamic generation. Since in mobile computing, the user context information is very dynamic by nature, the capability to dynamically detect this information at the beginning of each adaptation cycle is decisive to achieve acceptable results with the adaptation methodology.

3.1   Gathering the User Context

The *SMIL Media Adapter* follows the approach of using the Parlay middleware to obtain user context related information directly from the network [5]. The Parlay

Application Programming Interfaces (APIs) are a standardization effort carried out by the Parlay Group since 1998. These APIs enable application developers to access telecom network capabilities through an open interface. The final objective is to open up the network resources to trusted parties, such as service developers, content providers and service aggregators. The Parlay Group started in 2000 an update of their APIs to become Web services, with the intention of migrating to the all-IP convergence approach started at that time.

The appropriate Parlay APIs and Web services for obtaining the desired context information are: the *Terminal Capabilities API*, wich enables an application to synchronously retrieve the terminal capabilities of a specific terminal, as a CC/PP profile [6]; the *Terminal Status and Location Web Services*, which provide terminal status and location services, allowing applications to obtain the geographical location and the status (e.g., reachable or busy) of fixed, mobile and IP based telephony users; the *Connectivity Manager API*, which allows applications to constantly and efficiently obtain QoS monitoring information concerning the network conditions of user connections to service providers (restricted to an enterprise scale); and the *Presence Web Service*, which offers a synchronous and an asynchronous approach for obtaining presence and availability information.

3.2   SMIL Generation Process

The *SMIL Media Adapter* uses the XSL Transformations (XSLT) [7] of the Extensible Stylesheet Language (XSL), which is a language specified by the W3C consortium for defining XML documents transformations and presentations. XSLT allows the specification, in a standardized way, of functional transformations from one XML tree to another, which are specified in a document usually known as a style sheet. The *SMIL Media Adapter* defines one such style sheet, which establishes the transformation rules from the *MModel* XML tree to the SMIL XML tree. The use of a relatively simple approach for transforming the *MModel* specification into a concrete delivery format using a XSLT transformation is driven by the guarantee that the calculations for the visual layout and timing of the media items produces an interface *MModel* tree that is known to meet the current user context, as will be detailed later in this section.

Currently, most of the time-based formats are presentation formats. The SMIL was built as a Web presentation language, which supports hyperlinks to different parts of the presentation or to any external destination URI [8]. A drawback of the SMIL language is the lack of support for input processing (usually designated as forms processing in the Web world). The SMIL linking elements are not a suitable choice to manage user interactions over a SMIL interface, since they are interpreted directly by the SMIL player, at the client side, being completely hidden from the service provider, which is not desirable in a service provision context. The intrinsic lack of support for forms processing should not be seen as a real drawback of the SMIL language, since currently the focus of W3C specifications is to separate the forms processing from specific languages, creating a standardizing way of treating them. This standardization effort is materialized into the XForms standard [9], which may be considered as an autonomous module that contains forms semantic-related XML elements and attributes and should be integrated in different XML based languages, such as SMIL, extending these languages.

The *SMIL Media Adapter* internally uses the constraints theory to establish dependencies between user interface variables according to the user context information gathered. The main idea behind the constraint-based approach for the automatic generation of multimedia presentations is to use a constraint solver system to determine one (preferably the best) solution for a set of variables that are interrelated by constraints.

The constraint solver system chosen to be used in the context of the *SMIL Media Adapter* was the ECL^{i}PS^e constraint logic programming system [10], which not only offers a Java interface, but also the possibility to define application dependent constraints, which is a very useful feature for multimedia applications, where the relations between the different interveners cannot be easily specified using typical numerical domains constraints. In addiction, ECL^{i}PS^e supports the backtracking and unification features of logic programming, combining them with the domain reduction properties of constraint programming, resulting in what is usually called a Constraint Logic Programming (CLP) system. The use of the backtracking mechanism gives a dynamic characteristic to the specification of constraints. Alternative constraints can be specified when an initial constraint causes a failure, preventing the application from crashing or not providing any information.

The communication between the ECL^{i}PS^e system and the *SMIL Media Adapter* is made through a queue mechanism provided by the ECL^{i}PS^e/Java interface (see Fig. 3). Two information queues are defined (`ToEclipseQueue` and `FromEclipseQueue`), which allow the *SMIL Media Adapter* to respectively send to and retrieve information from the ECL^{i}PS^e.

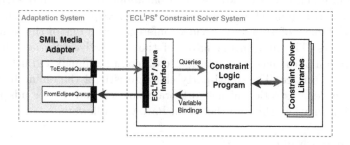

Fig. 3. Communication with the constraints solver system

When the internal ECL^{i}PS^e Constraint Solver Libraries find a solution for the constraint problem, the *SMIL Media Adapter* extracts it and updates the *MModel* focused part, namely with the spatial and temporal values found for each media item.

4   Parlay Middleware Usage Scenarios

As a proof of the concept we have implemented a prototype service with the objective of evaluating the most relevant research aspects proposed in this paper. An overview of the *Customer Care* service in presented in Fig. 4, which clearly shows one of the characteristics that is addressed by this service: the service ubiquitous access in terms of terminals and networks.

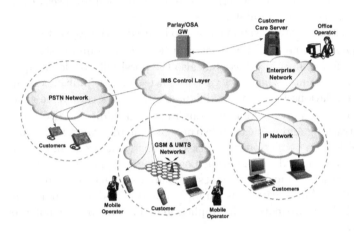

Fig. 4. Overview of the *Customer Care* service

The *Customer Care* service suitability for evaluating the use of telecommunications middleware in the service adaptation to the user context is directly related with the two features provided by the service: *interactive tutorials*, where the user interactively accesses information about products and services of a given supplier, organized as tutorials; and *online help*, where the user requests the establishment of an audio or videoconference with one of the available online operators. The multimedia flavor of the interactive tutorials enables the demonstration of the media adaptation to different terminals and networks used to access the service. The multi-party characteristic of the online help feature enables the demonstration of network transparency and service adaptation to location information, through the use of Parlay middleware.

4.1   Call Establishment Scenario

This scenario happens when a user requests online help from the *Customer Care* service. Initially, the service uses the Parlay Terminal Status Web service to determine the reachable online operators (see Fig. 5). Then, using the Terminal Location Web service, the *Customer Care* service determines the nearest available operator and send him an SMS, using the SMS Web service, notifying him of the user request.

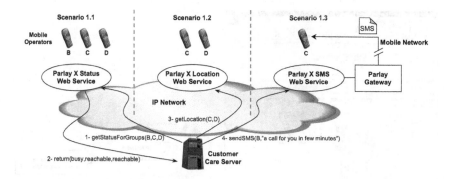

Fig. 5. Parlay terminal status(a), terminal location(b) and SMS(c) Web services usage

In the end of the scenario, the service transparently establishes a call between the user and the operator, using the Third Party Call Web service (see Fig. 6). The choice of calling the nearest available operator enables the reduction of the connection cost, which is an advantage for the user.

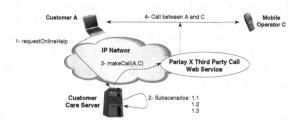

Fig. 6. Parlay third party call Web service usage

4.2   Multimedia Adaptation Scenario

This scenario happens when the user requests to access a product tutorial. The service initially uses the Parlay Terminal Capabilities API for obtaining the terminal characteristics, such as the screen dimensions and the audio capabilities (see Fig. 7). With this information, the *Customer Care* service adapts the SMIL product tutorial accordingly.

When the terminal is a laptop, the produced presentation has the spatial layout displayed in Fig. 7. In this case, no adaptation was performed, since the amount of text and the picture dimensions were all appropriate to fit in the screen dimensions. A different situation occurred when the terminal is a PDA, although the overall presentation structure shown in Fig. 7 is maintained. In this case, a primary adaptation operation is performed over text objects, adjusting the font size to an appropriate value, taking into account the small screen dimensions.

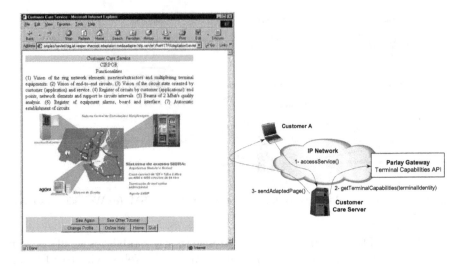

Fig. 7. Parlay terminal capabilities API usage

Then, because the width of some pictures of the tutorial is larger than the screen width, this fact forces the *SMIL Media Adapter* to adapt them, requesting the use of an image resize *media adapter*. The resize is performed if the percentage of the reduction does not go beyond a specified threshold, which is defined as a limit to preserve information consistency. If a specific picture needs a resize greater than the mentioned threshold, the *SMIL Media Adapter* takes the decision to drop it from the tutorial presentation.

As result of analysis, the approach based on the use of dynamic constraints, promoted by the *SMIL Media Adapter*, performs well with respect to the most common terminals that support multimedia presentations, guaranteeing consistent tutorial presentations even in the face of terminals with less capabilities.

5   Related Work

The work on the *MModel* can be seen as parallel to the definition of the User Interface Markup Language (UIML) [11], which is a declarative language, currently being standardized by OASIS, that derives its syntax from XML and enables the description of device-independent user interfaces. In contrast with UIML, the definition of the *MModel* did not have the ambition of being a standardized way to define user interfaces but only had the objective of defining a model simple enough to demonstrate the adaptation methodology.

In recent years, some research projects have been dedicated to the development of multimedia presentation systems following the constraint-based approach. *Cuypers* [12] is a research prototype system for the generation of Web-based multimedia presentations. Although our work was greatly inspired by this system, mainly because the system is designed to operate in the context of a client/server architecture and also because it is mostly targeted to the Web environment, the two approaches have differences. The most relevant is the dynamic integration of context information in the user interface generation process, promoted by the adaptation methodology proposed in this paper.

The integration of context information in telecommunications services and the development of context-sensitive applications have grown enormously in the present decade, mainly due to the increase mobility of users and to the research activities on ubiquitous and pervasive computing. The SmartRoutaari [13] is a sound example of a context-sensitive system. SmartRotuaari is operational at the city center of Oulu, in Northern Finland, and comprises of a wireless multiaccess network (WLAN, GPRS and EDGE), a middleware architecture for service provisioning, a Web portal with content provider interface and a collection of functional context-aware mobile multimedia services. The contextual information gathered by the SmartRoutaari system include the time, the location, the weather, the user preferences and the presence status. In contrast with our approach, the SmartRoutaari solution for gathering user context information is proprietary and has no facilities for the seamless expansion with independent third party services. This approach is not in line with the current standardization activities on telecommunications service provision, namely the 3GPP IMS standardization effort, which promotes the use of open APIs, such as Parlay, for opening operator networks to trusted third parties.

6   Conclusions

The work presented in this paper is a proposal to solve the problem of the dynamic adaptation of multimedia services. We presented a generic adaptation methodology suitable for the adaptation of telecommunications services. The methodology follows the *single source, multiple deliveries* approach, using a conceptual model (the *MModel*) for the user interface specification. The *MModel* enables a device independent specification of multimedia user interfaces, promoting a clear separation between service structure and service presentation. This model should be seen as a powerful way for the rapid construction of context independent representations of multimedia user interfaces, which should then be materialized into the most suitable formats.

We presented the most important implementation aspects of a *media adapter* prototype (the *SMIL Media Adapter*) specifically designed to enable the introduction of multimedia contents and to support time-based features in telecommunications services targeted to be used in the Web context. The *SMIL Media Adapter* relies on the use of open middleware, such as the Parlay APIs and Web services, to detect user contextual changes in mobile environments, which include the physical properties of the user terminal, the network state and the user location. These changes are then used to generate a set of constraints that the user interface should satisfy so that it may be properly displayed in the current conditions.

References

1. Camarillo, G., García-Martín, M.A.: The 3G IP Multimedia Subsystem: Merging the Internet and the Cellular Worlds. John Wiley & Sons, Chichester (2006)
2. Oliveira, J., Roque, R., Carrapatoso, E., Portschy, H., Hoványi, D., Berenyi, I.: Mobile Multimedia in VESPER Virtual Home Environment. In: Proceedings of the IEEE International Conference on Multimedia and Expo, Lausanne, Switzerland (August 26-29, 2002)
3. Oliveira, J., Roque, R., Dinis, M., Carrapatoso, E.: Provision of Mobile Multimedia over UMTS Middleware Platforms. In: Proceedings of the IST Mobile and Wireless Communications Summit, Aveiro, Portugal (June 15-18, 2003)
4. W3C: Synchronized Multimedia Integration Language (SMIL 2.1) Specification. Recommendation REC-SMIL2-20051213, Synchronized Multimedia Working Group (December 2005)
5. Parlay Group: Parlay Specifications (2003), http://www.parlay.org/en/specifications
6. W3C: Composite Capability/Preference Profiles (CC/PP): Structure and Vocabularies. Recommendation REC-CCPP-struct-vocab-20040115, Device Independence Working Group (January 2004)
7. Kay, M.: XSL Transformations (XSLT) - Version 2.0. Proposed Recommendation PR-xslt20-20061121, W3C (November 2006)
8. Bulterman, D.C.A.: SMIL 2.0, Part 1: Overview, Concepts and Structure. IEEE Multimedia 8(4), 82–88 (2001)
9. W3C: XForms 1.0. Recommendation REC-xforms-20060314, XForms Working Group (March 2006)
10. Apt, K., Wallace, M.: Constraint Logic Programming using ECLiPSe. Cambridge University Press, Cambridge (2006)
11. Phanouriou, C.: UIML: A Device-Independent User Interface Markup Language. PhD thesis, Virginia Polytechnic Institute and State University (September 26, 2000)
12. van Ossenbruggen, J., Geurts, J., Cornelissen, F., Hardman, L., Rutledge, L.: Towards Second and Third Generation Web-Based Multimedia. In: Proceedings of the 10th International World Wide Web Conference, Hong Kong, pp. 479–488 (2001)
13. Ojala, T., Korhonen, J., Aittola, M., Ollila, M., Koivumäki, T., Tähtinen, J., Karjaluoto, H.: SmartRotuaari - Context-Aware Mobile Multimedia Services. In: Proceedings of the 2nd International Conference on Mobile and Ubiquitous Multimedia, Norrköping, Sweden (December 10-12, 2003)

A Policy-Based Resource Reservation Service for Maritime Tactical Networks

David Kidston[1], Isabelle Labbé[1], Francis St-Onge[1], and Thomas Kunz[2]

[1] Communications Research Centre
Ottawa, Ontario, Canada
[2] Carleton University
Ottawa, Ontario, Canada

Abstract. Naval at sea (maritime tactical) networks are characterised by a dynamic, heterogeneous, and low-bandwidth environment. There is a critical need for Traffic Engineering (TE) mechanisms to support traffic prioritisation and resource optimisation in this environment. A desirable management service in this environment is end-to-end guaranteed bandwidth for critical application flows. Solutions such as RSVP are not appropriate for the maritime environment where links are error prone and easily overloaded. This paper describes the Resource Reservation Service (RRS), a policy-enabled flow-based TE management service developed specifically for the low-bandwidth, high-error rate, and mobility of the maritime environment. This service includes several novel features including multi-path probing, bi-directional reservations, and full policy control. The value of multi-path probing is demonstrated by simulation.

1 Introduction

Traffic engineering (TE) in maritime tactical networks represents a challenge for several reasons. Maritime networks are composed of heterogeneous links that are error-prone, failure-prone, high-latency, and offer relatively low bandwidth communication capacity. For these reasons traffic should be directed over links that support their QoS requirements while making best use of the network capacity available. This task is complicated by the navy's hierarchical command structure, which requires that network management authority be partially decentralised such that a subordinate level of network control remains available to the commander of each maritime node (ship). A final complicating factor for TE in this environment is the limited availability of skilled network operators. Automation of the management of communication resources is required to minimise the skill level required from operational personnel.

Policy systems are able to provide this automation by changing network behaviour to match currently stated policy. A Policy Based Traffic Management (PBTM) system was developed to support the automation of TE management services in the maritime environment [1]. Several services were developed, including a class-based adaptive routing service (forwarding depending on what delay, error, and bandwidth the type of traffic requires) and a class-based traffic prioritisation service (a DiffServ based scheme where traffic is prioritised depending on its value to the current mission).

D. Krishnaswamy, T. Pfeifer, and D. Raz (Eds.): MMNS 2007, LNCS 4787, pp. 149–160, 2007.

This paper describes another policy-enabled TE management service designed for the maritime environment, the resource reservation service (RRS). The RRS has several advantages over existing flow-based resource optimisation protocols. A distributed admission control scheme provides load balancing by probing multiple pre-computed routes at once. The use of time-outs and acknowledgements provides fault-tolerance. Bidirectional reservations are supported by making reservations in both directions at once. The RRS also coordinates its operation with the existing TE services to provide flow-appropriate routing and relative prioritisation when reservations fail.

The remainder of the paper is organised as follows. A description of the maritime environment provides an outline of TE management challenges in this area. This is followed by a description of the PBTM system which supports policy-based automation of the RRS by supporting routing and pre-emption decisions amongst other things. The four phases of the RRS operation are then described. Simulation results regarding the multi-route probing of the service follow. Finally, the paper ends with a discussion of related work, conclusions, and future work.

2 The Maritime Environment

Naval units (nodes) most commonly communicate in a combination of two modes [2]. First, they may communicate back to their strategic network using satellite communications (e.g. INMARSAT). This can be done in series to provide high bandwidth but high delay ship to ship communications. Second, ships may communicate directly with other ships via limited range radio (e.g. UHF LOS). Recently UHF/VHF relay technology has improved to the point that terrestrial radio systems may form mobile ad-hoc networks (MANETs). MANETs provide low bandwidth, low delay connectivity over a limited distance. A typical small task fleet deployment is shown in Fig. 1.

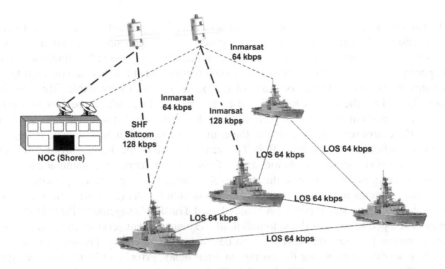

Fig. 1. Example of a Maritime Network

The maritime environment engenders several complicating factors that must be dealt with when designing a flow-based reservation service. These issues include: low bandwidth heterogeneous links; link failures engendered by node mobility; a hierarchical command structure which imposes strict but time varying traffic priority; and a lack of skilled network operators.

The RRS ensures that reservations do not use links that for reasons of limited bandwidth, delay, or error rate would not otherwise meet the QoS requirements of the requesting flow. These policies are provided by the class-based adaptive routing service (another TE management service). For instance, line of sight (UHF/VHF LOS) links pose a problem for the RRS since the media is shared and residual bandwidth cannot be reliably determined. There are currently no standards for QoS support in the Medium Access Control (MAC) layer of these media. Implementing QoS in these environments would involve probing, cross-layer communication, and/or instrumentation of the MAC with proprietary SNMP MIBs. These methods are not standardised and any attempt at direct measurement is likely to introduce significant overhead [3]. It is currently assumed that LOS links with more than 2 members within range are not suitable for reservations. When the link is dedicated and provides stable bandwidth, the residual bandwidth (the metric reserved by the RRS) can be determined by looking at the bandwidth available to be reserved and the amount currently reserved. This is the case for most satellite links where the media is not shared (i.e. a point-to-point link). Their operation can often be characterised as either available at full capacity or not available (binary). A policy-defined percentage of this nominal transmit capacity is set aside for reservations based on link type, connectivity, etc. at the discretion of a network architect. Residual bandwidth is then directly calculable by subtracting the currently reserved bandwidth from the link's reservation bandwidth pool. Note that the mechanism we use is the class-based traffic prioritisation TE service (DiffServ bandwidth sharing), so bandwidth that is unused by reservations will be shared amongst the remaining traffic classes.

The approach adopted for dealing with mobility is that reservations should be updated "periodically" and monitored "constantly." Existing reservations are probed at regular intervals. When a link on a reserved path fails, the reservation will be degraded to the policy-based default prioritisation level that was in force for that traffic prior to the reservation. This remains in effect until the reservation can be restored on a new route or the reservation is dropped and the user is informed of the error.

Reservation priority, as it is currently applied in fixed networks, reflects the needs and privileges of the particular application, workstation, or user. In the maritime environment all these factors must be considered, but in addition the current importance of the information being transported to the current mission (local importance) and the importance of the mission globally (domain importance) must be considered. The RRS uses a policy system to maintain a per flow priority based on these factors.

One final complication engendered by maritime networks is a lack of skilled operators to implement the required traffic engineering solutions. For this reason the RRS makes use of a policy system to automatically generate and distribute router configurations. The policy approach has the advantage that device configurations can be deployed quickly and in a coordinated fashion across the network. Finally the policy system provides authentication services which control who is allowed to submit reservations and at what level of priority through role-based security mechanisms.

3   The PBTM Policy System

The policy-based network management architecture upon which the PBTM is based has been previously described in [1,4] and is summarised here in Figure 2. The architecture is Web Services-based and fully distributed with all components residing on all nodes. The architecture is generic in that it is not specific to the maritime environment and can be extended to other service areas.

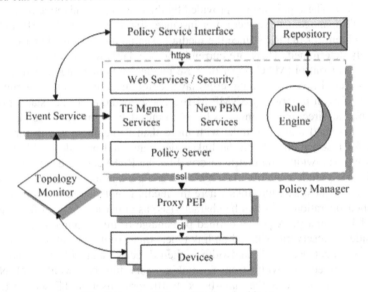

Fig. 2. Service Oriented Policy Architecture

The main components of the architecture are: the policy service interface, which accepts policy from operators while assigning roles to devices; the policy manager, which interprets high level policy and pushes low level policy out to policy-enabled resources (also known as PEPs); the proxy PEP, which takes the low level policy and configures their associated devices to conform with policy; repositories, which store the high level policies; a topology monitor, which notes changes in the network connectivity; and finally an event service, which helps to distribute events from the policy system and the underlying network (topology monitor).

As mentioned previously, the PBTM currently supports several TE services. The class-based traffic prioritisation service provides DiffServ-style traffic prioritisation for non-critical traffic. Load balancing is an important concern for resource optimisation and is enforced by the class-based adaptive routing service. Traffic prioritisation for critical flows is provided by the Resource Reservation Service (RRS). Together these management services provide an integrated solution to TE in this environment.

The PBTM system supports the RRS by providing policy supported decisions about reservation link bandwidth pool size, potential routing of the admitted flows (via the class-based adaptive routing service), prioritisation after reservation failure (via the class-based traffic prioritisation service), timeout and acknowledgement schemes, route selection, reservation restoration due to mobility or link failure, and the priority/pre-emption of reservations.

4 Main Algorithm

The Resource Reservation Service (RRS) uses distributed admission control to limit the number of flows that can use a pool of bandwidth reserved on each link in the route between source and destination. The goal of the RRS is to provide a guarantee of end-to-end QoS for a particular application flow. This sort of protection is most commonly useful for real-time applications (such as VOIP or video), but could also be used for critical data transfers (such as a specific image transfer or chat session).

The RSS consists of four phases. In the first phase, global link information is used to generate multiple routes between the source and destination of the requesting flow. The second phase of the algorithm probes the potential routes separately to determine if sufficient resources are available on all links. In the third phase, an acceptable path is selected and committed. Finally in the fourth phase the reservation is maintained until the flow terminates, the reservation lifetime ends, the reservation is ended manually, or the network can no longer support its requirements. Mobility is handled by assuming the network is stable for the period of call setup, and network maintenance handles topology changes while the reservation is active as described below.

Initialisation: The topology of the network is continuously updated using routing information available on the local router. OSPF, the routing algorithm of choice in maritime networks [2], regularly sends Link State Advertisements (LSAs) to distribute knowledge of the domain's connectivity information. Each router stores a complete set of the most recent LSAs in a Link State Database (LSDB). From the standard OSPF LSDB, the topology discovery module can extract: a list of current links in the domain with their associated cost metric, and node connectivity. Considering the relatively slow rate of mobility in maritime networks, the instability before OSPF can reconverge after a link failure is short compared to the operational time of the network. By using a predetermined OSPF link costs chart (an example is shown in Table 1.), the type and hence the characteristics of the links can be determined directly. Note that links with a shared medium such as UHF LOS are not suitable for reservations and are thus ignored by policy.

Table 1. Equating OSPF Cost to Link Type (an example)

OSPF Cost	Link type	Nominal BW (kbps)
750	INMARSAT	64
800	SHF SATCOM	128
1150	VHF/UHF LOS	64 (shared)
1300	UHF SATCOM	32 (shared)
1900	HF BLOS	9.6

In order to determine the bandwidth available for resource reservation on each link, the available bandwidth on each link is divided so that a percentage is assigned for reservations (which require admission control). The size of this reserved pool is based on policy and is currently 50% of the nominal bandwidth for all link types. Note that the reserved pool of bandwidth will be available for other traffic if not used by reserved traffic. This information is used for route generation and resource allocation as explained in the following subsections.

Phase One: When a user makes a request, topology information is used to generate a set of potential reservation routes dynamically. A partially disjoint routing algorithm is used to generate multiple routes in series as follows. The first route generated is the least-cost (highest bandwidth) route from source to destination (from the Dijkstra algorithm) while ignoring links that are not acceptable for the requested class of application (not enough bandwidth or counter indicated error or delay characteristics as defined in the adaptive routing policy). The second route is generated similarly, but ignores the highest cost (least bandwidth) link of the best route previously generated. The third route also uses the same algorithm, but ignores the highest cost links of the previous routes, etc. This can continue until no more routes are possible or the policy defined maximum number of routes for the reservation's priority is reached. This simple algorithm may be refined at a later date to include constraints such as error rates and latencies important in multimedia traffic. Once the routes have been generated, the generated routes are probed in parallel with each node on each route performing admission control (phase two). It is up to the destination to choose the route that will be reserved, assuming an acceptable route is available (phase three).

The main advantage of probing multiple paths is to discover the "best" path currently available. If several paths are acceptable the receiver will have a choice of selecting the reserved path such that the reservation can be made with minimal impact on the existing flows (least number of pre-empted flows). Another advantage is that probing multiple paths promotes load balancing. Where default routing forces all traffic over the "best" link, when multiple routes are considered, the route with the least loaded links can be identified for reservation. This type of selection allows the traffic to be balanced both at individual nodes and throughout the network.

Phase Two: Admission control in the proposed algorithm is similar to RSVP [5] but modified for the maritime environment. RSVP was found to be unsuitable for three reasons. First, RSVP assumes unidirectional reservations where most IP based applications are bidirectional. Second, RSVP uses the default routing to attempt reservations and does not probe multiple routes in parallel. In the low bandwidth maritime environment, the default route would be quickly overloaded and attempting alternate routes will increase the call acceptance rate. Third, although the RSVP standard has provisions for including policy control information; most implementations do not support this capability (for example, Cisco). This is required for communication with the RRS at each hop in the reservation to determine whether the flow should be admitted or not (depending on both local policy and the policy carried by the resource request). Finally it should be noted that RSVP was not designed for low bandwidth links. Its rate of signalling is high (although configurable) and it was not designed for robustness (it was mainly designed to be used over wired networks).

Instead of using RSVP for admission control, we have developed a proprietary robust signalling protocol. Admission control decisions are performed at each hop along the selected route(s). If sufficient resources exist for the desired link at the current node, the residual bandwidth of the link is noted in the probe and forwarded to the next node. Route probing is robust in that every probe message is acknowledged. Unacknowledged probes are resent after a policy configurable timeout. If a probe remains unacknowledged, the route is considered lost. Duplicate probes are ignored.

If insufficient resources are found at a node, the resources are re-checked to see if pre-empting lower priority flows would leave enough resources (pre-emption is explained below). If sufficient resources are still not available a failure message is sent to the destination, which will in turn inform the source once all probes have arrived. If sufficient resources are available, the request is forwarded to the next node in the route taking note of the flows that would be pre-empted if this route were used.

A copy of every resource request is stored at each node in the hope that a confirmation will eventually arrive. Only at that point will the resources be committed. If the confirmation has not arrived in a policy-defined amount of time, the "pending resource request" record is purged. It is important to realise that no change is made to active reservations or the router during phase two. The purpose of route probing is simply to determine if a reservation is possible along any of the generated routes. This may lead to the case where reservations are tentatively admitted but the resources are not available when the commit packet returns, because another reservation has committed first. We argue that these false admissions are preferable to the alternative of reserving resources during the initial probing. It is more likely that bandwidth reserved during probing will be wasted because downstream nodes are not able to handle the request. In other words, routes which have been probed are unlikely to be probed and committed on the same link before the original request has a chance to return and commit its bandwidth. Similarly, only one of the multiple probed paths will be reserved so there is no point in reserving resources on links that may not be used.

A novel capability of this algorithm is that a reservation in the reverse direction (destination to source) can be made at the same time as the forward direction (source to destination). Bidirectional reservations can be especially useful when the application has critical traffic in the reverse direction that needs protecting, such as VOIP calls or FTP downloads. The bandwidth requested need not be the same in both directions. Making bidirectional reservations reduces overhead and latency while ensuring that the reservation is bidirectional (it reserves at the same nodes at the same time for both directions on two different links).

Phase Three: Once one or more reservation probes have reached the destination, phase three, route selection, is performed. Several factors may influence the choice of route. Avoiding the pre-emption of existing flows is considered. In order to balance the load of the network, the minimal residual bandwidth of each route is considered. The residual bandwidth of each link on a route was noted during the route probing phase (phase two). In heavily reserved networks the number and priority of

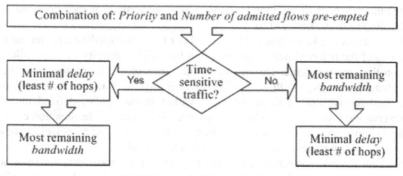

Fig. 3. Route Selection Algorithm

pre-empted flows along each route are also noted in the probes. Finally, the length of the route is also considered. The selection algorithm is presented in Fig. 3.

The selection algorithm first selects the route with the least number (and lowest priority) reservations pre-empted. If more than one route has the same number and type of pre-emptions, one of two possible selection methods are used. For real-time applications, delay is more important than raw bandwidth and therefore the flow should take the shortest route. Conversely, non real-time (data as opposed to delay focused) applications take the route with the highest minimum residual bandwidth. The rational for this is that real-time applications are more delay sensitive than they are bandwidth sensitive. Placing them on routes that are close to saturation may be advisable if the delay is reduced. Since delay is most often a factor of hop-count, the lower hop count is favoured for these applications. On the other hand, applications with heavy bandwidth requirements are more concerned with total data transmitted, a longer delay may be tolerated and thus routes with greater residual bandwidth are preferred.

Once the destination has decided upon a route, a commit message is sent back along that route, with each RRS updating the configuration of the router so that the flow is treated in the reserved class. In order to determine if a new request should actually be committed the RRS checks which reservations are using which local links.

If insufficient bandwidth is available in the reservation bandwidth pool for the identified link, the RRS will pre-empt existing flows only if it would free enough resources to admit the committing flow. Users assign a priority to a reservation when it is made which is then modified based on the current importance of the application, data, workstation and mission according to policy. Established but lower priority calls will be pre-empted in priority order lowest to highest and then largest to smallest in terms of bandwidth.

When a reservation is pre-empted all nodes along the pre-empted reservation's route are notified to release the related resources. Depending on the policy/priority of the pre-empted or unsuccessful reservation, a request may be reattempted at the source or may simply be dropped.

Phase Four: When a commit message reaches the source the reservation enters its active phase. Each committed reservation causes the dynamic creation of an explicit MPLS tunnel to force the identified flow down the reserved path. This tunnel is torn down when the reservation ends. Policing is applied on the flow to limit its data rate to the reserved bandwidth. This is to ensure that an admitted reservation will not degrade other reserved flows. Finally, bandwidth is guaranteed at each node end to end by defining a unique traffic class.

Reservations can be terminated by a number of events including termination by the user, end of the reserved period, pre-emption by a higher priority flow, or failure of a link on the reserved route. During the maintenance phase, keep-alive messages are sent along the reserved path at a policy-defined interval. Each RRS instance on the path must receive one of these messages within another policy-defined interval or the reservation is considered to have terminated. This "natural" termination causes the RRS to simply remove the reservation from its list, freeing the associated bandwidth and reversing any router configuration that has been made.

If a link fails or is degraded, due to mobility for instance, existing reservations must react to the changed topology. Fault management is achieved by eventually terminating reservations that use the failed link and potentially attempting to re-establish those reservations at the source (based on policy/priority). When a link is flagged by the routing protocol as no longer in the topology, the RRS will wait for a policy configurable amount of time before reacting to allow the link some time to recover. All reservations that are currently using a failed link will then be released. If the link is simply degraded (defined by policy), after the waiting period the service will recalculate whether admitted flows can still receive the resources they reserved on a degraded (reduced bandwidth) link. If not, pre-emption of the lowest priority flows continues until there is sufficient bandwidth available for the remaining reservations.

5 Simulation Results

The commercial tool OPNET [6] has been used to simulate the Resource Reservation Service (RRS). In an initial study of performance, the multi-probing feature of the RRS was measured including overhead introduced by the RRS, call acceptance, and pre-emption rate in a small (5 node) and larger (9 node) simulated maritime network. The (simulated) small network consists of four routers and four workstations and the larger network of eight routers and eight workstations. The routers use the base Cisco 3640 model with a modified OSPF stack that forwards the LSA graph to the appropriate RRS process in its associated LAN workstation. The workstations use the base Intel advanced model with the addition of a RRS process and packet generation process (used to initiate new requests locally). The routers are connected to their associated workstation with 10BaseT Ethernet and to each other by point to point links with bandwidth between 32 and 128 kbps as shown in Fig. 1. (for the small network). The larger network is composed of an additional 4 ships connected to the NOC. These network sizes and topologies were chosen based on current maritime deployments [2].

In order to remove the effects of a particular seed value, five runs at each load level are performed with different seeds. Statistics are averaged over those seeds. Simulation runs of 10,000 seconds have been used with 3 priority levels, 1 or 3 parallel probes, and with a reservation inter-arrival time for the network exponentially distributed and centered on 15s for low load and 7.5s for high load. These values were chosen to emulate a saturated network (low load) and an overloaded network (high load) Reservation sources and destinations are uniformly distributed between nodes. All reservations are for 8kbps with 50% of link bandwidth available for reservation. Reservations lifetimes are exponentially distributed with a mean of 270 seconds. In order to focus on the multi-routing aspect of the RRS, mobility has been disabled for this particular set of simulations. The results of the simulations are shown in Table 2.

The per-request (network wide) reservation overhead in bytes/call is high because it currently carries a complete reservation policy (encoded in XML) which is on average 3015 bytes of data. Compression of the XML document would improve both overhead and reservation setup time, which currently takes 2.5-3.5 seconds on average because of the low bandwidth environment. Reservation overhead includes each IP packet involved in a single request summed over each link on which it is sent. The average overhead of successful requests is shown. Note the difference in overhead between the low and high load of requests. The lower total overhead in high load networks is likely because when links become congested with requests, longer routes are rejected immediately at the source and thus the reservation request does not have to travel over as many links lowering the per-request overhead.

Table 2. Multi-Probing Simulation Results

Network Size	Load	Number of Routes Probed	Reservation Overhead (bytes/call)	Call Acceptance Rate (%)	Call Preemption Rate (%)
Small	Low load	3	13452	89.0	7.4
		1	3565	87.0	10.8
	High load	3	11114	69.6	19.4
		1	3544	71.7	20.4
Large	Low load	3	19028	87.0	7.4
		1	5836	83.2	7.6
	High load	3	15887	68.4	14.6
		1	5309	64.1	13.3

The call acceptance rate at low load (saturated network) is acceptable for the maritime environment, but not ideal. Even at high load (congested network) more calls are accepted than rejected. Further work will investigate the value of priority in preemption to give the most critical flows an event higher acceptance rate (where 99.9% would be more appropriate). As expected, the call acceptance rate is higher and call pre-emption rate lower for lower request loads. Also as can be expected, the preemption rate is higher for higher loads. The difference in these values based on the number of probes is almost negligible in the small network where there is a lack of alternate routes. However, in the larger network a definite advantage can be seen in improved call acceptance rates at the cost of higher overhead. Since RSVP is similar to RRS with a single probe, it is expected that this will remain the case. An investigation to directly compare the RRS and RSVP is currently being pursued.

6 Related Work

There has been very little research done to date investigating the TE requirements of maritime networks. A notable exception has been recent work in applying static Diff-Serv QoS to maritime networks [7], which showed that throughput and delay guarantees were hard to achieve in this environment. However, queuing and dropping mechanisms, if properly tuned, could provide limited service differentiation. The static nature of the DiffServ marking does not respect the dynamic nature of the maritime environment, where the importance attached to different information flows vary with time. It is however straightforward to implement and maintain. The RRS uses a policy system to accommodate changes in priority by automatically modifying the reservation priority of flows to meet their current mission value (as defined by policy).

RSVP-TE [8], a standard from the IETF, defines a traffic engineering enhanced version of the reservation protocol RSVP. RSVP-TE provides a mechanism by which MPLS label switched tunnels can be configured along a predetermined (explicit) route with or without a resource reservation being made at the same time. RSVP is used as a signalling protocol that can create and reroute label-switched tunnels. Rerouting may be required to bypass networks failures, congestion, and/or network bottlenecks.

If reservations are made, they can be pre-empted by higher priority reservations. All this is similar to the RRS. However the method for choosing a label-switched path is not specified in RSVP-TE. Also, reservations are unidirectional and are made in a single pass as a reservation message passes from node to node along the selected path from receiver to sender. The RRS allows bidirectional reservation to be made to ensure the delay/error characteristics of the label-switched path are symmetrical (an important characteristic for some types of flows). Finally, our work investigates a mechanism by which multiple potential routes are considered before selecting the most policy acceptable in order to increase the chance of call being accepted and to balance reservations over the network. RSVP-TE only considers the default route.

In terms of the policy system, hierarchical policy-based network management systems have been shown to be capable of providing user-configurable monitoring and automated configuration of MANETs [9]. The primary management services in their work include monitoring, data aggregation, and reporting. Our work also investigates the use of policy in network management in a similar environment but it focuses on TE management services.

7 Conclusions and Future Work

This paper describes the Resource Reservation Service (RRS), a policy-enabled flow-based bandwidth reservation service designed to support end-to-end QoS in maritime networks. Existing reservation schemes such as RSVP are not appropriate since links are error prone and easily overloaded. This service in addition to traffic prioritisation and adaptive routing management services are designed to provide Traffic Engineering (TE) mechanisms to support traffic prioritisation and resource optimisation in this heterogeneous, mobile, and low bandwidth environment.

The RRS provides several novel features to improve resource reservations in this environment. Since the RRS makes use of topology information available at every edge router to determine link types and connectivity, no additional overhead is required to generate routes from source to destination. Policy control ensures that multiple potential routes are generated that traverse links with sufficient raw bandwidth and have delay and error characteristics acceptable for the traffic type (according to operational policy). These routes are probed in parallel to increase the chance that a route will be found. When multiple acceptable routes are found, the route reserved is chosen to make the least impact on existing traffic, causing reservations to be balanced across the network. The use of acknowledgements, timers, and a retransmission scheme are used to mitigate the dynamic and error prone environment. For the same reason, the ability to make reservations for traffic in both directions at the same time is an advantage both to ensure bandwidth is simultaneously available and to reduce the time/bandwidth overhead compared to sequential reservations.

Simulations of the multi-probing aspect of the protocol show that, as would be expected, the call acceptance rate is higher and the call pre-emption rate is lower for lower request loads. Also, a lower overhead was observed with higher load, likely because as links become congested with requests, longer routes are rejected and reservations do not travel over as many links. The benefit of probing multiple paths becomes apparent in larger networks where there is a higher call admission rate.

While this service provides the basic mechanisms required for an efficient and robust TE service for critical flows in maritime networks, there are still many avenues for future work. Currently resource requests are unicast (one source and one destination). A multicast resource request may also be possible if RSVP-type mechanisms were to be used to merge multiple reservations, a useful capability for video conferencing and other broadcast communications. Another potential enhancement would be the use of MPLS route protection mechanisms to support the reservation of alternate parallel paths for very high-priority flows. The alternate routes on "warm standby" would be reserved in advance in anticipation of link outages with an immediate switchover when the primary reserved route fails. Finally, a more comprehensive evaluation of the RRS is planned by comparing the RRS with alternative resource reservation mechanisms such as RSVP [5] (designed for fixed networks) and INSIGNIA [10] (designed for MANETs).

Acknowledgements

This work was supported by Defence R&D Canada (DRDC).

References

1. Kidston, D., Labbé, I.: A Service Oriented Framework for Policy-Based Management of Maritime Mobile Networks. In: MILCOM 2006, Washington, D.C., USA (October 2006)
2. Maritime Tactical Wide Area Networking (MTWAN), ACP 200 Project, AUSCANZUKUS Unclassified (available through author) (July 2003)
3. Jorgenson, M., Reichelt, C., Johnson, T.: Operation of the Dynamic TDMA Subnet Relay System with HF Bearers. In: MILCOM 2005, Atlantic City, NJ, USA (October 2005)
4. Labbé, I., St-Onge, F., Kidston, D., Roy, J.-F.: A Policy System for Traffic Management in Maritime Tactical Networks, DRDC Technical Report TR-2007-005 (January 2007)
5. Braden, R., et al.: Resource ReSerVation Protocol (RSVP) – Version 1 Functional Specification, IETF RFC 2205 (September 1997)
6. OPNET: web site, (last accessed July 11, 2006), http://www.opnet.com/
7. Barsaleau, D., Tummala, M.: Testing of DiffServ Performance over a U.S. Navy Satellite Communication Network. In: MILCOM 2004, Monterey, CA (October-November 2004)
8. Awduche, D., et al.: RSVP-TE: Extensions to RSVP for LSP Tunnels, ITEF RFC 3209 (December 2001)
9. Chadha, R., et al.: Policy Based Mobile Ad Hoc Network Management. In: POLICY 2004 (June 2004)
10. Lee, S-B., Ahn, G-S., Campbell, A.: Improving UDP and TCP Performance in Mobile Ad Hoc Networks with INSIGNIA. IEEE Communications Magazine, pp. 156–165 (June 2001)

Autonomic Resource Management for Multimedia Services Using Inventory Control

Ramy Farha and Alberto Leon-Garcia

University of Toronto, Toronto, Ontario, Canada
ramy.farha@utoronto.ca, alberto.leongarcia@utoronto.ca

Abstract. The proliferation of real-time multimedia services has triggered attempts by service providers to seek ways to reduce the cost of managing those services, while satisfying customer demands for the resources involved in the service delivery. A key issue is to avoid costly service interruptions in such real-time multimedia services. In this paper, we propose the use of the inventory control approach from the Operations Research community to remedy to this problem. We show two possible inventory control models to manage the resources involved in real-time multimedia service delivery. We also perform extensive simulations to compare the advantages and disadvantages of the two inventory control models for resource management of real-time multimedia services.

1   Introduction

Recent years have witnessed a proliferation of real-time multimedia services delivered to customers. In parallel, the number of wireless customers asking for such services has also increased. Service providers offering such services are therefore faced with the challenge of offering real-time multimedia services to customers with desirable Quality of Service (QoS) characteristics [1]. In order to achieve this, real-time multimedia service providers are exploring novel techniques to automate resource management for their services. The goal is to obtain a self-managing network infrastructure, which adapts to changes in customer demands, satisfying the needs for networking, computing, and storage resources.

Inventory control is commonly used in the Operations Research community to analyze inventory systems of industries and businesses, placing and receiving orders when needed to meet demands for a given product [2]. An analogy between inventory control and autonomic resource management for multimedia real-time services, is that of balancing the two extreme cases: Having a small amount of resources leads to costly service interruptions, thus leading to customer dissatisfaction, while having a large amount of resources leads to idle capital expenditures, thus leading to lower profits for service providers. An important factor in the formulation and solution of a resource inventory model is whether the demand (per unit time) for a resource is deterministic (known with certainty) or probabilistic (described by a probability distribution). Since the first assumption is too optimistic in a real-world environment, we will turn our

D. Krishnaswamy, T. Pfeifer, and D. Raz (Eds.): MMNS 2007, LNCS 4787, pp. 161–172, 2007.

attention to probabilistic inventory models. In this paper, we will use inventory control for autonomic resource management of multimedia real-time services.

The rest of this paper is structured as follows. In section 2, we summarize some related work. In section 3, we describe two inventory control models we examine in this paper for autonomic resource management of multimedia real-time services. In section 4, we show how the inventory control models are applied to a situation involving multimedia real-time service providers. In section 5, we show some simulation results. In section 6, we conclude this paper.

2   Related Work

The use of inventory control to solve problems for real-time multimedia services is a relatively new concept. One paper [3] considered applying inventory control to capacity management for utility computing. A framework consisting of theoretical foundations, problem formulations, and quality of service (QoS) forecasting is presented. While the paper considers inventory control to solve a problem in the IT world, it does not tackle the problem explored in this paper.

However, adaptive resource management for wireless networks offering real-time multimedia services is not a new idea. Several papers have been written on the issue. One paper used flow and admission control algorithms for efficient resource utilization in wireless networks [4]. This approach is based on control theory concepts to offer network-aware multimedia applications in wireless networks. Another paper [5] proposed bandwidth adaptation in case of insufficient bandwidth in order to allocate the desired bandwidth to every multimedia connection originating in a cell or being handed off to the cell.

The main differences between previous approaches and the one proposed in this paper are that a) we consider predictive rather than reactive mechanism, b) we do not need to manage at the granularity of individual multimedia connections as the overhead might become prohibitive, and c) we do not interfere with the regular operation of the existing service instances which are active in a given cell (by adapting their bandwidth or dropping some using priority schemes).

3   Inventory Control

The developed models for probabilistic inventory control in Operations Research [2] are broadly categorized under continuous and periodic review situations. We will focus on the continuous review model, where the inventory is being monitored on a continuous basis so that a new order can be placed as soon as the inventory level drops to the reorder point. A continuous review inventory system for a particular resource is based on two critical numbers: reorder point R and order quantity y. The inventory policy is a simple one: whenever the inventory level of the resource drops to R units, place an order for y more units to replenish inventory. All inventory problems seek to answer two questions: *when* to order, and *how much* to order.

The costs involved in the Inventory Control problem are:

- Purchasing Cost: Based on the price per unit of the resource. It may be constant or variable.
- Setup Cost: Represents the fixed charge incurred when an order is placed. This cost is independent of the size of an order.
- Holding Cost: Represents the cost of maintaining the inventory in stock. It includes the cost of storage, maintenance, and handling.
- Shortage Cost: Represents the penalty incurred when we run out of stock. It includes potential loss of income, as well as the more subjective cost of loss in customer's goodwill. It can also include the lost revenue opportunity and the cost of possible delays resulting from the shortage in a given resource.

Determining the best inventory control approach revolves around making a managerial decision on the desired service level. We will consider two possible continuous review probabilistic inventory models in this paper and compare their advantages and shortcomings. The first model, which we will refer to as Model 1, uses a buffer stock to account for the probabilistic demand. The second model, which we will refer to as Model 2, is a more exact model which includes the probabilistic demand directly in the formulation. In the first model, the goal is to minimize the number of shortages encountered during operation. In the second model, the goal is to minimize the total expected cost during operation.

The assumptions of the continuous review probabilistic inventory models are:

1. Each use of the model involves a single resource.
2. The inventory level is under continuous review.
3. The only decisions to be made are to choose R and y.
4. There is a lead time L between the time when the order is placed and when the order quantity is received. This lead time L can be either fixed or variable.
5. The demand for resources from the inventory during the lead time L is uncertain. However, the probability distribution $f(x)$ of the demand is stationary with time, and the corresponding expected demand per unit time is given by D.
6. If a stockout occurs before the order is received, the excess demand is backlogged, so that the backorders are filled once the order arrives. Therefore, the excess demand is not lost, but is instead held until it can be satisfied once enough resources are delivered to replenish the inventory.
7. The fixed setup cost is denoted by K, and is incurred each time an order is placed. But except for this setup cost, the cost of the order is proportional to the order quantity y of a resource with unit cost c.
8. The holding cost h is incurred for each unit of resource in the inventory per unit time.
9. When a stockout occurs, the shortage cost p is incurred for each unit of resource backordered per unit time until the backorder is filled.

3.1   Model 1

Model 1, shown in Fig. 1, reflects the probabilistic nature of the demand by using an approximation that superimposes a constant buffer stock on the inventory level throughout the entire planning horizon. The size of the buffer is determined such that the probability of running out of stock during lead time L does not exceed a given value. We define the following additional parameters:

- x_L: random variable representing demand during lead time L.
- μ_L: average demand during lead time L.
- B: buffer stock size.

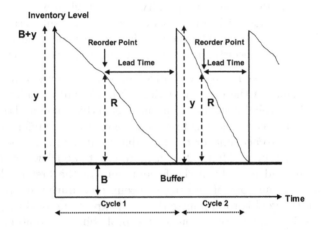

Fig. 1. Continuous Review Probabilistic Inventory Model 1

As mentioned before, the demand x during the lead time L is random with probability distribution $f(x)$. The buffer stock B needs to be found for a given probability of stock shortage. This maximum allowable probability of running out of stock during the lead time L is given by α. The probability statement used to determine B can be written as:

$$P\{x_L \geq B + \mu_L\} \leq \alpha \tag{1}$$

3.2   Model 2

Model 2, shown in Fig. 2, allows for a shortage of demand. The reorder level R is a function of the lead time L between placing and receiving an order. The optimal values of y and R are determined by minimizing the expected cost per unit that includes the sum of all costs incurred in this inventory model.

The elements of the cost function are:

1. **Setup Cost:** The approximate number of orders per unit time is $\frac{D}{y}$, so that the setup cost per unit time is $\frac{KD}{y}$.

2. **Expected Holding Cost:** The average inventory is given by:

$$I = \frac{y + E(R-x) + E(R-x)}{2} = \frac{y}{2} + R - E(x) \tag{2}$$

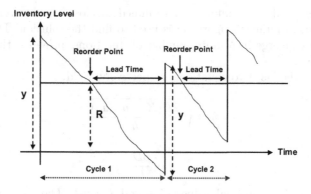

Fig. 2. Continuous Review Probabilistic Inventory Model 2

The expected holding cost per unit time thus equals hI. The formula is based on the average of the beginning and ending expected inventories of a cycle, $y + E(R - x)$ and $E(R - x)$, respectively. As an approximation, the expression ignores the case where $R - E(x)$ may be negative.

3. **Expected Shortage Cost:** Shortage occurs when $x > R$. Thus, the expected shortage quantity per cycle is given by:

$$S = \int_{R}^{\infty} (x - R)f(x)dx \tag{3}$$

Because p is assumed to be proportional to the shortage quantity only, the expected shortage cost per cycle is pS, and based on $\frac{D}{y}$ cycles per unit time, the shortage cost per unit time is $\frac{pDS}{y}$.

The resulting total cost function per unit time is given by:

$$TCU(y, R) = \frac{DK}{y} + h\left(\frac{y}{2} + R + E(x)\right) + \frac{pD}{y}\int_{R}^{\infty}(x - R)f(x)dx \tag{4}$$

The solutions for optimal y^* and R^* are determined from:

$$\frac{\partial TCU}{\partial y} = -\frac{DK}{y^2} + \frac{h}{2} - \frac{pDS}{y^2} = 0 \tag{5}$$

$$\frac{\partial TCU}{\partial R} = h - \frac{pD}{y}\int_{R}^{\infty}f(x)dx = 0 \tag{6}$$

We thus get the following solutions for the optimal values of y and R, denoted by y^* and R^*:

$$y^* = \sqrt{\frac{2D(K + pS)}{h}} \tag{7}$$

$$\int_{R^*}^{\infty}f(x)dx = \frac{hy^*}{pD} \tag{8}$$

Because y^* and R^* cannot be determined in closed forms from the above two equations, a numeric algorithm is used to find the solution. The algorithm is proved to converge in a finite number of iterations, provided that a feasible solution exists.

For $R = 0$, the last two equations, respectively, yield:

$$\hat{y} = \sqrt{\frac{2D(K + pE(x))}{h}} \tag{9}$$

$$\tilde{y} = \frac{pD}{h} \tag{10}$$

If $\tilde{y} \geq \hat{y}$, unique optimal values of y and R exist. The solution procedure recognizes that the smallest value of y^* is $\sqrt{\frac{2KD}{h}}$, which is achieved when $S = 0$. The steps of the algorithm are:

Step 0. Use the initial solution $y_1 = y^* = \sqrt{\frac{2KD}{h}}$, and let $R_0 = 0$. Set $i = 1$, and go to step i.

Step 1. Use y_i to determine R_i from the second equation. If $R_i \approx R_{i-1}$, stop; the optimal solution is $y^* = y_i$, and $R^* = R_i$. Otherwise, use R_i in the first equation to compute y_i. Set $i = i + 1$, and repeat step i.

4   Application of Inventory Control

Having introduced some approaches to traditional inventory control, we now turn our attention to their possible applications for management of resources in next generation network infrastructures. With the increasing trend towards virtualization of physical resources to deal with heterogeneity, and with the rise of on-demand computing through the exchange of virtual resources as commodities on a market of service providers, we envision service providers in the future to exchange virtual resources (networking, computing, and storage) in an open market based on demand. Thus, the use of inventory control models to improve the performance of such markets is investigated. More specifically, we consider the use of the inventory control model in the context of service providers dealing with multimedia and real-time services that should not be interrupted because of lack of resources as customers move across cells in next generation networks. Fig. 3 shows the application of the inventory model for management of real-time multimedia services in wireless networks managed by a given service provider which owns a stock of physical resources hosting virtual resources managed by the inventory control system.

In traditional work on resource management, we assume that orders are placed as needed between the service providers and that resources purchased are instantaneously replenished. However, in practice, a lead time elapses between the time at which an order is placed and the time at which the virtual resource amount ordered is delivered. Hence, the policy would be to use the continuous

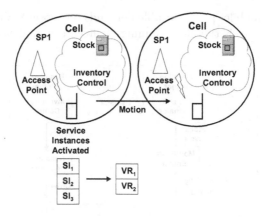

Fig. 3. Example of the Inventory Model for Wireless Real-Time Multimedia Services

review probabilistic inventory model to order virtual resources whenever needed to avoid real-time multimedia service interruptions. Since demand varies in unpredictable ways, we use collected historical data to approximate the distribution of this demand put on service providers for a given virtual resource, in order to find the expected demand during the lead time. The empirical distribution could be found by summarizing the raw data gathered over a training period where the demand for a given virtual resource is studied. The summary is in the form of an appropriate frequency histogram and allows the service providers to determine the associated empirical probability distribution functions of demand.

The inventory control provides autonomic resource management to allow resources to be ordered when needed, as shown in Algorithm 1. The resources are used by service instances activated by the customers for the services they had bought, hence service providers need to keep track of each virtual resource consumption and make appropriate decisions on *when* to order and *how much* to order in order to avoid service interruptions to the customers. In case of mobile customers, the variation in demands for a given resource is driven by customers moving between cells managed by the same or different service providers.

Fig. 4 shows how inventory control models can be incorporated in an autonomic loop for management of virtual resources by service providers subjected to variable demands by fixed and mobile customers. We consider the use of the inventory model in the context of service providers owning several resources needed by the various real-time multimedia services offered by this service provider. Assuming that the service provider has a stock of N virtual resources needed by V services. The virtual resources are referred to as: VR_1, VR_2, ..., VR_N. The stock of virtual resource VR_i at time t is denoted by $A_t(VR_i)$ and needs to be constantly monitored. Initially, the stock of virtual resources is formed by buying from other service providers offering virtual resources, or by using previously owned virtual resources amounts. Let the initial amounts of the N virtual resources be referred to as: $A_0(VR_1)$, $A_0(VR_2)$, ..., $A_0(VR_N)$. Customers, whether fixed or mobile, place variable demands on those N Virtual Resources. Each service provider is therefore running N inventory models in parallel.

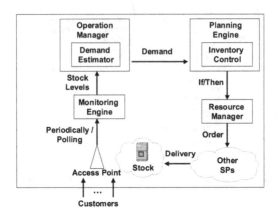

Fig. 4. Inventory Control Autonomic Loop

Algorithm for Autonomic Resource Management using Inventory Control
Training Period
```
For each Virtual Resource VRᵢ:
Run network for a training period
Generate empirical distributions f(xᵢ) based on statistical data on
demand collected in training period
Deduce mean demand per unit time Dᵢ
Deduce initial order policy [If/Then]: If A₀(VRᵢ) < Rᵢ, order yᵢ
```
Inventory Control Period
```
Turn Inventory Control policy ON:
Monitor Virtual Resource VRᵢ stock
Continuously update empirical distributions f(xᵢ) based on
statistical data on demand collected on the fly
Update estimate of mean demand per unit time Dᵢ
Update order policy [If/Then] at time t: If Aₜ(VRᵢ) < Rᵢ, order yᵢ
When inventory level of VRᵢ drops below Rᵢ, order yᵢ
```

Algorithm 1. Pseudo Code for Inventory Control

5   Simulation Results

To study the performance of the two inventory control models for autonomic resource management of multimedia real-time services, we built a custom simulator using the Java programming language. We divide the network infrastructure into several cells over a city, modelled as a rectangular grid, which has main and secondary streets, with one or more access points in each cell, allowing both fixed and mobile access over several access network technologies based on the customer's mobile device capability. Access independence is made possible through fixed mobile convergence, proposed in the IP Multimedia Subsystem (IMS) [6].

We also emulate the movement of mobile customers at a given speed which depends on whether the cell is mainly spanning a main street in the city, or a secondary speed, with an exponentially distributed sojourn time in each cell, and transfer the activated service instances and the amounts of virtual resources they need to new access points as the customers move between cells. Note that, as the mobile customers move to new cells, if they cannot find a bootstrap access point supporting their mobile device's access network technologies, they have to terminate their existing service instances which were previously activated and were still running, and continue their motion, waiting to move to a new cell which might have access points supporting any of the mobile device's access network technologies to reactivate those service instances.

We create customer entities connecting to access points through physical resources, to activate the service instances corresponding to real-time multimedia services bought from service providers. The virtual resources in the network infrastructure are distributed on physical resources which are geographically spread in the cells. Each physical resource hosting a given service has a random capacity for each virtual resource used in the network infrastructure. The customers buy several services from the real-time multimedia service providers and activate several instances of such services. The service instances are activated according to start times which follow an exponential distribution, and are kept active for service times which follow another exponential distribution.

The holding, shortage, and unit of resource costs are kept constant for the duration of a given simulation. We monitor the inventory level of the stock of virtual resources at each time step, and update the empirical distributions of the virtual resource demands. The order policies for different virtual resources are updated on a periodical basis using the most updated demand distributions. The total cost calculated for each simulation is given by the sum of the purchasing costs, the setup costs, the holding costs, and the shortage costs, which are all calculated on a unit time basis, and then added to the total cost.

The parameters used in the simulations are as follows. The unit time step is set to 1 second. The training time is set to 1000 seconds, where data is collected, and empirical distributions of the demand on a service provider are deduced. The policy is reviewed every 20 seconds. The lead time is chosen to be 10 seconds. In problems where the costs are varied, the holding costs, shortage costs, and setup costs are proportional. The shortage cost is chosen to be 100 times the holding cost, and the setup cost is chosen to be 100 times the holding cost. The unit cost is chosen to be equal to the shortage cost. The reason for this choice is that while Model 1 always works, Model 2 only produces a unique and optimal solution when $\tilde{y} \geq \hat{y}$, thus for a fair comparison we need to set the costs appropriately for both inventory control models to operate normally. We run each simulation for 20000 seconds.

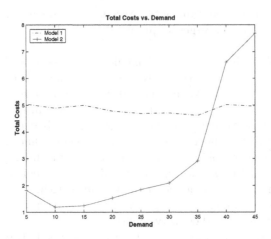

Fig. 5. Total Costs vs. Demand for both Inventory Models

Fig. 5 shows the variation in the total costs incurred by the service provider for both models as the demand increases. The holding cost is set to 10, so the unit cost is set to 10, the shortage cost is set to 1000, and the setup cost is set to 100000. The observation here is interesting. For higher demands, Model 1 seems to perform better than Model 2 because of the lower costs incurred on the service provider, even though Model 2 was designed for reduction of costs. The problem is that for high demand, the cycle time in Model 2 reduces to lower than the lead time, and in extreme cases, can become lower than a unit time. This leads to consistent shortage in Model 2, and therefore while Model 1 orders a large amount of resources, Model 2 is paying the price for shortage and this contributes to its total cost increasing.

Fig. 6 shows the variation in the total costs for low and high demands as the costs per unit time are increased in both inventory models. Initially, the holding cost is set to 1000, so the unit cost is set to 1000, the shortage cost is set to 100000, and the setup cost is set to 10000000. The total costs for both models increase as all the costs are increased by a factor of 1 to 9. For Model 1, the probability of "no shortage" is set to 0.9. For low demand (Fig. 6a), the demand is set to a maximum of 5 resource units per unit time from a given customer. Model 1 outperforms Model 2 in this setup. For high demand (Fig. 6b), the demand is set to a maximum of 50 resource units per unit time from a given customer. Model 2 outperforms Model 1 in this setup. Thus, we can conclude that the performance of one model versus the other depends not only on the demand for a given resource, but also on the costs chosen in the network, as these costs affect the design of model 2 and the values chosen for y^* and R^*.

Fig. 7 shows the inventory level variation as a function of time for both inventory models. For Model 1 (Fig. 7a), the "no shortage" probability was chosen to be 0.9. As expected, the inventory level drops from the initial value of 50000 resource units at the start time as demand for that resource starts in the network.

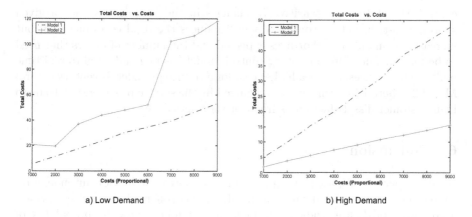

a) Low Demand   b) High Demand

Fig. 6. Total Costs vs. Costs for Low and High Demand for both Inventory Models

When the threshold value is reached, an order is placed for an additional 50000 resource units. As seen in the figure, few orders are needed, and the inventory level is always positive, i.e. no shortages have occurred. For Model 2 (Fig. 7b), the inventory level drops from the initial value of 50000 resource units at the start time as demand for that resource starts in the network. When the threshold value R^* is reached, an order is placed for an amount y^* of resource units. As seen in the figure, several orders are needed, and the inventory level is always fluctuating around zero, so several shortages have occurred.

We performed several other experiments on the two inventory control models. However, due to space limitations, we will not present them here. The main conclusions from the experiments are that inventory control Model 1 is more predictable, while inventory control Model 2 is less controllable. While inventory

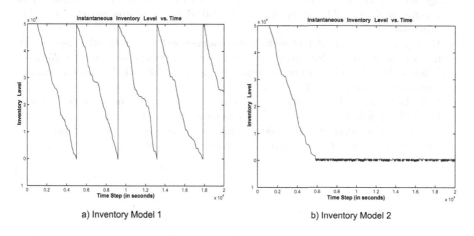

a) Inventory Model 1   b) Inventory Model 2

Fig. 7. Inventory Level Variation with time for Both Inventory Models

control Model 1 seems sensitive to changes in the holding costs for a given shortage cost, inventory control Model 2 reduces the total costs incurred, but increases the number of shortages expected and the number of orders that need to be placed. Therefore, inventory control Model 1 is more adapted to real-time multimedia services, but at a higher cost for a service provider. Inventory control Model 2 is better in terms of costs incurred by the service provider, but leads to high customer dissatisfaction as frequent shortages occur.

6   Conclusion

In this paper we proposed to apply inventory control models for autonomic re-source management of real-time multimedia services offered by a service provider. Two such models are studied: the first aims at minimizing the probability of resource shortages occurring, while the second aims at minimizing the costs in-curred by service providers. Results have shown that while the first model is more appropriate for customers, it increases costs for service providers. On the other hand, the second model is more appropriate for service providers, but leads to customer dissatisfaction. A more detailed study of how demand, policy update period, and cost variation affect the performance of the two models is still needed. However, this paper shows that inventory control is a promising approach for autonomic resource management of real-time multimedia services.

References

1. Ye, J., et al.: A comprehensive resource management framework for next generation wireless networks. IEEE Transactions on Mobile Computing, 249–264 (2002)
2. Hillier, F.: Introduction to Operations Research. McGraw-Hill, New York (2001)
3. Hellerstein, J., et al.: A framework for applying inventory control to capacity man-agement for utility computing. In: 9th IFIP/IEEE International Symposium on Integrated Network Management, pp. 237–250. IEEE Computer Society Press, Los Alamitos (2005)
4. Banerjee, N.L., et al.: Adaptive resource management for multimedia applications in wireless networks. In: Sixth IEEE International Symposium on the World of Wireless Mobile and Multimedia Networks, pp. 250–257. IEEE Computer Society Press, Los Alamitos (2005)
5. Seth, M., et al.: Adaptive resource management for multimedia wireless networks. In: IEEE 58th Vehicular Technology Conference, pp. 1668–1672 (2003)
6. 3rd Generation Partnership Project, Technical Specification Group Services and Systems Aspects : IP Multimedia Subsystem (IMS): Stage 2. 3GPP TS 23.228. (2003)

A Quality of Service Assessment Technique for Large-Scale Management of Multimedia Flows[*]

J.L. García-Dorado[1], J. Aracil[1], J.A. Hernández[1], S. Lopez-Buedo[1],
J.E. López de Vergara[1], P. Reviriego[2], G. Huecas[3], S. Pavón[3],
and J. Quemada[3]

[1] Universidad Autónoma de Madrid, Spain
jl.garcia@uam.es
[2] Universidad Carlos III de Madrid, Spain
[3] Universidad Politécnica de Madrid, Spain

Abstract. This paper presents the concept and preliminary experiments of a system for assessing on the Quality of Service of multimedia flows. The goal is to devise a mechanism that allows a service provider to take action whenever poor quality of service is detected in the delivery of multimedia flows. Such procedure is fully automatic since it is based on a goodness-of-fit test between source and destination packet interarrival histograms. If the null hypothesis of the test is accepted the flow is marked as in good standing, otherwise it is marked as anomalous and the network management system should take action in response. The proposed technique is analyzed in terms of hardware complexity and bandwidth consumption. The results show this technique is feasible and easily deployable at a minimum hardware and bandwidth expense.

1 Introduction and Problem Statement

Multimedia networks are very challenging to operate and manage. Indeed, the assurance of quality of service implies the surveillance of a very large number of flows, possibly thousands. This is due to the tremendous growth of multimedia applications over the past few years, which is expected to remain steady in the near future.

With such a large number of flows, it is essential to implement *automatic procedures for quality of service management* that actually save operators to take action manually. Ideally, flows would be marked as either "pass" or "fail" and such binary decision would trigger the appropriate corrective mechanisms automatically. In this paper, we provide a technique that tackles the former problem, since the latter is out of the scope of this paper.

Besides overall latency, quality in multimedia applications is primarily measured with two different metrics: data loss and jitter [1]. In our proposal, we focus on obtaining a single metric that actually captures *how similar incoming and outgoing multimedia flows are*. In other words, we wish to evaluate the amount of

---

[*] The authors would like to acknowledge the support of the Comunidad Autónoma de Madrid to this work, under project *e-Magerit (S-0505/TIC/000251)*.

D. Krishnaswamy, T. Pfeifer, and D. Raz (Eds.): MMNS 2007, LNCS 4787, pp. 173–176, 2007.
© IFIP International Federation for Information Processing 2007

distortion suffered by a multimedia flow as it traverses a given path across the network. To do so, we propose to perform a goodness-of-fit test [2] between the interarrival time probability distributions of the multimedia flow at the ingress and egress points of the path under study. Note that such procedure allows us to merge the above-mentioned two metrics (i. e. data loss and jitter) into a single one, since it is clear that the packet interarrival time series will be distorted by data loss and jitter.

The advantages of the proposed technique are manifold: On one hand, there is no need for time synchronization between the monitored endpoints. The measurement devices at the path entry and exit points are only required to calculate histograms, yet remaining low system complexity, as shown in the next section. In addition, this technique is non-intrusive and consumes nearly no bandwidth. Unlike RTCP [3], there is no need to periodically report to the transmitting end about the observed jitter, which results in bandwidth consumption and it is difficult to implement in channels with limited outbound bandwidth from the client. Finally, our method is mathematically rigorous, since it is based on well-known and reliable statistical techniques.

2   System Architecture

The system architecture is depicted in fig. 1. Let us consider a given ingress-egress pair of nodes. The ingress measurement node builds a histogram with the interarrival times of a given multimedia flow, and so does the egress measurement node. Each node transmits its histogram to a centralized network management node, which performs a goodness-of-fit test between them all. Such node thus marks flows as "pass" or "fail" for a given significance level.

Clearly, this approach paves the way for autonomic network management, where, as stated in [4], a multimedia system can self-optimize the traffic of the flows sent to users to achieve a given objective QoE (Quality of Experience) based on feedback information about that traffic. This capability is very important for Video-on-Demand (VoD) scenarios, where users pay for receiving multimedia contents.

Moreover, this information can also be used to perform admission control and let new users start new multimedia sessions. If the current set of flows over the network passes a given QoS test, then a new flow can be admitted. Otherwise, no new sessions will be allowed in order to avoid higher QoS degradation. Furthermore, it is possible to use this information for capacity planning of networks with such multimedia constraints.

Concerning the physical implementation of the proposed solution, histogram calculation is a low-complexity task that can be easily handled by any cheap FPGA-embedded microprocessor, such as MicroBlaze [5]. Even for small FPGAs, this processor occupies few resources of the device. For example, MicroBlaze uses less than 15% of XC3S1200E [6], and costs less than US\$10. For instance, if $\sqrt{N_s}$ bins are used, where N_s is the number of samples, the amount of memory required to store one such histogram would be $\sqrt{N_s} \cdot \log_2{(N_s)}$ bits. For a typical 10 minute session, using 500-byte packets and a high quality 1Mbps multimedia

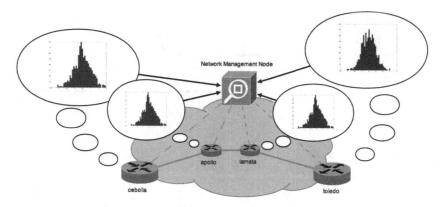

Fig. 1. Architecture and testbed scenario

stream, the average histogram size would be 6.5 Kb. Current low-cost FPGAs have internal memories typically two orders of magnitude bigger, and they also feature glueless interface to conventional DRAMs. For example, a 32 MB DDR memory like MT46V16M16 [7] is currently priced under US$5, thus making completely viable a FPGA-based low-cost solution capable of storing tens of thousands of such histograms.

3   Results and Conclusions

The authors have used the ISABEL application as testbed for the performance evaluation of our proposed technique. ISABEL [8] is an advanced collaborative work application that supports video, audio and data to create collaborative sessions adapted to the users' needs.

In our performance evaluation, we set ISABEL to collect packet interarrival times at all intermediate nodes in the network. This way permits us to perform a quality-of-service test on a per-hop basis. With N_s measurements, we perform the standard χ^2 goodness-of-fit test, with $\sqrt{N_s}$ histogram bins. It is worth pointing out that the number of bins can be modified in order to focus on a particular range of interarrival times, or as a way to demand a higher fidelity between the matching histograms.

Specifically we consider the traffic generated by the source "cebolla" node (see fig. 1). Fig. 2 shows the cumulative distribution function (CDF) for the interarrival times between packets sent by the "cebolla" node to the "apollo" node, which are then forwarded by "apollo" to "lamata", and finally transmitted from "lamata" to "toledo" node.

Table 1 analyzes the QoS degradation as the number of hops increases, for a particular flow under study. It turns out that "apollo" and "lamata" pass the χ^2 test for low values of α but the "toledo" node does not. Thus, we can conclude that "toledo" node is suffering anomalies and action should be taken if it repeatedly shows such behavior.

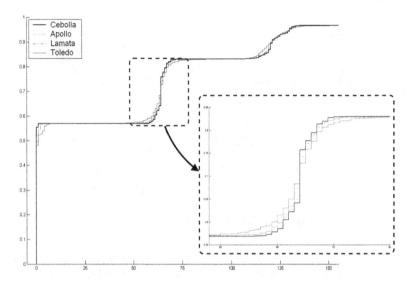

Fig. 2. CDF of packet interarrival time (in milliseconds) in all the nodes

Table 1. χ^2 test between the interarrival packet times

Node	Significance level (α)	Null hypothesis (H_0)
apollo	0.01	√
lamata	0.02	√
toledo	0.05	X

References

1. Claypool, M., Riedl, J.: The effects of high-speed networks on multimedia jitter. In: SCS Euromedia Conference (1999)
2. Montgomery, D.C., Runger, G.C.: Applied Statistics and Probability for Engineers. John Wiley and Sons, Chichester (1999)
3. Schultzrinne, H., Casner, S., Frederick, R., Jacobson, V.: RTP: A transport protocol for real-time applications. Internet proposed standard RFC 1889 (January 1996)
4. López, D., de Vergara, J.E.L., González, F., Sánchez-Macián, A.: An OWL-S based architecture for self-optimizing multimedia over ip services. In: Proc. 1st IEEE Int. Workshop on Modelling Autonomic Communications Environments, IEEE Computer Society Press, Los Alamitos (2006)
5. Xilinx Inc.: Microblaze Product Brief (2005)
6. Xilinx Inc.: Spartan-3E FPGA Family Data Sheet (2007)
7. Micron Technology Inc.: 256 Mb DDR SDRAM Datasheet (2006)
8. Quemada, J., et al.: Isabel: an application for real time collaboration with a flexible floor control. In: Proc. Int. Conference on Collaborative Computing: Networking, Applications and Worksharing (2005)

MPTC – A Minimum-Energy Path-Preserving Topology Control Algorithm for Wireless Sensor Networks[*]

Xian Zhou, Yun Li, Weiliang Zhao, Zhanjun Liu, and Qianbin Chen

Special Research Centre for Optical Internet & Wireless Information Networks
Chongqing University of Posts & Telecommunications
Chongqing, China, 400065
zhouxian219@Gmail.com

Abstract. The topology control strategies of wireless sensor networks are very important to reduce the energy consumptions of sensor nodes and prolong the life-span of networks. In this paper, we put forward a minimum-energy path-preserving topology control (MPTC) algorithm. MPTC not only resolves the problem of exceeding energy consumption because of the unclosed region in SMECN[2], but also preserves at least one minimum-energy path between every pair of nodes in a communication network. At last, we demonstrate the performance improvements of our algorithm through simulation.

Keywords: wireless sensor networks, topology control, minimum energy property, k-redundant edges.

1 Introduction

Wireless sensor network can be deployed in wide variety of civil and military applications. Because the power of sensor nodes are limited, so network protocols that minimize energy consumption is a major design goal for wireless sensor networks. As one of the key techniques, Topology control can design power-efficient algorithms that maintain network connectivity and optimize performance metrics such as network life and throughput.

At present, there are a number of documents carrying on the research on the topology control [3],[4],[5],[6],[7],[8]. The work most closely related to ours is that of Li (Erran) Li et al. [2], they propose an effective topology control algorithm, which is called a small minimum-energy communication network (SMECN). But SMECN has a flaw about the unclosed region which could result in exceeding energy consumption. We put forward a new topology control algorithm- Minimum-energy Path-preserving Topology Control (MPTC) which not only resolves the problem, but also ensures the connectivity of network which has minimum-energy path property.

[*] Supported by the Research Grants by the Science & Tech. Commission of Chongqing (CST2006BB2370), the Science and Technology Research Project of Chongqing Municipal Education Commission of China (KJ070521), and Ph.D Grand of CQUPT (A2007-07).

D. Krishnaswamy, T. Pfeifer, and D. Raz (Eds.): MMNS 2007, LNCS 4787, pp. 177–182, 2007.
© IFIP International Federation for Information Processing 2007

2 Model

We assume that all nodes in the wireless sensor network are deployed in two-dimensional area, where no two nodes are in the same physical location. Each node knows its own location, and has a unique identification code. A transmission between node u and v takes power $p(u,v) = td(u,v)^n$ for some appropriate constant t, where $n \geq 2$ is the path-loss exponent of outdoor radio propagation models [1], and $d(u,v)$ is the distance between u and v. In this paper, we designate n equals 4.

When each node of the network uses its biggest power in working, this topology is called the biggest power topology(G_{max}). A $PATH(u,v) = (u = u_0, \cdots u_n = v)$ in G, the consumed energy when messages delivered through this path is $C(PATH(u,v)) = nc + \sum_{i=0}^{n-1} P(u_i, u_{i+1})$, c is the consumed energy when a node receives messages.

3 The MPTC Algorithm

According to the SMECN[2], the direct-transmission regions(DTR) of the nodes can be divided two different types: closed region and unclosed region. If u can find its transmitted power p_u ($p_{max} > p_u > 0$) that satisfies $F(u, p_u) \supseteq \eta$, u's DTR is a closed region. (Fig. 1(a) shows closed region). Otherwise, $F(u, p_u) \not\supseteq \eta$ when p_u ($p_{max} > p_u > 0$), u's DTR is a unclosed region. (Fig .1(b) shows unclosed region.). The DTR of the nodes at the verge of the wireless network are almost unclosed region. SMECN will set p_{max} as the node's transmitted power when the node's DTR is an unclosed region, which makes these nodes consume more energy.

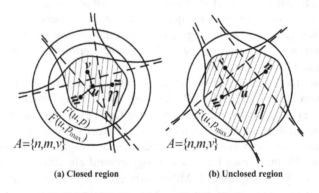

(a) Closed region   (b) Unclosed region

Fig. 1. Closed region and unclosed region

Different from SMECN[2], MPCT sets the transmitted power of nodes without judging whether the nodes' transmission region covers its direct- transmission region.

The detail of MPTC algorithm is shown in Fig.2, which consists of the following main steps.

Aoglrithm MEPN

$P(u) = P_{max}$;
$M = \varnothing$;
Broadcast"Hello"message with power P_{max} and gather Acks;
$NBR(u) = \{v \mid p(u,v) \le P_{max}\}$; // $NBR(u)$is a set of all the nodes in $F(u, p_{max})$
while $NBR(u) \ne \varnothing$ do
    p=Increase(p);
    Broadcast"Hello"message with power p and gather Acks;
    N=$\{v \mid Loc(v) \in F(u,p), v \notin M, v \ne u\}$; // N consists of the new nodes in the current iteration
    $M = M \cup N$;   // M inculdes all the nodes in $F(u,p)$
    $NBR(u) = NBR(u) - N$;
    for each $w \in NBR(u)$ do
      for each $v \in N$ do
        if $C(u,w) > C(u,v,w)$ then // judge whether the edge(u,w) is a two-redundant edge
          $NBR(u) = NBR(u) - \{w\}$;
$P(u) = p$;   // After $NBR(u) = \varnothing$, u sets its final transmitted power (p)
$N(u)$=$\{v \mid Loc(v) \in F(u,p), v \ne u\}$; // $N(u)$is a set of u's neighbors in $F(u,p)$

Fig. 2. Algorithm MPTC running at node u

Define the graph $G = (V, E)$ by taking $(u, v) \in E$ iff $v \in Nbr(u)$, as constructed by the algorithm in Fig.2. Thus, the following theorem holds.

Theorem 1. If the G_{max} can ensure the connectivity of the wireless network, then the subgraph $G = (V, E)$ can also ensure the connectivity of network and has the minimum-energy property [2].

Proof- **Connectivity:** We assume that there is a $PATH(u,v)=(u=u_0,...,u_n=v)$ in G_{max}. According to MPTC algorithm, if $edge(u_i, u_{i+1})$ is not a two-redundant edge[2], we reserve the this edge in G. Otherwise, if $edge(u_i, u_{i+1})$ is a two-redundant edge, there are $PATH^*(u_i, u_{i+1})=(u_i, w_i^1, \cdots, w_i^m, u_{i+1})$ in G, and $C(PATH^*(u_i, u_{i+1})) < C(edge(u_i, u_{i+1}))$. So, if u_i and u_{i+1} are connected in G_{max}, they are also connected in G. We can find a path like $PATH^*(u,v)=(u=u_0, w_0^1, \cdots, w_0^{m_0}, u_1, w_1^1, \cdots, w_1^{m_1}, \cdots, u_{n-1}, w_{n-1}^2, \cdots, w_{n-1}^{m_{n-1}}, u_n = v)$ in G. The above process prove that for a given pair of nodes u and v, if there is a path between them in G_{max}, there is also a path between u and v in G. Therefore, if G_{max} is connected, so is G.

Proof- **The minimum-energy property:** We assume there is a minimum-energy path between u and v in G_{max}, $PATH(u,v)=(u=u_0,...,u_n=v)$, which is not in G. There is at least an $\text{edge}(u_i, u_{i+1})(i = (0, \cdots, n-1))$ in $\text{PATH}(u,v)$ which is not included in G . Due to the connectivity of G , there is another $\text{PATH}^*(u_i, u_{i+1}) = (u_i, w_i^1, \cdots, w_i^m, u_{i+1})$ in G to connect u_i and u_{i+1} . According to MPTC algorithm, it is not hard to show $C(\text{PATH}^*(u_i, u_{i+1})) < C(\text{edge}(u_i, u_{i+1}))$, so there is another $\text{PATH}^*(u,v) = (u = u_0, \cdots, u_i, w_i^1, \cdots, w_i^m, u_{i+1}, \cdots, u_n = v)$ in $G_{\max}$ and $C(\text{PATH}(u,v)) > C(\text{PATH}^*(u,v))$, which means that $\text{PATH}(u,v)$ is not a minimum-energy path between u and v in $G_{\max}$. It is contrary to the foregoing assumption. Hence we can conclude G has the minimum-energy path property.

4 Evaluations

A. Simulation Environment

The simulation is conducted on simulator NS-2[9]. We generated 10 random network with 100 nodes. The nodes are randomly placed in a rectangular region of 1000m $\times$ 1000 m. Each node has a maximum transmission range of 200 m and is equipped with 20J of energy at beginning of the simulation. We randomly set 4 CBR flows at sending rate of 5 packets/sec, each packet size is 512 bytes. We use AODV[10] as routing protocol.

B. Simulation Results

We firstly concentrate our research on topology structure. Fig. 3 shows the networks' topology structure controlled by MaxPower, SMECN and MPTC respectively. Compared with the subnetworks controlled by SMECN and MPTC, the MPTC's subnetwork is smaller than that of SMECN, which can decrease the collision and save energy of nodes.

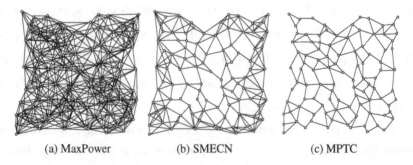

(a) MaxPower   (b) SMECN   (c) MPTC

Fig. 3. The topology structure controlled by MaxPower, SMECN and MPTC

We simulate the average remaining energy of nodes in the path of flows after 300s simulation time. Fig.4(a) shows the simulation results for MPTC, SMECN and

MaxPower, respectively. We can see that the average energy decrease rate of MPTC is significantly lower that that of SMECN and MaxPower Fig.4(b) shows the average degree of nodes for MPTC, SMECN and MaxPower, respectively. From Fig.4(b), we can conclude the average degree of MPTC is evidently lower than that of SMECN. The average degree of MPTC is only 70%~75% of SMECN. After about 270s, the average degree of MaxPower is decrease to 0, which means the most nodes in the network have no neighbor because a lot of nodes have been dead.

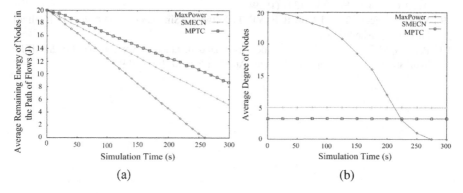

(a)   (b)

Fig. 4. (a) Average remaining energy of nodes (b) Average degree of nodes

5 Conclusion

Topology control can reduce the consumptions of sensor nodes, optimize the performance of networks and prolong the life span of the networks through adjusting the transmission power of sensor nodes. Our paper puts forward a new topology control algorithm of wireless sensor networks–MPTC. It not only avoids the exceeding energy consumption which results from the unclosed region in SMECN, but also ensures the connectivity of network which has minimum-energy path property. Finally, we have shown the performance improvements of MPTC over SMECN and MaxPower through simulation.

References

1. Rappaport, T.S.: Wireless Communications: Principles and Practice. Prentice-Hall, Englewood Cliffs[M], NJ (1996)
2. Erran, L., Halpern, J.Y.: A Minimum-Energy Preserving Topology-Control Algorithm[J]. IEEE Transaction on Wireless Communications 3(3), 910–921 (2004)
3. Erran, L., Halpern, J.Y., Bahl, P.: A Cone-Based Distributed Topology-Control Algorithm for Wireless Multi-Hop Networks[J]. IEEE/ACM Transactions on Networking 13(1), 147–159 (2005)
4. Yin, B., Shi, H., Shang, Y.: A Two-Level Strategy for Topology Control in Wireless Sensor Networks[A]. In: ICPADS 2005. Proceedings of 11th International Conference on Parallel and Distributed Systems, pp. 358–362 (2005)

5. Chen, B., Jamieson, K., Balakrishnan, H., Morris, R.: Span: An energy-efficient coordination algorithm for topology maintenance in ad hoc wireless networks[J]. Mobile Computing and Networking 8(5), 85–96 (2002)
6. Liu, J., Li, B.: Distributed topology control in wireless sensor networks with asymmetric links[J]. IEEE GLOBECOM 2003 3(8), 1257–1262 (2003)
7. Busse, M., Haenselmann, T., Effelsberg, W.: A Topology and Energy Control Algorithm for Wireless Sensor Networks [A]. In: MSWiM 2006, pp. 317–321 (2006)
8. Rodoplu, V., Meng, T.H.: Minimum energy mobile wireless networks. IEEE J. Select. Areas Commun. 17, 1333–1344 (1999)
9. VINT Project. The UCB/LBNL/VINT Network Simulator-ns (Version2). [Online], http://www.isi.edu/nsnam/ns
10. Perkins, C.E., Royer, E.M.: Ad-hoc on-demand distance vector routing. In: 2nd IEEE Workshop Mobile Computing Systems Applicat, pp. 90–100 (1999)

QoS Management for Distributed Multimedia Services

Ralf Seepold, Natividad Martínez Madrid, and Javier Martínez Fernández

Departamento de Ingeniería Telemática
Universidad Carlos III de Madrid, Leganés (Madrid), Spain
{ralf.seepold,natividad.martinez,javier.martinez}@uc3m.es

Abstract. Currently, several multimedia devices support the UPnP protocol allowing automatic detection of devices, connection of devices and agreement on a certain quality of the communication established between a server of content (Media Server) and a player of content (Media Renderer). The focus of this paper is to add to the UPnP standard quality of service (QoS) some elements to incorporate better performance in the local networks. All these additions are compatible with the current standard.

1 Introduction

Nowadays, a wide variety of devices have in theory the capability to interact with each other. A solution for device interfacing is proposed by the UPnP (Universal Plug and Play) Forum [1]. With the help of the UPnP standard, new devices can be quickly detected, services can be used and devices are capable to start a direct communication. Within this group a specific architecture has been proposed that supports multimedia applications (UPnP AV architecture [2]) allowing for exchange of multimedia data from one device to another without any mediator.

For example, a trailer of a cinema movie offered by a Multimedia Server can be displayed in home-cinema equipment or on a mobile phone. Both so called Media Renderers have very different capabilities to display the video contents but from both of them it is expected that the video is shown in an acceptable quality. The crucial aspect remains: the provisioning of a service and fixing service quality that is required to enable the service in the dynamic environment of a network. This article proposes a solution that allows device integration into a home network, service registration in a home network platform and multimedia service delivery with Quality of Service (QoS) with a UPnP for a better performance in QoS management for local networks.

2 Quality of Service Extension of the UPnP Standard

The UPnP AV is directly linked to the UPnP QoS architecture [3], acting the audiovisual control point as the client of the QoS manager. The management of multimedia devices in a home network, and the distribution of the generated traffic with QoS have some requirements:

D. Krishnaswamy, T. Pfeifer, and D. Raz (Eds.): MMNS 2007, LNCS 4787, pp. 183–186, 2007.

1. Automatic discovery and configuration of multimedia devices
2. Request for establishment of traffic with QoS from the audiovisual control point to the QoS manager
3. Calculation of the path in a centralized or distributed way
4. Allowance of different mechanisms to specify the QoS (prioritized or parameterized)
5. Possibility of different admission control strategies: centralized (decided by the QoS manager), distributed (decided by the devices) or hybrid.

Only requirements 1 and 2 would be automatically guaranteed by using the UPnP AV and QoS architectures. The establishment of traffic with QoS is a stateless service. This means that the list of devices in the network is the only information kept by the QoS manager between two invocations of the service. All other information regarding topology of the network, characteristics of the network and the devices, or already admitted traffic flows, will be erased and recalculated for each invocation. While this strategy might have sense in a network with a very high degree of device mobility, the kind of home media networks addressed in this work are relatively stable, and therefore it makes sense to store different information regarding its state.

Furthermore, UPnP QoS V2 is only addressing the management of QoS for prioritized traffic, but there is no way to express other types of parameters (bandwidth, allowed delays, etc.) to administrate the resources.

The proposed extended functional model for the QoS architecture allows the QoS manager to store state information and to check it, having thus a better performance. As in the standard architecture, the service of establishment of traffic with QoS is requested by a client control point, typically audiovisual. The *QoS Manager* receives the request and checks first of all within the *QoS Policy Holder* the priority to be assigned to the traffic according to its policy rules. The diagram of the functional model is shown in Figure 1.

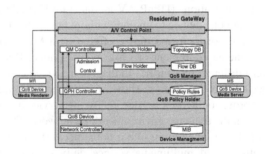

Fig. 1. Extended Functional Architecture for one Local Network

The QoS Manager is the main element, and is divided into four main modules:

The **QoS Manager Controller** receives the original request and orchestrates the interaction with the other internal and external components.

The **QoS Topology Holder** serves requests the paths between two devices in the network. In order to do this, it queries during setup the available multimedia devices and stores all information necessary to describe the topology of the network. After storing this information for each subsequent path query, it does not need to interact again with the devices, but just calculates the route according to the stored topology. All previously calculated paths are cached in a table to speed up the reply time. The topology and path table are kept stable between QoS requests, unless a device is added or removed. In this case, the tables should be recalculated.

The **QoS Flow Holder** gives support to the Admission Control component. It stores the dynamical information about the flows being transmitted at a given moment, including information about the path they are following, their priorities and parameters. In the current version of the standard, this information is not stored in any central place, so the manager has to query all devices in the path for their current state before admitting a new flow. This component would allow its flow querying and updating. Each time a new flow is admitted, an entry is added in the flow table. Correspondingly, each time a flow finishes, its entry is removed from the table. The first assumption is actually also made in the standard UPnP QoS architecture, and the second one is not considered to be too restrictive for the proposed scenario.

The **QoS Admission Control** component performs the traffic admission control, being therefore the main component of the manager. Its tasks include: Distribution and adaptation of QoS requirements along the traffic path, relevant for parameterized QoS; Orchestration of the admission control.and Decision in case of traffic rejection.

The **Device Management** module encapsulates the functionality of the residential gateway as an UPnP QoS Device, according to the standard service specification.

The scenario described is based on the standard architectures UPnP audiovisual (unmodified) and UPnP QoS (modified to be able to store state and take into account parameterized QoS). Both architectures assume that all devices are on the same local network. If the devices are located in different local networks connected though a residential gateway, the solution can be an easy variant of the previous scenario.

An AV control point in a single local network can only discover (and announce himself to) Media Servers and Media Renderers inside his own network. The same applies to the QoS Manager, which acts as control point of the QoS Devices. The proposed solution takes advantage of the fact that the residential gateway is a device connected to both networks, and thus provides both the audiovisual control point and the QoS Manager with the QoS Policy Holder. Figure 2 shows a communications module with the mentioned services and with a different functionality that the standard.

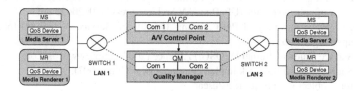

Fig. 2. Extended Functional Architecture for more than one local network

The QoS Manager will also perform its functionality in similar way to the one presented in the first scenario, except that it will have to add the network identifier to the device information, and that the residential gateway itself will always be on the path if the source and destination of the traffic are in different local networks.

3 Implementation and Conclusions

The different scenarios have been tested with a gateway that offers a hardware platform running on Linux. The system was started on the embedded pc. On top of the operating system, an OSGi framework [4] (Oscar [5]) has been selected. This decision has been taken because we wanted to have a backup position when access to the source code is required. As a bundle (an OSGi application) an UPnP control point has been adopted and integrated into the OSGi framework. The Control Point of Cidero [6] has been selected for the test. The media server (CyberMediaGate [7]) has been installed as well in the gateway. Finally, a special bundle has been designed to launch both applications in the framework.

External to the gateway two configurable switches have been connected. These switches offer accessibility in the different home LANs. UPnP Renderers and UPnP Media Servers have been installed in computers running Windows, Linux or mobile devices like the Nokia N93. A Nokia 770 has been used as a remote control.

Now the QoS Manager can perform admission control. The extension of the traffic descriptor allows a fine grained tuning of the possible multimedia flows according on the device's capability (stored in the profile data and derived from the current load).The presented approach extends the current UPnP standard with features that provide establishment of traffic with QoS from the audiovisual control point to the QoS manager, calculation of the path in a centralized or distributed way, allowance of different mechanisms to specify the QoS (prioritized or parameterized), the possibility to enable different admission control strategies: centralized (decided by the QoS manager), distributed (decided by the devices) or hybrid.

Acknowledgments. The work has been partly funded by the projects PLANETS (MEDEA+ A306 funded by the Spanish Ministry of Industry; FIT-330220-2005-111), MUSE (IST-Program; MUSE-IST 026442) and MARTES (ITEA 04006, funded by the Spanish Ministry of Industry under FIT-340000-2006-166).

References

1. Universal Plug and Play (UPnP) Forum (June 2007), http://www.upnp.org/
2. Universal Plug and Play (UPnP) Forum, UPnP AV Architecture: 1, (June 2002), http://www.upnp.org/specs/av/UPnP-av-AVArchitecture-v1-20020622.pdf
3. Universal Plug and Play (UPnP) Forum, Quality of Service V 2.0 (October 2006), www.upnp.org/specs/qos/
4. Open Service Gateway Initiative (OSGi) Alliance (2007), http://www.osgi.org
5. Open Source OSGi framework implementation, Oscar (June 2007), http://forge.objectweb.org/projects/oscar/
6. Cidero Software Solutions for the Digital Home (2007), http://www.cidero.com
7. Reference Implementation of UPnP AV, Satoshi Konno, Tokyo, Japan (June 2007), http://www.cybergarage.org/net/cmgate/java/index.html

Distributed Self Fault-Diagnosis for SIP Multimedia Applications

Kai X. Miao[1], Henning Schulzrinne[2], Vishal Kumar Singh[2], and Qianni Deng[3]

[1] Intel Corporation, 2200 Mission College Boulevard,
Santa Clara, CA 95052-8119, USA
`kai.miao@intel.com`
[2] 450 Computer Science Building, Department. of Computer Science, Columbia University
New York, NY 10027, USA
`{hgs,vs2140}@cs.columbia.edu`
[3] 1954 HuaShan Road, Department. of Computer Science, Shanghai Jiaotong University
Shanghai 200030 P.R. China
`deng-qn@cs.sjtu.edu.cn`

Abstract. IP real-time multimedia applications present a challenging environment for network and service management, which requires a new approach. DYSWIS (Do You See What I See), proposed in this paper, is peer-to-peer distributed management architecture for multimedia network and service management, characteristic of active fault probing and identification based on protocol and functional scripting and rules.

Keywords: Fault, SIP, VoIP, Internet, IP, quality, QoS, diagnosis, SNMP, P2P.

1 Introduction

In spite of the recent growth in Internet multimedia communications, service availability and voice quality of IP-based multimedia applications still falls behind when compared to traditional PSTN voice services, as shown in a recent study [1]. In contrast to PSTN, the Internet decentralizes network intelligence and allows end user devices and local networks to grow significantly in capability and complexity. Yet, the world is still dominated by a centralized service and management model, as in PSTN. In this model, we assume all network elements can be professionally (centrally) managed, a service provider is able to "see" and control every network element, including a user device, and all failures are hard failures thus easily detectable. All these assumptions are obviously no longer true for IT multimedia services and the centralized control model of the past is no longer able to effectively handle the complexity of today's IP network for multimedia services, as is evidenced by failed efforts to solve the service quality problem of VoIP.

In particular, existing network management approaches are limited in cases like residential users for whom there is no IT admin, communications in a rural community where only extremely limited IT support is available, and corporate users having

D. Krishnaswamy, T. Pfeifer, and D. Raz (Eds.): MMNS 2007, LNCS 4787, pp. 187–190, 2007.

certain transient problems such as telecommuters using networks not owned by their employer. Traditional problems management is based on a model of "ownership" – by either an IT department or a service provider. In IP multimedia service environment, however, there are many useful service scenarios where a service or device can not be fully owned by a provider or IT. Automatic problem management, including self fault diagnosis and automatic problem fixing capabilities, is crucial and so is a standard based fault diagnosis mechanism so that problems can always be found no matter where they occur. Such a standard is apparently beyond SNMP's capability.

Even for a multimedia service clearly owned by a provider or IT department, managing user devices can be very hard in a world where convergence and divergence of networks and user devices appear to be happening at the same, which makes managing a multi-media service or a user device is a huge challenge. Traditional network management cannot reach into certain user devices and thus cannot easily exclude certain failure causes, in consideration of the fact that many user devices such a PC or SIP phone today are not managed.

In the complex world of IP multimedia services, faults can be very elusive, even for experienced IT experts. The same visible problem to a user or an IT admin can be caused by many different root causes, for example, from DHCP address allocation failures (apparently common in large-scale wireless networks) to NAT time-outs and various ISP failures. Harder-to-diagnose "dynamic" network elements such as NATs with binding time-outs or limited binding tables make the traditional management approaches quite ineffective for fault identification.

Following the above discussion, we propose a new and generic distributed network management framework that leverages distributed resources in a network. We call the basic approach *"Do You See What I See"* (**DYSWIS**) [2]. DYSWIS treats each node as a potential source of network management information, gathering data about network functionality and component function availability, performance, and failures. Each participating (DYSWYS) node has a certain capability level for fault diagnosis, from basic failure detection and maintenance of failure history records to the ability to invoke a set of standardized or customized network probing tools within the system (e.g., ranging from versions of "ping" and "traceroute" to more application-specific probing tools) for specific network and application layer protocols and the abilities to learn and track network fault behavior, intelligently create and manage diagnostic tests and perform inference modeling and analysis of faults. Other nodes can ask DYSWIS nodes to report on its view of certain network nodes and services.

In the next section, we will provide more details about DYSWIS.

2 DYSWIS Architecture and Components

Figure 1 shows the fault-diagnosis framework we are proposing consisting of a number of regular nodes and DYSWIS nodes in a network. A DYSWIS node is capable of local fault detection, communicating fault information with other nodes about network faults, and storing network fault history information.

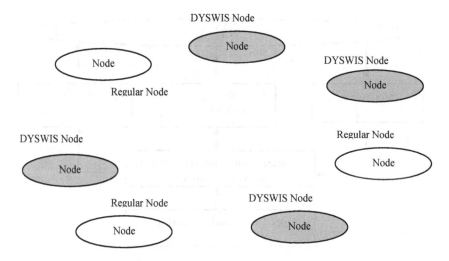

Fig. 1. *DYSWIS – "Do You See What I See"* – Fault Diagnostic Framework

A DYSWIS node is capable of actively testing or probing functions for the purpose of fault identification in a network, which may include gathering properties associated with a multimedia call or collecting historical information. For example, if SIP call set up fails, a node would go through a set of steps, such as sending a ping to the proxy, trying a SIP test server or reaching other nodes on other protocols, to see if the problem is with server reachability, a firewall that blocks SIP messages or general network reachability problems.

DYSWIS nodes are distributed over the network where a multimedia call is made, because, often, the only way to detect a fault is to run tests from multiple vantage points in the network. A problem as experienced by a user can be "far away" from the fault that causes the problem. A local DYSWIS node can work with a remote DYSWIS node to more effectively identify where the fault resides.

DYSWIS architecture can operate in both centralized (client/server) mode and p2p mode. It needs a mechanism for a manager to gather data collected by measurement points in a network, but also needs to function in peer mode when there is no central manager. In p2p mode, each node could monitor its local communications and then trigger a query to peers, following a set script and set of rules, depending on the observed condition.

An extensible set of building blocks in DYSWIS nodes can test protocol functionalities not only along the "path" of a call but also across the network stack, as faults can occur anywhere in the network stack. In addition, a functionality fault needs to be measured and characterized by different performance levels, in addition to hard failures.

Within a DYSWIS node, as shown in Figure 2, the fault management system can be seen as consisting of several key components: monitoring, probing, sharing via a communication mechanism to exchange results (i.e., DYSWIS protocol), a rule-based language or engine that invokes monitoring or probing or sharing, and a database that contains history data, dependencies and rules associated with multimedia calls, etc.

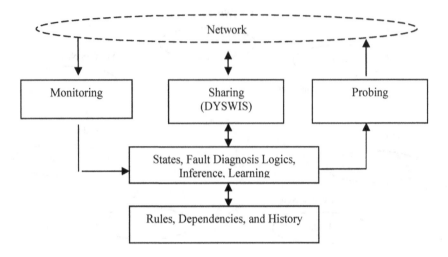

Fig. 2. Functional Components in DYSWIS Fault Diagnosis Framework

3 Work in Progress

Research is being currently carried out at Columbia University and Shanghai Jiaotong University, following the proposed DYSWIS architecture: 1) Extensive analysis has been done on dependency relationships in SIP multimedia call flows (protocol) and scenarios (functional). Fault detection algorithms have been developed on a real system built with SIP server and client components. 2) Packet sniffing software tools for inspecting multimedia application packets have been developed for media fault detections and analysis. 3) Analysis on fault probing operations based on call conditions described in a scripting language is also underway. 4) Investigation is also underway on how to apply the proposed approach to p2p and s/c models for fault diagnosis in general.

References

1. Keynote VoIP Competitive Intelligence Study, Keynote Systems, TMCnet (July 11, 2005), http://www.tmcnet.com/usubmit/2005/jul/1161904.htm
2. Sculzriinne, H.: Managing (VoIP) Applications, Columbia University (July 2005), http://www.cs.columbia.edu/~hgs/papers/2005/IRTF-management.ppt

Hierarchical QoS-Aware Routing in Multi-tier Wireless Multimedia Sensor Networks

Stephane Lohier[1], Gilles Roussel[1], and Yacine Ghamri Doudane[2]

[1] Université Paris-Est - IGM, 75420 Marne-la-Vallée Cedex – France
[2] ENSIEE-LRSM, 18, allée Jean Rostand, 91025 Evry Cedex – France
lohier@univ-mlv.fr, roussel@univ-mlv.fr, ghamri@ensiie.fr

Abstract. The Wireless Multimedia Sensor Networks (WMSN) are a particular case of Wireless Sensors Networks (WSN) as they present a lower density, a limited mobility, require more important resources and need QoS control to transport the multimedia streams. In this paper, we propose, starting from a reference architecture of WMSN, a first approach for hierarchical self-organizing routing ensuring a certain level of QoS.

1 Introduction

The emergence and the development of WMSN [1] are related to the availability of low-cost and low-consumption CMOS cameras. For this new kind of networks the applications are numerous: monitoring of public or private places (concerts, borders, companies, houses...); detection, recognition and tracking of objects; automobile traffic management (speed control, car parking assistance...); industrial process control (visual inspection, automated actions...).

In these particular sensor networks, the main concerns are not only the scalability and the energy but also the QoS needed by multimedia streams: delay guarantees for the real time flows; bandwidth on the links related to the tolerable compression ratio; limited loss ratios. Besides, the routing problem on WSN [2] is different from that met on MANET (many-to-one and not many-to-many); the type of routing (hierarchical or data-centric) and the QoS metrics are strongly related to the application (application aware). Moreover, for WMSN, we have to consider specific factors: low mobility, low density, heterogeneous sensors, specific nodes capabilities for the processing and the storage.

Figure 1 described our proposal for a multi-tier architecture inspired by the work of I.F. Akyldiz [1]. In this heterogeneous and hierarchical architecture, each tier corresponds to a category of video sensors with increasing capabilities in term of camera resolution, processing, storage and transmission. For the first tier, the sensors can be CMUCam (weak resolution of 160x255) coupled with microcontrollers allowing a minimum processing and not very greedy transmissions like in ZigBee, Bluetooth or UWB standards. The second tier can be made up of webcam and microcontrollers with more processing, more storage and mixed transmissions, ZigBee and 802.11 for instance. The last tier is connected to the sink (multimedia server) and includes high resolution cameras coupled with laptop. An implementation example of this type of architecture is presented in [3].

D. Krishnaswamy, T. Pfeifer, and D. Raz (Eds.): MMNS 2007, LNCS 4787, pp. 191–195, 2007.
© IFIP International Federation for Information Processing 2007

For each tier, our proposal is to organize the topology in clusters with Cluster Head (CH), Cluster Routers (CR) allowing multi-hop routing when necessary, and Cluster Terminals (CT), only able to capture video information and to transmit it. In order to limit the interferences, the nearby clusters can use distinct transmission channels. The sensors of the various levels can be moved but are not permanently mobile.

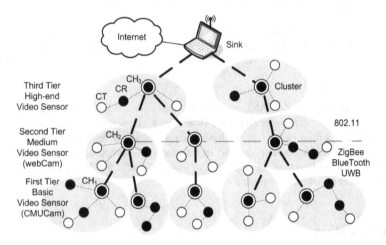

Fig. 1. Multi-tier Architecture of WMSN

Moreover, the processing, essentially carried out in the CHs and towards the collector, includes specifics operations like data aggregation (images from different scenes in the same flow) and data suppression (redundant images from various sensors). For all these reasons (clustered architecture, many-to-one flows, heterogeneous capabilities, processing into the CHs) we believe that a hierarchical routing is the most suited.

The following sections present a first approach for QoS-aware hierarchical routing inside clusters, whatever is the tier, and between the clusters of the various tiers. The QoS routes setup is a first step of our solution. Indeed, the network organization must remain evolutionary according to the periodic requests of nodes to join/leave a cluster and to the needs of the sink-application which will select, starting from descriptors, interesting flows (image of a particular zone with a selected resolution…). Thus, the objective here is not to guarantee a QoS constantly but to choose and receive pictures of a sufficient quality (soft QoS) by dynamically optimizing the links quality, the processing in the nodes and the choice of the sources.

2   Intra-cluster QoS Routing

The proposed QoS routing in each cluster is proactive and includes 6 stages for the cluster self-organization and the routes setup procedures (figure 2):

1. Each node self-determines its possible role (CH, CR or CT) in a cluster according to fixed or periodically re-evaluated criteria:

– sufficient storage and energy (comparison with specific thresholds for each role);
– for CH:
  • transmission capacities (need for the corresponding interfaces);
  • computation capacity for aggregation, suppression, compression....
2. Each CH initiates a cluster (scan channels, select a channel, select a cluster id...).
3. CR and CT carry out a research for a cluster:
– CR/CT broadcast a message for discovery: *Cluster_Discovery_Request (Scan Channels...)*;
– response of the nearby CHs (and/or CR in case of multi-hop) with a *Cluster_Discovery_Response (Cluster Description...)*.
4. Estimation of a cost for the concerned links (use of a function integrating the selected QoS metrics, see section 4) starting from the exchange of the *Cluster_Discovery* messages of stage 3.
5. CR and CT choose a CH (or a CR) according to the previous QoS estimate and join a cluster:
– CR/CT send a message *Cluster_Join_Request (Cluster id...)*;
– response of the selected CH (or CR) with a *Cluster_Join_Response (Cluster id, Network addresses...)*.

The associations of the CRs and the CTs are carried out in a recursive way: for the multi-hop routing, a CT out of the CH range has to wait for the association of a nearby CR to obtain an answer and thus to join in its turn a cluster.
6. The CR informs its CH (or its nearby CR which is closer to CH) of its router's role:
– CR send a message *Cluster_Router_Request (Cluster id...)*;
– Response of CH (or CR) with a *Cluster_Router_Response (Cluster id, Network address block...)*. In its response, the CH specifies the address block (or the sub-block for the response of a CR) which can be used by the CR for its CT (or its lower level CR).

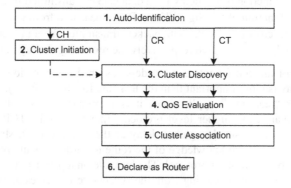

Fig. 2. Intra-cluster Routing Algorithm

After one or several exchange cycles, each CR or CT knows the address of its CH or its nearby CR (the one with the lower cost toward the CH); each CH or CR has a routing table for all its nodes. The routing is hierarchical: all the data go towards CH. According to the network dynamicity, the various stages are periodically re-launched.

3   Inter-tier QoS Routing

The routing between the CHs of the various tiers (figure 1) proceeds in 5 stages according to the same hierarchical and recursive principle:

1. The CH_1 (CH of first tier) broadcast to know the CH_2.
2. The CH_1 choose a CH_2 according to a cost estimated on the links (see section 4).
3. The CH_2 broadcast in their turn on the corresponding interface to know the CH_3.
4. The CH_2 choose a CH_3 according to a cost estimated on the links.
5. The CH_3 broadcast to know the sink. In this last case, the cost is also computed to evaluate if, according to its position and its environment, the CH_3 can obtain a sufficient QoS on the link towards the sink.

After sufficient exchanges, each CH_i knows the address of its CH_{i+1} or of the sink (transmitted with the broadcast response). Each node of each cluster can thus transmit towards the sink and conversely (the sink knows the CH_3 which knows the CH_2...).

4   Estimation of the Links Cost

During the messages exchange of the discovery stage (between CT/CR and CR/CH or between CH_i and CH_{i+1}), the cost on each possible links is periodically estimated and compared (i) with a threshold to decide if the node is under the conditions (range, noise, contentions...) to obtain a sufficient QoS and (ii) with the costs on the other links to choose the most efficient CR/CH. The cost function on a link between two nodes i and j (j being the closest to the sink) can be expressed according to the chosen QoS metrics:

$$C_{ij} = c_1 \times f(delay_{ij}) + c_2 \times f(SNR_{ji}) + c_3 \times f(e_{ij}) + c_4 \times f(energy_i) + c_5 \times f(energy_j)$$

- $f(delay_{ij})$ is a function of the delay for a data packet transmitted from i towards j;
- $f(SNR_{ji})$ is a function of the Signal/Noise Ratio measured from j towards i;
- $f(e_{ij})$ gives the error rate for the data packets transmitted from i towards j;
- $f(energy_i)$ and $f(energy_j)$ give respectively the remaining energy in i and j.

The choice of the coefficients c_1 to c_5 depends on the application and the type of traffic (the delay is more important than the loss rate for streaming...).

Besides, for "real time" applications, it is necessary to control the end-to-end delay. Rather than using higher level protocols like RTP and RTCP which involve overload, we can evaluate this global delay at the routing level, starting from the delay on each link and the knowledge of the route towards the sink, both information being provided by our routing protocol. The loss rate on a path from a CT towards the sink can also be evaluated, starting from the successive loss rates and the knowledge of the route.

5   Conclusion

In this paper, we presented a first approach for QoS routing in the WMSN. Insofar as the nodes are very few, not very mobile, and heterogeneous in term of resources, a hierarchical routing passing by "Cluster Head" is the most suitable. To introduce QoS, we proposed a cost function, estimated on a hop and which can be extended on several hops or the complete route towards the sink. The continuation of this study will be directed to (i) the complete specifications and the tests of the routing algorithm and the cost function, in connection with the possible MAC layers (ZigBee, UWB, 80211) and (ii) the specification of the data exchanges and processing after the first stage of QoS routing.

References

1. Akyildiz, I.F., et al.: A survey on wireless multimedia sensor networks. Computer Network (2006)
2. Akkaya, K., Younis, M.: A survey of routing protocols in wireless sensor networks, Ad Hoc Network (Elsevier) (2005)
3. Kulkarni, P., Ganesan, D., Shenoy, P.: The Case for Multi-tier Camera Sensor Networks. In: NOSSDAV. Proceedings of the Fifteenth International Workshop on Network and Operating Systems Support for Digital Audio and Video (2005)

Author Index

Lecture Notes in Computer Science

Sublibrary 5: Computer Communication Networks and Telecommunications

For information about Vols. 1– 4479
please contact your bookseller or Springer

Vol. 4195: D. Gaiti, G. Pujolle, E.S. Al-Shaer, K.L. Calvert, S. Dobson, G. Leduc, O. Martikainen (Eds.), Autonomic Networking. IX, 316 pages. 2006.

Vol. 4124: H. de Meer, J.P.G. Sterbenz (Eds.), Self-Organizing Systems. XIV, 261 pages. 2006.

Vol. 4104: T. Kunz, S.S. Ravi (Eds.), Ad-Hoc, Mobile, and Wireless Networks. XII, 474 pages. 2006.

Vol. 4074: M. Burmester, A. Yasinsac (Eds.), Secure Mobile Ad-hoc Networks and Sensors. X, 193 pages. 2006.

Vol. 4033: B. Stiller, P. Reichl, B. Tuffin (Eds.), Performability Has its Price. X, 103 pages. 2006.

Vol. 4026: P.B. Gibbons, T. Abdelzaher, J. Aspnes, R. Rao (Eds.), Distributed Computing in Sensor Systems. XIV, 566 pages. 2006.

Vol. 4003: Y. Koucheryavy, J. Harju, V.B. Iversen (Eds.), Next Generation Teletraffic and Wired/Wireless Advanced Networking. XVI, 582 pages. 2006.

Vol. 3996: A. Keller, J.-P. Martin-Flatin (Eds.), Self-Managed Networks, Systems, and Services. X, 185 pages. 2006.

Vol. 3976: F. Boavida, T. Plagemann, B. Stiller, C. Westphal, E. Monteiro (Eds.), NETWORKING 2006. Networking Technologies, Services, and Protocols; Performance of Computer and Communication Networks; Mobile and Wireless Communications Systems. XXVI, 1276 pages. 2006.

Vol. 3970: T. Braun, G. Carle, S. Fahmy, Y. Koucheryavy (Eds.), Wired/Wireless Internet Communications. XIV, 350 pages. 2006.

Vol. 3964: M.Ü. Uyar, A.Y. Duale, M.A. Fecko (Eds.), Testing of Communicating Systems. XI, 373 pages. 2006.

Vol. 3961: I. Chong, K. Kawahara (Eds.), Information Networking. XV, 998 pages. 2006.

Vol. 3912: G.J. Minden, K.L. Calvert, M. Solarski, M. Yamamoto (Eds.), Active Networks. VIII, 217 pages. 2007.

Vol. 3883: M. Cesana, L. Fratta (Eds.), Wireless Systems and Network Architectures in Next Generation Internet. IX, 281 pages. 2006.

Vol. 3868: K. Römer, H. Karl, F. Mattern (Eds.), Wireless Sensor Networks. XI, 342 pages. 2006.

Vol. 3854: I. Stavrakakis, M. Smirnov (Eds.), Autonomic Communication. XIII, 303 pages. 2006.

Vol. 3813: R. Molva, G. Tsudik, D. Westhoff (Eds.), Security and Privacy in Ad-hoc and Sensor Networks. VIII, 219 pages. 2005.

Vol. 3462: R. Boutaba, K.C. Almeroth, R. Puigjaner, S. Shen, J.P. Black (Eds.), NETWORKING 2005. XXX, 1483 pages. 2005.